成都市哲学社会科学规划办公室一般项目"一带一路视新'空间'传承与发展研究"（项目编号 2019R36）研究成果

四川非遗文化整合与传承

郝雯婧　王雪梅　许志强　著

西南交通大学出版社

·成　都·

图书在版编目（ＣＩＰ）数据

四川非遗文化整合与传承 / 郝雯婧，王雪梅，许志
强著. 一成都：西南交通大学出版社，2021.11
ISBN 978-7-5643-8299-5

Ⅰ.①四… Ⅱ.①郝… ②王… ③许… Ⅲ.①非物质
文化遗产 – 研究 – 四川 Ⅳ.①G127.71

中国版本图书馆 CIP 数据核字（2021）第 205824 号

Sichuan Feiyi Wenhua Zhenghe yu Chuancheng
四川非遗文化整合与传承

郝雯婧　王雪梅　许志强　著

责 任 编 辑	梁　红
助 理 编 辑	李　欣
封 面 设 计	原谋书装
出 版 发 行	西南交通大学出版社
	（四川省成都市金牛区二环路北一段 111 号
	西南交通大学创新大厦 21 楼）
发 行 部 电 话	028-87600564　028-87600533
邮 政 编 码	610031
网　　　　址	http://www.xnjdcbs.com
印　　　　刷	成都蜀通印务有限责任公司
成 品 尺 寸	170 mm × 230 mm
印　　　　张	19.75
字　　　　数	300 千
版　　　　次	2021 年 11 月第 1 版
印　　　　次	2021 年 11 月第 1 次
书　　　　号	ISBN 978-7-5643-8299-5
定　　　　价	89.00 元

前言

　　我国各族人民在长期生产生活实践中创造的丰富多彩的非物质文化遗产，代表着各族人民与群众生活密切相关的、世代相承的各种传统文化，表现形式和文化空间。非物质文化遗产是人类无形的文化遗产，代代相传的是群体的价值。其中蕴含的是人类鲜活的文化历史传统，是一个国家和民族文化软实力的重要资源，更是民族精神、民族情感、民族历史、民族气质、民族凝聚力和向心力的有机构成和重要表征。加深人们对非物质文化遗产的认识，保护和弘扬优秀的非物质文化遗产，对传承人类文化的伦理基础、维系社会的价值核心和取向具有重要意义。

　　但随着全球化趋势的加强和现代化进程的加快，我国的文化生态发生了巨大变化，非物质文化遗产的生存状况受到越来越大的冲击，加强我国非物质文化遗产的保护与传承工作已经是刻不容缓。

　　目前，四川省已有联合国教科文组织非遗名录项目 7 项，国家级非遗代表性项目 153 项、省级 611 项。四川省非物质文化遗产资源丰富多样，以古蜀文化与藏、羌、彝民族文化为核心，具有历史文化源远流长、区域文化特色显著、历史遗产荟萃丰富、古蜀文化兼容多元、民族文化绚丽多姿等特点，充满独特的魅力。虽然四川省非遗文化保护与传承呈现出较好的发展态势，但由于当前经济、社会等各方面的原因，四川省非遗文化保护与传承工作仍面临着环境、人才、资金、发展等的制约和不足。

本书全面客观分析四川非遗文化的整合及传承现状，认真研究其呈现出的规律、特征，以及所面临的困境和难题，其目的是为四川非遗传承与保护提供有价值的参考。四川非遗文化的保护，关键在于延续非遗的"生命活力"，在发展中促进传承。如何将各式各样丰富的非遗资源有效整合，从而寻求我省非遗文化保护与传承的战略和途径，已成为我省非遗保护传承工作中必须认真考虑的关键。

本书分为上、下篇。上篇为理论研究，共分为7个章节：首先阐述了非物质文化遗产的相关概念，再在探究四川非遗文化保护与传承现状的基础上发掘过程中所存在的不足之处，然后对于新时代四川非遗文化的整合与传承进行对策研究以及"一带一路"视域下非遗文化融合发展的模式与路径研究，最终提出四川非遗文化活态传承与发展的多维重构，助力四川非遗文化"走出四川"。并以蜀绣为例完成了案例研究。下篇则为四川省世界级与国家级非物质文化遗产项目列表、中英文简介和四川省省级非物质文化遗产名录列表。

本书能够顺利出版，要感谢很多支持并帮助我们的朋友，是你们的支持与鼓励让我们一直有动力完成这本书。

目录

上 篇

下　篇

上篇

第一章
非物质文化遗产相关概念

非物质文化遗产是人类无形的文化遗产，非物质文化遗产传递的是群体的价值。其中蕴含的是人类鲜活的历史文化传统，是一个国家和民族文化软实力的重要资源，更是民族精神、民族情感、民族历史、民族气质、民族凝聚力和向心力的有机构成和重要表征。深刻认识非物质文化遗产的性质，保护和弘扬优秀的非物质文化遗产，对传承人类文化的伦理基础、维系社会的价值核心和取向具有重要的意义。

一、非物质文化遗产的提出

1972 年 11 月 16 日，在巴黎召开的联合国教育、科学及文化组织大会第 17 届会议通过了《保护世界文化和自然遗产公约》（简称:《公约》），第一次正式指明"文化遗产"的含义及范围，开启了全人类共同保护世界文化和自然遗产的序幕，是文化和自然遗产确定、保护、保存、展出和传承的全面规划和计划的总政策。

1948 年的《世界人权宣言》、1966 年的《经济、社会及文化权利国际公约》和《公民权利和政治权利国际公约》、1989 年的《保护民间创作建议书》、2001 年的《教科文组织世界文化多样性宣言》和 2002 年的《伊斯坦布尔宣言》，均强调了非物质文化遗产不容忽视的重要意义：非物质文化遗产与物质文化遗产、自然遗产相互依存，是人类文化多样性的熔炉和可持续发展的重要保证。社会经济不断发展，全球化和社会转型为各群体之间开展新的对话创造了条件，同时也加大了对人类赖以生存和延续的自然文化资源的需求压力。但与之不匹配是缺少对自然文化资源的有效保护，尤其是与人民生活生产密不可分的大量非物质文化遗产。因此，联合国教科文组织于 2003 年 9 月 29 日至 10 月 17 日在巴黎举行的第 32 届会议上对原 1972 年的《公约》进行了有效的补充，充实了非物质文化遗产方面的新规定以及各项计划，并宣布"人类口头遗产和非物质遗产代表作"计划，认定了非物质文化遗产是密切人与人之间的关系，以及人与人之间进行交流和了解的要素，需要受到人类的共同保护。同时，承认了人 —— 无论是原住民、社会各群体还是个人，在非物质文化遗产的生产、保护、延续和再创造方面发挥的重要作用，从而为丰富文化多样性和人类创造性做出贡献。至此，具有国际约束力的保护非物质文化遗产的准则性多边文件正式形成。

二、非物质文化遗产的含义

相对于有形的可传承的物质遗产而言，非物质文化遗产又被称为"口头遗产"或"无形遗产"，它指的是源于某一种文化传统，涵盖语言知识、口头文学、音乐舞蹈、手工技艺、风俗习惯等各方面的全部创作形式，由某一群体或特定个体所表达，并被认为是符合该文化期望的文化与社会特性的表达形式。

根据《保护非物质文化遗产公约》定义：非物质文化遗产（Intangible Cultural Heritage）指的是被各社区、群体、团体或个人所视为是其文化遗产的各种实践、表演、表现形式、知识体系和技能，及其有关的工具、实物、工艺品和文化场所。各个群体和团体随着其所处环境、与自然界的相互关系和历史条件的变化，不断使这种代代相传的非物质文化遗产得到创新，同时使他们自己具有一种认同感和历史感，从而促进了文化多样性，激发了人类的创造力。因此可以这样总结，《保护非物质文化遗产公约》所定义的"非物质文化遗产"包括以下五个方面：① 口头传统和表现形式，包括作为非物质文化遗产媒介的语言；② 表演艺术；③ 社会实践、仪式、节庆活动；④ 有关自然界和宇宙的知识和实践；⑤ 传统手工艺。

基于《保护非物质文化遗产公约》的国际条款，中国于 2011 年 6 月颁布了《中华人民共和国非物质文化遗产法》（简称：《非遗法》），针对中国非物质文化遗产的保护、传承、开发与发展实际，进行了相应的中国化改造。根据《非遗法》规定：非物质文化遗产是指各族人民世代相传并视为其文化遗产组成部分的各种传统文化表现形式，以及与传统文化表现形式相关的实物和场所，即《非遗法》所规定的非物质文化遗产包括：① 传统口头文学以及作为其载体的语言；② 传统美术、书法、音乐、舞蹈、戏剧、曲艺和杂技；③ 传统技艺、医药和历法；④ 传统礼仪、节庆等民俗；⑤ 传统体育和游艺；⑥ 其他非物质文化遗产。《非遗法》补充说明道，属于非物质文化遗产组成部分的实物和场所，凡属文物的，适用《中华人民共和国文物保护法》的相关规定。

三、中国非物质文化遗产法的出台及解读

中国各族人民在漫长的历史发展中所创造的非物质文化遗产，绚丽多姿、异彩纷呈，是中华文化的瑰宝，是中华文脉的重要象征，也是发展国家文化软实力的重要资源。非物质文化遗产深深植根民间，世代传承于人民的生产生活之中，与人民群众的生产生活息息相关，与积淀于人们心中的文化印记紧密相连，蕴含着中华民族文化的精华，体现了中华民族薪火相传、自强不息的民族精神。保护非物质文化遗产，深入挖掘和充分展示非物质文化遗产的深刻内涵和重要价值，对增强中华民族的自信心和凝聚力，弘扬以爱国主义为核心的伟大民族精神，发挥着重大的作用。

中国的非物质文化遗产保护工作，萌芽于清末政府在学习借鉴国际做法基础上对物质文化遗产的保护，而立法保护真正开启于 20 世纪 90 年代。历经多年的探索与发展，2011 年 2 月 25 日，中华人民共和国第十一届全国人民代表大会常务委员会第十九次会议通过公布《中华人民共和国非物质文化遗产法》。这部法律的出台是为了继承和弘扬中华民族优秀传统文化，促进社会主义精神文明建设，加强非物质文化遗产保护和保存工作。

《非遗法》共六章四十五条，自 2011 年 6 月 1 日起施行。法律明

确，国家对非物质文化遗产采取认定、记录、建档等措施予以保存，对体现中华民族优秀传统文化，具有历史、文学、艺术、科学价值的非物质文化遗产采取传承、传播等措施予以保护，至此中国非遗保护工作真正有法可循。

法律规定，保护非物质文化遗产，应当注重其真实性、整体性和传承性，有利于增强中华民族的文化认同，有利于维护国家统一和民族团结，有利于促进社会和谐和可持续发展。

（一）出台背景

20世纪末，全国人大教科文卫委员会在通过数年对云南、四川、贵州、重庆、广西等地的民间艺术、传统工艺等进行调查后，向文化部提出了研究起草民族民间传统文化保护法的建议，并经文化部反复论证研究后，于2002年8月向全国人大教科文卫委员会报送了民族民间文化保护法的建议稿。

2003年10月，联合国教科文组织通过了《保护非物质文化遗产公约》。2004年8月，中国全国人大常委会批准加入《保护非物质文化遗产公约》。为了更好地与国际公约接轨，2005年开始，国家文化部成立了非物质文化遗产保护法立法工作小组，在总结实践经验、广泛调查研究的基础上，起草了《中华人民共和国非物质文化遗产保护法（草案送审稿）》，于2006年9月报请国务院审议。国务院法制工作机构在审查草案送审稿的过程中，会同有关部门进行了认真的修改和完善。2010年6月，温家宝总理主持召开国务院第115次常务会议，讨论通过了《中华人民共和国非物质文化遗产法（草案）》，并提请全国人民代表大会常务委员会审议。草案先后经过十一届全国人大常委会第十六次、第十八次和第十九次会议的三次审议，于2011年2月25日最终获表决通过，并予以公布，即中国现行的《中华人民共和国非物质文化遗产法》。

　　近年,中国的非物质文化遗产保护工作取得了积极的进展。自2005年开始的全国性大规模非物质文化遗产普查工作以来,通过大量走访民间艺人、普查文字记录、汇编普查资料和收集珍贵实物资料,中国基本完成了对全国范围的非物质文化遗产资源的统计。在党和政府的高度重视下,中国非物质文化遗产保护已然跻身世界前列。国务院先后于2006年、2008年、2011年、2014年和2021年公布了五批国家级项目名录,共计1557个国家级非物质文化遗产代表性项目。同时,将非遗项目分为十大门类:民间文学,传统音乐,传统舞蹈,传统戏剧,曲艺,传统体育、游艺与杂技,传统美术,传统技艺,传统医药,民俗。2007年、2008年、2009年、2012年、2018年,国家文化主管部门先后命名了五批国家级非物质文化遗产代表性项目代表性传承人,共计3068人。截至2018年12月,中国被列入联合国教科文组织非物质文化遗产名录(名册)项目共计40项,总数位居世界第一。其中,人类非物质文化遗产代表作32项(如昆曲、古琴艺术、新疆维吾尔木卡姆艺术和蒙古族长调民歌等);急需保护的非物质文化遗产名录6项(如羌年、中国木拱桥传统营造技艺、中国活字印刷术等);优秀实践名册1项(福建木偶戏后继人才培养计划)。非物质文化遗产项目的入选,体现了中国日益提高的履约能力和非物质文化遗产保护水平,对增强遗产实践社区、群体和个人的认同感和自豪感,激发传承保护的自觉性和积极性,在国际层面宣传和弘扬博大精深的中华文化、中国精神和中国智慧,都具有重要意义。

　　与此同时,中国社会各界和广大群众保护非物质文化遗产的意识大大增强,非物质文化遗产保护工作产生的社会影响日益增长。非物质文化遗产保护工作是一项长期而艰巨的任务,全球化进程中,随着工业化、城市化、国际化的步伐加快,源于农耕文明、主要靠口传心授方式传承的非物质文化遗产的生存土壤及生态环境受到了严重冲击，面临着巨大的生存危机。非物质文化遗产的保护工作任重道远，需要通过立法明确相关保护制度，促进全社会全人类的共同保护。《中华人民共和国非物质文化遗产法》的出台，成为了中国非物质文化遗产保护的一个里程碑，标志着中国非物质文化遗产保护进入了依法保护的阶段。立法前，中国在非物质文化遗产保护方面已经做了大量的探索工作（如非遗普查、传承人保护、文化生态区保护等），而《非遗法》给予保护工作以法律依据。只有"依法保护"，才能真正进行强有力的科学保护，推动中国非遗保护工作不断前进。

（二）主要内容

《中华人民共和国非物质文化遗产法》共六章四十五条。第一章为"总则"，明确了本法的对象，对不同的非物质文化遗产分别采取不同的保护原则和措施。第二章为"非物质文化遗产的调查"，规定了县级以上人民政府开展非物质文化遗产调查的工作职责，对境外组织或个人在中华人民共和国境内进行非物质文化遗产调查也做出了具体规定。第三章为"非物质文化遗产代表性项目名录"，规定了建立非物质文化遗产代表性项目名录的政府层级、程序规范以及对名录项目的各种保护措施，并确立了对非物质文化遗产代表性项目集中、特色鲜明、形式和内涵保持完整的特定区域实行区域性整体保护的制度。第四章为"非物质文化遗产的传承与传播"，确立了非物质文化遗产代表性项目的代表性传承人认定制度和支持措施，规定了各级人民政府及其部门负责宣传非物质文化遗产、鼓励支持开展相关科研活动、设立专题博物馆和传承场所、支持合理利用非物质文化遗产代表性项目开发文化产品和文化服务等职责，以及学校、新闻媒体、公共文化机构等在教育、传播非物质文化遗产方面的责任等。此外，第五章还对违反本法有关规定的行为明确了相应的法律责任。

《非遗法》在《公约》基础上进一步落实了中国的非物质文化遗产各项规定，是《公约》的具体落地和显性拓展。《非遗法》有针对性地极大地丰富了《公约》中较广义和泛指的内容，为中国非物质文化遗产的保护工作提供了相对切实可行的操作方向，占据着中国非物质文化遗产保护各类法律体系中举足轻重的主导地位。要说《公约》体现的是国际的共同精神意志，《非遗法》则表明的是中华民族本身的信念财富，适应于中华民族文化的或显性或隐性的政策法律、观察于中国非物质文化遗产保护的各项地方措施和行动之中，提出了中国非物质文化遗产保护的基本原则，填补了中国非物质文化遗产保护的法律空白。

第一，《非遗法》具体化了《公约》对非物质文化遗产的概念。《非遗法》指出非物质文化遗产是指各族人民世代相传，并视为其文化遗产组成部分的各种传统文化表现形式，以及与传统文化表现形式相关的实物和场所。非物质文化遗产世代相传，在各社区和群体适应周围环境以及与自然和历史的互动中，被不断地再创造，为这些社区和群体提供认同感和持续感，充分显示了对文化多样性和人类创造力的尊重。

《非遗法》规定的非物质文化遗产的概念，既遵从了《公约》所体现的基本理念，又侧重强调了中国非物质文化遗产本身所具有的三个关键特点：

一是非物质文化遗产是世代相传的。非物质文化遗产是在一个地区、一个族群内通过口传心授或者不断反复进行等方式世代相传延续下来的，具有活态传承的特点。例如，中国传统节日春节，具有几千年历史，世代相传至今，已经成为中华民族的一项重要文化遗产，每一名炎黄子孙都把春节作为每年的重要节日进行庆祝。换句话说，春节这一非物质文化遗产就是通过从古至今的每年庆祝的方式相传下来的。

二是非物质文化遗产与人民群众的生产生活密不可分。非物质文化遗产是人民群众在生产生活中创造的，其本身就是人们生产生活的一部分，如刺绣、编织、剪纸、风筝、酿酒等非物质文化遗产都来源于人们的日常生活，又如民俗活动，本身就是人民群众日常生活中形成的各种风俗习惯。

三是非物质文化遗产由文化表现形式及相关的实物和场所组成。文化总是以各种形式表现出来，中国传统文化具有非常丰富的表现形式，如传统音乐、舞蹈、戏剧、曲艺和杂技等人们喜闻乐见的表演艺术，它们本身就是一种文化表现形式。作为一种表现形式，其本身是非物质的，但却离不开物质的载体，所以实物和场所也是非物质文化遗产的组成部分。例如，非物质文化遗产的传统戏剧在演出时所使用的行头、道具，伴奏乐器等都是实物，另外还有戏剧演出舞台，即场所。

第二，《非遗法》将《公约》原有的范围由五个拓展为六个，并在拓展中有针对性地将范围转化成适用于中国非物质文化遗产的内容。尤其将《公约》中所谓的"表演艺术"转变为"传统美术、书法、音乐、舞蹈、戏剧、曲艺和杂技"，以及"传统体育和游艺"，是《非遗法》对《公约》的中国特色化发展。中国历史悠久、民族众多，各民族的表演艺术形式丰富多彩、底蕴深厚，例如雕塑、剪纸、盆景技艺、木版年画、刺绣、灯彩等的传统美术；汉字书法和少数民族文字书法等传统书法；民歌、弦索乐、丝竹乐、吹管乐、鼓吹乐和吹打乐等乐器音乐，以及说唱音乐、戏曲音乐等传统音乐；使用于各种仪式性场合的传统舞蹈，大到国家的祭祀、朝会、出战、庆功、王室更替，小到百姓婚丧嫁娶、播种收割等均有适用于该仪式的舞蹈；以及用歌舞演故事为主体的综合舞台艺术形式等传统戏剧。据资料记载，中国的传统戏曲有 390 多种，如今还在传承的大约有 260 多种，如京剧、曲剧、昆曲、沪剧、评剧、黄梅戏、越剧等。还有以民间讲唱文学为基础的传统曲艺，将讲唱文学、音乐、表演三者融合在一起的中国传统艺术，包括相声、评书、大鼓等。而起源于秦朝"角抵戏"的传统杂技，经过几千年的传承发展，已从简单的技巧表演发展为有乐队、舞蹈、灯光等配合的综合表演艺术。

第三，《非遗法》规定了中国非物质文化遗产保护的原则和措施，将《公约》原有的"保护"概念拓展为对不同非物质文化遗产分别进行"保护"与"保存"两方面的内容。

《公约》的全称为《保护世界文化和自然遗产公约》，名称中的"保护"一词在中文中指的是"尽力照顾使其权益不受损害"。而中国《非遗法》的名称为《中华人民共和国非物质文化遗产法》，并没有加入"保护"二字，为的是避免由于"保护"一词的意思局限性，导致公众产生对所有的非物质文化遗产不加区分地一律进行保护的误解。

因此《非遗法》的第三条规定中提出：国家对非物质文化遗产采取认定、记录、建档等措施予以保存，对体现中华民族优秀传统文化，具有历史、文学、艺术、科学价值的非物质文化遗产采取传承、传播等措施予以保护。条款明确了中国非物质文化遗产保护工作的基本原则，即是对不同对象选用不同的"保护"或"保存"的方式，使其不受损失或不发生变化。

第四，《非遗法》在原有《公约》的基础上，增加规定了中国公共文化机构等在非物质文化遗产工作方面的责任，强调了中国非物质文化遗产保护的公共文化自觉性与全社会的参与性，确定了特定机构应当结合具体业务，开展非物质文化遗产保护的法律义务。例如第三十五条所规定的"图书馆、文化馆、博物馆、科技馆等公共文化机构和非物质文化遗产学术研究机构、保护机构以及利用财政性资金举办的文艺表演团体、演出场所经营单位等，应当根据各自业务范围，开展非物质文化遗产的整理、研究、学术交流和非物质文化遗产代表性项目的宣传、展示"。

非物质文化遗产的保存与保护除了需要唤起社会大众的文化自觉，更需要具备较强的专业性和科学性，因此非物质文化遗产的整理、研究、展示、交流、宣传需要合适的依托和专业的平台。按照条款规定，中国的公共文化机构、专业学术机构、利用财政性资金举办的演艺团体等，应当充分发挥其在非物质文化遗产保护中的作用，以推进非物质文化遗产的传承与传播。国务院办公厅《关于加强我国非物质文化遗产保护工作的意见》还指出，各级图书馆、文化馆、博物馆、科技馆等公共文化机构要积极开展对非物质文化遗产的传播和展示，通过举办展览、论坛、讲座等活动，使公众更多地了解文化遗产的丰富内涵。

首先，公共文化机构具有非物质文化遗产保护义务。

公共文化机构的功能之一，就是收集、加工、整理、科学管理具有一定价值的实物、文献等资源，以便公众参观、学习和使用。图书馆、文化馆、博物馆、科技馆作为主要的公共文化服务机构，能够也应当为保护非物质文化遗产发挥重要作用。

第一，图书馆作为公共文化服务体系的重要组成部分，承担着保存人类文化遗产、开展社会教育、传播公共知识以及开发智力资源的重要职责。国际图书馆统计标准将图书馆划分为国家图书馆、高等院校图书馆、其他主要的非专门图书馆、学校图书馆、专门图书馆和公共图书馆六大类。基于此，图书馆可以通过多种形式来落实保护非物质文化遗产义务，如关注并采购有关非物质文化遗产的图书、音像资料；开辟专区，将馆藏中的有关非物质文化遗产的部分集中展示；组织专门力量，摘录、分析、研究馆藏中有关非物质文化遗产的资料，并进行系统性再加工；举办有关非物质文化遗产的报告、展览等。

第二，文化馆是普及科学文化知识、开展社会教育、提高群众文化素质的文化活动场所。目前中国县级以上地方政府基本都有文化馆，其主要职能是：举办丰富多彩、形式多样的展览、讲座、培训等，促进精神文明建设；开展群众喜闻乐见的文化活动和流动文化服务；指导群众业余文艺团队建设，辅导和培训群众文艺骨干；组织并指导群众文艺创作，开展群众文化工作理论研究；开展对外民间文化交流等。文化馆开展非物质文化遗产保护，应该注意发挥自身服务基层、贴近群众的特点和优势，尤其注重收集、整理、研究本地区的非物质文化遗产，并开展相应的普查、展示、宣传活动。

第三，博物馆是历史记忆的储藏库，主要通过实物的收藏、研究、陈列、展览来保存和宣传历史文化，实现对人们的爱国主义教育、乡土教育、历史教育、文明礼仪教育。博物馆所收藏、陈列的物品、资料都是历史文化的载体，具有不可再生性和不可替代性。现代博物馆按照主藏品和定位的不同可分为历史类、遗址类、艺术类、纪念类、自然科学类、民族民俗类、综合类、专题类等。对于保护非物质文化遗产，博物馆可以扮演重要的角色。因此，博物馆落实保护非物质文化遗产的义务，可以重点收集、利用、展示与非物质文化遗产相关的实物、空间场所，并在此基础上开展其他形式的保护活动。

第四，科技馆的功能主要是通过科学性、知识性、趣味性相结合的展览，反映科学原理及技术应用，培养公众的科学思想、科学方法和科学精神。对于非物质文化遗产来说，其中包含了大量科技性的内容，科技馆可以在陈列布局中重点规划、实施这些与非物质文化遗产有关的展览。

其次，有关学术研究机构、保护机构、利用财政性资金举办的演艺机构亦具有非物质文化遗产保护义务。

非物质文化遗产学术机构包括专题研究所、社会科学研究机构、开设非物质文化遗产学术研究课程的高等学校等，其特点是拥有丰富的知识和智力资源，有研究的积累和理论视野，能够推动保护工作有序深入地开展。但与此同时，非物质文化遗产的保护机构需要具有很强的专业性和实践性，利用财政性资金举办的演艺机构对类似戏剧、音乐等非物质文化遗产项目的传承具有不可替代作用。这些机构应当充分发挥自身的特色和优势，相互交流，根据各自业务范围，开展非物质文化遗产的整理、研究、学术交流和非物质文化遗产代表性项目的宣传、展示。

四、四川省非物质文化遗产政策及解读

自 2011 年《中华人民共和国非物质文化遗产法》颁布实施以来，四川省按照国家"保护为主、抢救第一、合理利用、传承发展"非物质文化遗产保护的十六字方针，持续发力，推动四川省非遗立法工作。省委、省政府相继出台了《四川省非物质文化遗产条例》《关于传承发展中华优秀传统文化的实施意见》《四川省传统工艺振兴实施计划》《四川省非物质文化遗产传承发展工程实施方案》等法规和规范性文件，初步构建起具有四川特色的非遗保护工作新格局。

2017 年 6 月 3 日，四川省第十二届人民代表大会常务委员会第三十三次会议通过《四川省非物质文化遗产条例》并于 2017 年 9 月 1 日起施行。《条例》将全省非遗保护工作经验上升为政府意志和责任，并纳入法制化保障体系。同时为深入贯彻中央办公厅、国务院办公厅印发的《关于实施中华优秀传统文化传承发展工程的意见》（中办发〔2017〕5 号）精神，延续中华优秀传统文化中四川文化发展脉络，提升人民群众文化素养，坚定文化自信，增强四川文化软实力，结合四

川省实际颁布《关于传承发展中华优秀传统文化的实施意见》，在坚持传承发展为主要目标基础上，梳理出四川省传承发展优秀传统文化主要项目，其中四川省非物质文化遗产传承发展工程被列为了主要项目之一。

随着四川省非物质文化遗产的保护传承工作的展开，四川省非遗保护与传承发展体系得到不断完善，2018年《中国传统工艺振兴计划》提出，计划在四川省实施一批传统工艺振兴重点项目、建设一批传统工艺产品孵化基地、培训一批传统工艺优秀工匠、打造一批具有鲜明四川特色的传统工艺精品，形成具有四川特色的传统工艺振兴体系，并公布四川省第一批传统工艺振兴目录。2019年《四川省非物质文化遗产传承发展工程实施方案》制定并印发，具体要求加大非遗保护传承创新发展力度，推动非遗保护传承见人见物见生活，让非遗保护成果更好地惠及广大民众，为加快建设文化强省旅游强省做出更大贡献。同时提出非物质文化遗产的传承发展目标：到2025年全省非遗保护工作体制机制更加健全，非遗保护名录体系更加完备，国家级和省级非遗项目得到有效保护，最终使四川非遗保护传承、发展利用水平步入全国前列。至此，具有四川省特色的非遗保护传承与发展的政策保障与工作方案得以初步构建。相比其他地区而言，四川省的非物质文化遗产保护工作最大的特点是活态传承，非遗传承发展坚持"创新传承、融合发展、彰显特色、见人见物见生活"四个统领基本原则，保护与利用并举。在加大保护力度的同时促进非遗资源转化，创新非遗形态和表达方式，提高四川非遗传承创新能力，发挥非遗资源优势和多重价值，促进与旅游深度融合与发展。要求在文旅融合大背景下，保护和利用各地特色非遗资源大力发展地方文化旅游业，将四川独特的非遗资源转化为具有地方特色的产品和服务。挖掘传统民俗节庆活动的文化内涵，例如四川省成都市崇州市道明镇竹艺村、四川省德阳市绵竹年画村等以刺绣、年画、竹编、陶艺等为主要特色的传统乡镇和传统村落，以及非遗小镇、非遗特色乡村的建设工作。四川非遗文化传承和保护以打造旅游目的地为目标，围绕观光旅游、乡村旅游、生态旅游、休闲旅游等方面开发特色非遗旅游线路及非遗产品，提升食、住、行、游、购、娱各个旅游环节的文化内涵，扩大诸如"自贡灯会""彝族火把节""羌年"等国家级、省级非遗项目的知名度和影响力，加强四川独有非遗项目的推广力度，推动非遗"走出去"，彰显巴蜀文化和四川以藏羌彝为代表的民族文化的独特魅力，打造具有地方特色和民族特色的文化旅游品牌。同时，尊重非遗传承人群的主体地位和创造性表达权利，加大传承人培训力度，提升传承人的传承能力和内生动力，促进非遗融入当代生活，使四川非遗"看得见摸得到"，以"见人见物见生活"来持续增强其生命力和传承活力，并实现非遗发展和振兴。

第二章
四川非遗文化保护与传承现状

四川省非物质文化遗产资源丰富多样，以古蜀文化与藏、羌、彝民族文化为核心，以历史文明渊源深厚、区域文化特色显著、历史遗产荟萃丰富、古蜀文化兼容多元、民族文化绚丽多姿等为特点，文化魅力独特。近年来，四川非遗保护硕果累累。目前，四川省已有联合国教科文组织非遗名录项目7项，国家级非遗代表性项目153项、省级611项。历届中国成都国际非物质文化遗产节成功举办，"文化和自然遗产日"宣传展示活动高潮迭起、精彩纷呈。

一、非遗文化保护传承机制逐步完善

非物质文化遗产属于不可再生的珍贵资源，随着时代的发展和现代化进程地推进，加强非物质文化遗产的保护工作刻不容缓。近年来，四川省按照国家"保护为主、抢救第一、合理利用、传承发展"的非物质文化遗产保护工作方针，各地各部门高度重视，以强大的责任感和紧迫感，结合具体实际采取切实措施，持续推动四川省非遗文化保护传承机制的逐步完善。

（一）制度建设以保障非遗工作的科学保护与传承

近年来，四川省各级政府与文化行政部门高度重视四川省非物质文化遗产保护与传承工作的制度建设，着力建立健全科学的、具备根本性、全局性、稳定性和长期性的制度体系，以保障各项工作的稳步推进。四川省先后出台了多项法规、规章和规范性文件，如《四川省非物质文化遗产条例》《关于传承发展中华优秀传统文化的实施意见》《四川省传统工艺振兴实施计划》《四川省非物质文化遗产传承发展工程实施方案》等法律法规和规范性文件。通过规范非遗工作的主体、内容、程序等内容，用律法的约束性保障四川省非物质文化遗产的保护与传承工作，构建科学的规则体系和运行机制，维护四川非遗工作的规范性，引领和推动四川非遗的科学传承与发展。

此外，四川省各地也纷纷制定适用于自己的地方非遗保护工作实施细则，四川省从省政府到地方单位形成由上至下多极化的非遗工作运作机制，构建起了极具四川特色的非遗保护工作新格局。例如凉山州、阿坝州、甘孜州、绵阳市北川县等地先后出台了适用于本地区的非遗条例，依法开展保护工作并已积累了一定的经验。多项科学的法律法规和规范性文件为四川省的非遗保护工作提供了强制手段和制度保障，确保各项工作严格落实、有效运转。

同时，建立健全执行制度，各级文化行政部门充分发挥主导作用，与有关单位分工负责，加强协调，切实履行职能。根据有关法律法规和政府赋予的职能，制定责任清单，明确路线图、时间表，形成主体清晰、权责统一、各司其职、各负其责的工作格局，保证非遗工作各项任务的具体落实，实施行业管理，合力推进四川省非物质文化遗产的保护与传承工作。

（二）财政支持以提供非遗保护的资金保障

近年来，国家十分重视对非遗保护的财政保障。"十三五"期间，"国家非物质文化遗产保护利用设施建设"被列入"十三五"时期文化和自然遗产保护设施建设规划，国家发展改革委安排中央预算对全国的非遗保护利用基础设施建设提供投资支持。四川省亦从经费投入方面对全省的非遗保护与传承进行支持，同时积极推进政府购买服务，为非遗保护相关工作提供资金保障。

一是加大对四川非遗保护的投入经费，将非物质文化遗产保护传承工作纳入国民经济和社会发展规划,将保护传承经费列入财政预算。对四川省非物质文化遗产项目代表性传承人与非物质文化遗产项目申报给予补助，对非遗代表性项目的收藏、展示和传播活动提供场地与经费资助。特别对受众较广泛、活态传承较好的非遗项目，通过认定传承人、培育或扶持传承基地等方式，实行传承性保护，并资助传承人和传承基地在开展传承活动时所必要的经费。如今，省财政用于非遗保护的专项资金达每年1800余万元，对每个省级传承人每年给予5000元传习补助经费。成都、绵阳、泸州、攀枝花等市州还专门设立了传承人专项补助经费。

二是积极推进政府购买服务。四川各级地方人民政府和文化主管部门将非物质文化遗产传播与农村文化、社区文化、校园文化、企业文化、家庭文化建设相结合，丰富地方优秀公共文化产品服务与供给。与此同时，为进一步支持文化惠民工程，支持非物质文化遗产的传承，将满足地方群众公共文化服务需求的非遗代表性项目的传承与展示活动列入地方人民政府向社会力量购买公共文化服务的指导性目录。各级财政部门通过调整支出结构、盘活存量资金等方式，加大政府购买公共文化服务力度，以购买公共文化演出方式支持非遗展演等活动，在满足群众日常文化需求的同时，有益于文化惠民、艺术普及和非遗传承。

三是探索四川省非遗产业化发展模式，利用商业价值与产品收入以反哺非遗。针对具有市场需求与开发潜力的非遗传统技艺、美术、医药类等特色项目，在保护非物质文化遗产核心价值的基础上，发挥资源特殊优势，进行非遗再创造，开发文创产品，获得收益的同时实现非遗的可持续传承。

（三）汇聚社会合力以提供非遗保护的社会保障

四川省的非遗保护传承坚持全员参与性，把四川非遗传承发展的各项任务落实到农村、企业、社区、机关、学校等城乡基层，全社会形成合力。各类文化单位与文化阵地平台均担负起守护、传播和弘扬四川非遗文化的职责。各企业和社会组织积极参与非遗文化资源的开发、保护与利用，生产丰富多样、社会价值和市场价值相统一、人民喜闻乐见的优质非遗文化产品，扩大中高端产品和服务的供给。同时，充分尊重工人、农民、知识分子的主体地位，发挥社会各群体的积极作用，形成人人传承发展非遗文化的生动局面。

二、非物质文化遗产保护初见成效

全省各市县积极组织非遗项目申报国家级、省级非遗项目名录，积极推进乡村国家级、省级非遗代表性传承人抢救性记录工程并取得显著成效。近年来四川省积极利用非遗资源、音乐舞蹈、传统手工技艺等亮丽名片，加大非遗保护与乡村振兴、脱贫攻坚地有机结合。全省传统工艺振兴计划稳步实施，不断为非物质文化遗产发展增动能、添活力。

（一）出台条例，组织管理

自 2005 年中国启动非遗保护工作，至今已逾 16 年。经过不懈努力，四川省以非遗代表性名录项目多、代表性传承人多、资源类型丰富，成为全国的非遗资源大省。四川省省委、省政府结合全省实际情况，采取多项措施落实与持续推动四川非遗保护工作，四川省绝大部分地方都建立了非遗文化安全巡查、机构人员保障、配套资金落实等专项制度。同时，逐步完善省、市（州）、县三级非遗保护工作机构和工作队伍，并陆续公布了一批非遗保护规划。

四川省考虑到四川非遗保护任务重的地区大多为少数民族地区和连片贫困地区，提出将非遗护工作与脱贫攻坚、乡村振兴相结合的战略思路，加大四川非遗的保护与传承工作力度，厘清非遗资源存量，落实非遗保护措施，培养非遗后继人才，培育非遗创新发展，开发非遗商业产品，建立非遗生态保护区，打造非遗文化旅游目的地。

2017 年，颁布与实施四川省非遗保护重要文件《四川省非物质文化遗产条例》，在充分总结四川非遗保护工作经验与教训的基础上，注重基本概念、保护原则、工作程序与上级主管部门的法规对接，立足全省保护工作实际，强调非遗工作全民参与，具有较强的针对性和可操作性。除此之外，在国家和省级文化及相关部门的指导下，四川省结合国家文化传承与非遗保护各项法律、法规和规范性文件，编制出《关于传承发展中华优秀传统文化的实施意见》《四川省传统工艺振兴实施计划》《四川省非物质文化遗产传承发展工程实施方案》等文件章程，从原则、目标、文化规划、开发项目、实施步骤、具体措施以及保障机制等方面全方位对四川省非遗代表性项目的保护与传承工作进行了阐述。同时，实施省级非遗代表性传承人记录工程（2018—2020），对 65 岁以上省级非遗代表性传承人进行抢救性记录；建立非遗资源数据库，对已有非遗档案进行数字化转换。为抢救保护、传承弘扬四川非遗文化提供了科学客观、切实可行的理论保障。

（二）非遗认识不断提高，保护传承意识持续增强

非物质文化遗产与人们社会生活息息相关，非物质文化遗产保护工作是一项长期、复杂和艰巨的综合性系统工程，并非一朝一夕能够完成。四川省各地区针对不同非遗项目和地方特色，根据实际情况采取与之适应的保护措施，调动和发挥各方面的积极性，完善保护与传承机制，营造积极的保护与传承环境，不断延续四川非遗的生命活力。

以"保护为主、抢救第一、合理开发、充分利用"为指导方针，四川省不断加强对非物质文化遗产保护工作的协调和管理对具有重要价值的非遗代表性项目与传承人，在政策与资金上给予重点扶持；设置非遗传习所与生态保护区，展示与传播特色非遗项目；鼓励非遗传承人开班授徒，培养一批新型的传承人等。同时加大宣传，合理利用，积极推动非遗与文化产业、文化旅游结合，开发旅游产品，形成四川各地独具特色的地域文化品牌。在全省各项工作推进过程中，保护与传承效果较为显著，社会参与度越来越高，宣传活动广泛开展，对非物质文化遗产的保护意识渐入人心，为传承四川文脉，繁荣文化，促

进社会经济发展做出了积极的贡献。

（三）非遗文化资源的挖掘与整理

《四川省非物质文化遗产条例》确立了"县级以上人民政府"在非遗保护中为"责任主体"。县级以上地方人民政府文化主管部门负责非物质文化遗产调查，全面掌握其种类、数量、分布、生存环境、保护现状等情况。在非遗文化资源的挖掘与整理实施过程中，以挖掘特色、整合资源和提升价值为核心内容，有效延展四川非遗文化的生命力。

一是摸清非遗文化资源家底。组织开展全省非遗文化资源普查，对非遗文化资源种类、存量、分布、存在环境和保护现状等进行调查；对非物质文化遗产资源进行备案登记，为进一步研究和探索非遗文化提供依据。

二是开展非遗文化资源整理分类。坚持"普查、宣传、保护、传承"八字方针，开展全省各类非遗文化资源的分类整理和登记造册等工作。建立四川非遗文化资源库，完善全省非遗项目代表性目录及传承人普查、修复和保存工作机制；建造一批四川特色的非遗文化展室、传习所、传习中心等。

三是挖掘非遗文化资源特色。结合四川省的实际情况，有针对性地对非遗项目开展深入、系统、客观的调查与挖掘，对一系列古老的尤其是以巴蜀文化和藏羌彝少数民族非遗资源所承载的历史文化追根溯源进行整理、研究，理清历史发展脉络，科学分析和深度挖掘全省各地各类非遗文化的特色，优化四川非遗文化资源配置水平。

四是整合非遗文化资源。坚持开放融合理念，发挥四川非遗资源的集聚效应，全面统筹全省非遗文化建设，整体推进四川非遗文化资源有效整合和要素合理配置，着力推动四川省非遗文化资源利用转化向优质高效转变，着力提高四川非遗文化产业规模化、集约化、专业化发展水平。

五是提升非遗文化价值。创造性转化四川非遗文化资源，大力提升传统手工技艺、民俗活动、民间文学、民间音乐、民间舞蹈、传统美术、人生礼俗、民间信仰等非遗文化的价值，探索多种途径，因地制宜地让四川非遗文化资源"活"起来，提升其有效利用和创造转化水平。牢固树立"文化+"的概念，发展非遗文化新业态，培育非遗文化原创力，充分发挥非遗文化促进四川精神文明建设、推动非遗经济转型发展和提质增效的作用。

三、非遗文化活动深入开展

（一）深抓非遗宣传展示，让非遗走进生活

为促进四川非遗文化走进人民群众的生产和生活，四川省各界充分利用文化和自然遗产日、中国成都国际非遗节、中国非遗博览会等重大非遗文化节，组织非遗项目参加各类展示交流活动，宣传展示四川非遗魅力和保护成果。

一是建设中国非物质文化遗产主题公园。2007年，中国非物质文化遗产主题公园落户四川省成都市金牛区两河城市森林。按照"传承历史文脉、保护文化遗产、融入生活方式、守望精神家园"的原则，公园建设坚持"与生态保护相结合、与产业化相结合、与市场化相结合"，着力打造成文化内涵丰富、生态环境优美、人文与自然和谐相处的中国非物质文化遗产保护基地、全国文化产业示范基地、国家AAAA/AAAAA级文化旅游景区、青少年爱国主义教育基地。按照国务院公布的中国第一批非物质文化遗产项目分成民间文学、民间音乐、民间舞蹈、传统戏剧、曲艺杂技与竞技、民间美术、传统手工艺、传统中医、民俗10大类别，主题公园划分为10个聚落，即中国民间文

学聚落、中国民间音乐聚落、中国民间舞蹈聚落、中国地方戏剧聚落、中国曲艺聚落、中国传统竞技聚落、中国民间美术聚落、中国民间工艺聚落、中国中医药聚落和中国民俗风情聚落，每一个聚落都代表一种类别。按照保护性原则、独特性地域性原则、阶段性原则、产业化原则，在每一类别中选择 2～10 个具有代表性并能实现互动体验效果的文化产业项目。主题公园内还打造了"百卷楼""百工坊""百戏城""百草堂""百趣园""百闲河""百味街""百客栈"等"八百工程"。不仅如此，主题公园还重视突出人的参与性，通过功能分区和特色项目立体展示非遗文化，形成独特的文化感观和景区吸引力，主要分为展示区、体验区、展销区、文化景观区和商业服务区五大功能区。如今，非物质文化遗产国家公园已然承担了保护、研究、展示各类非物质文化遗产的载体功能，成为中国非物质文化遗产集中展示区，是中国成都国际非物质文化遗产节的重要组成部分，在遗产节期间承担举办一系列丰富多彩展演活动的任务。

二是办好中国成都国际非物质文化遗产节。2006年经国务院批准，在国家文化部的大力支持下，中国成都国际非遗节落户四川成都。中国成都国际非遗节是全中国唯一以非遗为主题的大型国际文化节，也是联合国教科文组织持续参与主办的国内唯一的国际文化活动，更是四川省唯一的国家级文化艺术节。两年一届的成都国际非遗节，向人们呈现来自世界各国和全国各地精彩纷呈、独具魅力的非物质文化遗产，向国际社会彰显中国政府在非遗保护领域所做的巨大努力以及取得的丰硕成果,对于提升公众的非遗保护意识和全社会参与非遗保护的水平，做出了积极而重要的贡献。中国成都国际非遗节以非遗为主题，形成国际非遗论坛、非遗国际大展、传统表演艺术展演、非遗项目竞技、非遗节分会场活动、非遗社区实践、非遗节国际推广七大类品牌活动。成都国际非遗节期间活动丰富、形式多样、贴近民众，主要包括天府大巡游、非遗博览会、国际论坛、戏剧精品展演、分会场及配套活动等，吸引广大民众和中外游客踊跃参加。

四川省以高度的文化自觉和文化自信，抢占世界和全国非遗保护的主动权和制高点，让非遗节真正成为"文化的盛会和民众的节日"。非遗节的持续举办，对于扩大对外文化交流，扩大中华文化影响力，宣传展示中国特别是四川的优秀传统文化保护成果，在提升四川国际知名度和美誉度方面，发挥了积极重要的作用。

三是契合文化与遗产日，促进非遗走进生活。每年 6 月份的第二个星期六，是我国的"文化和自然遗产日"。2020 年文化和自然遗产日四川非遗宣传展示活动的主题为"非遗传承 健康生活"，期间开展了 240 余场四川非遗宣传展示系列活动，重点突出了非遗在人民大众生活中发挥的重要作用，围绕非遗走近民众生活、守护民众健康，展示我省非遗独特魅力及保护成果，普及非遗知识和健康生活理念，大力弘扬中华优秀传统文化，坚定文化自信，营造全社会共同参与、关注、保护和传承优秀传统文化的浓厚氛围，推动优秀传统文化传承和非遗创新实践。

由于受疫情影响，2020 年非遗宣传展示活动以网络平台为主、线上线下相结合的方式开展。"文化和遗产日"期间，全省各地各具特色、内容丰富的非遗宣传展示活动，或通过互联网，或深入社区、走近乡村，将优秀传统文化的精髓带到民众身边，营造全社会共同参与、关注、保护和传承优秀传统文化的浓厚氛围。例如，6 月 13 日至 7 月 12 日，四川省图书馆举办了《非遗传承 健康生活 —— 中医药之美主题展》，期间还每周举办健康系列线上讲座、沙龙，将中医药健康知识带到了群众身边；成都在街子古镇举办了首届成都非遗美食节；南充、广元、德阳等地组织了各区（县）领导在非遗购物节中为本地非遗产品代言，进行直播带货活动；甘孜州在成都宽窄巷子举办了《雪域匠心》影像展暨非遗手工艺品、文创产品展示、展播、展销，还开展了网络直播带货活动；阿坝州组织了全州非遗扶贫工坊负责人进行电商平台展示展销培训，并在茂县古羌城举办主场展示展演活动。

2020 年，疫情开拓线上非遗传播与传承新的"云"的示范。第一，以"云上·四川非遗影像展"为代表的"云展演"，分"非一般的匠心""非一般的韵律""非一般的味道" 3 个篇章，向广大观众呈现非遗传统技艺精品视频、《蜀风遗韵》非遗精品展演、川菜知识及经典菜品制作教程等精彩内容；第二，川渝两地非遗保护积极融入成渝双城经济圈国家战略，在活动期间紧密合作，同步在淘宝上线川渝非遗好物专场，并以"拼接海报"和"视频稿件"的形式实现川渝非遗"云相聚"，传递巴蜀两地联动打造非遗品牌、共同保护传承非遗的心声和理念；第三，还有首届"四川非遗购物节"的举办，联合了四川省在阿里、京东、拼多多、东家、快手、美团、苏宁等 10 余家电商平台，汇聚了全省 100 余位非遗传承人、139 个非遗扶贫就业工坊、500 余家非遗店铺及相关企业、5000 余种四川非遗特色产品共同参与非遗"云消费"。不仅如此，淘宝、拼多多还推出了四川非遗购物专场，美团举办了非遗美食节活动，携程也上线了"跟着非遗游四川"四川非遗之旅精选产品。

（二）非遗进社区，公共文化融入非遗元素

一是推动非遗融入生活。四川省大力实施传统工艺振兴计划，积极推动制定《四川省传统工艺振兴实施计划》，积极践行非遗保护"见人见物见生活"的理念，承办了全国竹编、刺绣等传统工艺技艺大赛，支持各级非遗代表性传承人带徒授艺，加强四川非遗新生代传承人的培养。中央美术学院驻四川成都传统工艺工作站正式设立，将按照"跨界融合、品牌引领"思路，推动四川传统工艺振兴，推进以传统工艺

为特色的文创产业集聚发展。川北大木偶将传统工艺与现代科技完美融合，创作的"熊猫大队长"形象闪亮平昌冬奥会闭幕式"北京八分钟"，为中国和四川赢得荣誉，让四川的名字响彻全世界。

二是公共文化融入非遗元素。四川省文化历史悠久、底蕴厚重，各类非遗文化资源富足，省委、省政府高度重视非遗文化的弘扬宣传与保护工作，结合地方实际情况，在多地的公共文化融入非遗元素，将非遗成为真正的"见人见物见生活"、人民群众主动积极参与的基本文化生活。

例如在阿坝州茂县，非遗文化即是人人参与的公共文化。作为茂县羌民族的公共文化核心，茂县非遗文化已经融入人民群众的生活中，非遗元素几乎处处可见。近年来，茂县大量开展各种非遗民俗活动，结合"羌年""瓦尔俄足""转山会"等茂县非遗项目举办羌语比赛、羌族选美、羌族服饰设计大赛等；大量民间文化协会、民间文艺表演队伍、文化服务志愿者参与其中，更不用说茂县非遗"羌族萨朗"与市民广场舞融为一体的"坝坝舞"，在极大丰富茂县人民群众精神文化生活的同时，茂县非遗文化也得到了保护与传承。

三是促进文旅融合发展。有效发挥民俗文化优势，把保护民俗文化和发展经济有机结合，与建设幸福美丽家园有机结合，同发展文化旅游产业有机结合，用旅游带动民俗资源的保护传承，实现文化与经济社会发展协调互进，带动当地群众就业增收。将非遗资源与当地民俗节庆活动结合，举办藏历年、羌历年、绵竹年画节、彝族火把节、都江堰放水节等各类民俗节庆活动，实现了民族文化与旅游的有机融合，实现了非遗保护与旅游业发展的良性互动，提升了四川文化旅游业的影响力和竞争力。

四是非遗助推文化脱贫。全省各地将非遗资源与振兴传统工艺、乡村振兴、文化产业发展有机结合，在有效保护的基础上，充分发挥蜀绣、羌绣、竹编、唐卡等传统工艺带动贫困地区群众就近就业、居家就业的独特优势，实施技艺创新、人才培养，吸引当地群众主动参与传统技能学习培训，非遗助推扶贫已形成气候和良好态势。

（三）加强传承人培养传承，不断增强非遗传承发展后劲

非遗项目代表性传承人是非物质文化遗产的重要载体，是保护和弘扬民族文化的重要阵地，因此保护传承人是非遗保护工作最核心的任务。只有做好传承人才培养才能真正有效地不断增强非遗传承发展后劲。

一是开展非遗传承人群培养。四川省大力实施国家文化和旅游部、教育部、人力资源社会保障部"中国非遗传承人群研修研习培训计划"，极大地提高了非遗传承人的传承实践能力，增强了非遗项目发展后劲。通过开展研培计划促进非遗保护成果转化，例如四川大学成立了非遗研究中心，成都纺织高等专科学校开设了"刺绣设计与工艺"新专业，为四川非遗保护传承提供了理论和人才支撑。

二是开展非遗专业人才培养。邀请非遗专家、大师、传承人等举办非遗培训班，提高非遗工作者的工作能力和业务水平，培养具有专业知识、专业技能、专业精神的非遗保护工作队伍，不断增强管理能力，逐步推进非遗保护传承工作。

三是开展非遗进校园活动。四川省各级文化、教育部门主动担当起弘扬民族优秀传统文化的责任，中小学结合当地非遗资源和特色，推动民间文学、传统音乐、传统舞蹈、传统戏剧、传统技艺等非遗项目进校园，部分地区还编辑了《蜀绣》《青城武术》《皮影》《羌绣》《唐卡》等职业技能培训教材，丰富拓展了校园文化，培养了青少年的民族文化自信，提升了文化艺术素质。

（四）非遗活动地方开花

不仅四川省省委、省政府高度重视、大力保护四川非物质文化遗产的保护与传承，全省各地也纷纷结合地方特色，开展各式各样不同的非遗活动，可谓四川非遗"地方开花"。

1. 达州：非遗保护体系不断完善

四川省达州市有"巴人故里"之称，非遗文化数量众多、内容丰富。积极推进非物质文化遗产社会传承，圆满完成"四川省首届民间艺术节"的"民间文化手艺广场汇"展览活动及"达人秀"演出活动等。因为非遗保护工作是一项时间跨度大、涉及专业多、工作任务重的系统工程，为方便常态化开展非遗保护工作，达州市文体广电新闻出版局文化遗产保护科制定更加科学合理的保护规划，建立健全非遗保护制度和保护体系，树立全民保护意识；开展好文化遗产日和各种非遗专题活动，把非遗编项目排成群众喜闻乐见的文艺作品，让非遗进入公共文化场所，成为大众文化；让非遗走进校园、走进课堂、走进社区、走进乡村，代代传承。同时，将调动社会各方面的积极性，鼓励、吸纳社会力量广泛参与，在人、财、物上给予必要的支持，加大非遗工作保护和传承力度。

2. 内江："传承人补助"激励非遗保护传承

2018年，四川省内江市根据地方特色出台《内江市市级非遗项目代表性传承人考核办法（试行）》，进行非遗"传承人补助"，每年对内江所有市级非遗项目代表性传承人开展非遗活动、授徒、宣传等方面情况进行考核，按考核结果评分高低给予不同等级的补助。考核不达标，不发放补助，连续两年考核不达标的还将撤销其传承人称号，营造了尊重传承人、弘扬传承优秀传统文化的良好氛围。

设置"传承人补助"，有效解决传承人的后顾之忧，使他们能更加专心地从事技艺的传承，提高传承人保护非遗的积极性，引导全社会关心、重视非遗传承保护，更好地激励和鞭策传承人主动学习专业知识，努力开展传承、授徒、交流等活动，推动非遗保护形成更多成果，有利于鼓励支持非遗项目代表性传承人开展工作。

3．茂县：非遗进校园，普及教育课堂

为推进羌族非遗的保护与传承，大力弘扬羌传统文化，丰富茂县广大学生的非遗知识，丰富和活跃校园文化生活，本着非物质文化遗产保护"从娃娃抓起"的理念，四川省阿坝州茂县文体广电新局联合县教育部门启动了"羌文化进校园"工程，即"非遗进校园"活动，展开了一系列非遗普及教育活动工作，使得茂县学子切实感受羌民族优秀的传统文化的魅力，了解非物质文化遗产保护的重要意义。

以普及羌族非遗文化为宗旨，茂县成立领导小组，制定切实可行的实施方案，组织非遗传承人进校园，举办校园成果展，先后在叠溪镇小学校、黑虎小学校等地成功推进"非遗进校园"活动，在校园内掀起学习、保护、弘扬羌族文化的热潮。不仅如此，茂县还对全县 200余名音、体、美教师进行了集中培训，培训内容包括萨朗舞、羌族民歌以及传统体育项目等，以培训的方式深化茂县教师队伍进一步了解羌族文化；专项拨款，鼓励非遗传承人进入学校承担羌笛、羌族萨朗、羌绣、羌语等的教授工作；搜集、整理适用于学生学习和传唱的羌族民间故事和羌族歌曲，编辑成册分发至各个学校；编创、录制羌笛演奏基本教学方法及羌族萨朗基本步法教学视频以更直观有效地教导学生等。

羌族民族非物质文化遗产，代表着羌族历史文化所取得的成就。茂县"非遗进校园"的活动，拉近了学生与传承人的距离，增进了学生对羌族非物质文化遗产的了解，增强了学生的民族自豪感，激发学生对文化的热爱的同时，也提高了学生对羌族文化遗产的认知水平、保护意识和传承信念。非遗进校园，让学校成为充满文化气息的育人场所，不仅能开阔青少年的视野，更能使非遗保护与传承工作"后继有人"，使传统文化得以薪火相传，具有深远的意义和非凡的价值。

4. 叙永：传承"非遗文化"助力脱贫梦

四川省泸州市叙永县枧槽苗族乡以丰富的扎染、蜡染、苗绣等"非遗"文化资源为突破口，将发展特色民族文化产业与精准扶贫结合，通过县级专业合作社平台，对留守在家的贫困群众开展技术培训，采取"合作社+村资公司（工坊）+农户"的方式，带动覆盖苗乡100余户、400多人贫困群众，实现人均增收500元以上，从而精准确保贫困群众脱贫增收。在地处川南深山中的贫困村，留守的苗族妇女在精准脱贫中，加入到叙永县扎染蜡染苗绣专合社，重拾民族手工技艺，融合现代审美元素，一件件精美的作品，不仅将扎染、蜡染和苗绣等非遗文化传承起来，也勾画出苗乡脱贫梦。

5. 彭山：专项经费保护非遗传承人

非物质文化遗产的保护与传承，其核心在于对传承人的保护。及时足额发放非遗传承人保护经费，目的就是鼓励非遗传承人保护传统技艺并发扬光大，使非物质文化遗产永久地传承、保留下去。作为全国有名的长寿之乡四川省眉山市彭山区，投入大量资金对地方非遗代表性项目传承人进行有效的保护。以"长春号"南味豆腐乳传统制作技艺为例，其起源于清嘉庆十四年（1809），后由在彭山经商的陕西渭南人李仲云之子李长春潜心钻研、发扬光大，创名"长春号"。由于传统手工艺制作精湛，产品享誉全川，名扬全国，曾被誉为川人食品中的"天府之花"。但随着社会需求量不断增大，传统的手工制作逐渐被食品工业机械化生产所取代，致使传统的"南味豆腐乳"制作技艺长期受到挤压，传统技艺传无后人，制作技艺逐渐萎缩。为保护这一宝贵的非物质文化遗产，彭山区做好申报和保护工作，于2009年6月，"长春号"南味豆腐乳手工制作工艺入选四川省级"非遗"保护名录。除此之外，对"长春号"南味豆腐乳传统制作技艺传承人潘福祥更颁发省级非物质文化遗产传承项目保护经费，专项用于此项非遗技艺的保护传承。

6. 彭州：亮相法国，积极推荐非遗"走出去"

四川省彭州市有3 000多年的历史，是古蜀文化的发源地，聪明、智慧的彭州人民开创了历史悠久的湔江文化，为我们留下了宝贵的非物质文化遗产。近年来，彭州市把握非遗保护的"广度"，积极构建非遗保护"宣传体系"，不仅积极组织参加中国成都国际非遗节，宣传和展示彭州市非遗保护传承成果，更不断推荐彭州非遗项目走上去、走出去。

2019年6月14—16日，首届中法历史文化名城对话会 —— "巴蜀古国 魅力四川"在法国枫丹白露宫举行。糖画彭州市级传承人李贵云、剪纸彭州市级传承人庄丛灿现场进行了技艺展示，分别为法国友人现场制作糖画，进行人物头像剪影。在场的法国友人纷纷感叹神奇的东方文化，饶有兴趣地体验了一番彭州非遗。

四、非遗文化艺术创作繁荣发展

（一）创作优秀文艺作品

充分挖掘优秀传统文化的思想价值和艺术价值，结合时代特点和要求，运用丰富多样的艺术形式进行当代表达，规划并推出一批重大革命和历史题材、现实题材、爱国主义题材、青少年题材等优秀文艺作品，体现四川特色、讲好四川故事、传播四川声音。实施川剧振兴和地方戏曲曲艺保护传承、巴蜀书画艺术传承发展等工程，做好地方戏曲"像音像"工作，支持戏曲和书画艺术精品创作生产。组织编写传承发展优秀传统文化幼儿读物，创作系列绘本、童谣、儿歌、动画等。加强对中华诗词、音乐舞蹈、书法绘画、曲艺杂技和历史文化纪录片、动画片、出版物等的扶持。实施网络文艺创作传播计划和巴蜀网络文学书写计划，加强网络文化产品创作生产，推动网络音乐、网络动画、网络剧、微电影、微视频等传承发展优秀传统文化；组织巴蜀经典民间故事动漫创作生产；推进文艺作品展演展览平台建设，推动传统文艺和网络文艺创新性融合；加强文艺评论，改革文艺评奖，促进优秀文艺作品创作与传播。

例如，为填补羌民族没有系统、完整、规范的民间文学和音乐歌曲集的空白，四川省阿坝州茂县文体广电新局收集、整理、出版了《中国羌族民歌集》《羌笛演奏教程》《羌族民间故事集》等系列丛书，以及《中国羌族经典歌曲系列》音乐视频光碟；创作了大型羌族原生态歌舞剧《羌魂》进行全国非遗调演的专场演出及全国巡演；编创的《肩铃舞》《腰带舞》《羌族多声部》《跳甲》等剧目成为羌族独树一帜的民俗文化品牌，多次应邀前往欧洲各国、韩国、新加坡等国以及中国台湾等地区参加文化交流，并代表羌族参加中央电视台晚会，对外展示了羌族地区浓厚的文化底蕴和悠久的历史。

（二）加强非遗丛书研究出版工作

编辑出版了《四川省非遗名录图典》《四川非物质文化遗产》《羌族文化传承人口述史》等。在国家级、省级非遗项目中，针对濒危项目、特色项目、影响广泛项目和年老体弱传承人等优先进行调查，采用数字化手段，利用录音、录像等手段，及时加以抢救和重点保护。设立四川非遗微信公众号，吸引了众多粉丝关注。运用互联网宣传非遗，举办"聚焦四川非遗·全国网络媒体四川采风活动"，在国内外产生了广泛深远的影响。

五、非遗文化创新融合效益增收

近年来，越来越多的人开始关注和学习中华优秀传统文化与非遗文化，但不少相关文化产品尚缺乏吸引力，一个重要原因就在于其呈现方式与体验方式过于单一，互动性差，缺少趣味和韵味。随着数字技术及新媒体的发展，不仅文化的生产方式、储存方式、表现方式发生了变化，文化的传承方式、传播方式、体验方式也发生了变化。这为推动非遗文化创造性转化提供了前所未有的机遇，以创新融合达成效益增收的新的发展趋势。期间，要注重创新非遗文化传播的内容、形式和渠道，充分利用技术和创意含量高的载体与形式对非遗文化资源进行转化，努力让非遗文化"活"起来，打造知名文化品牌，让人们在形象化、互动化的感知中爱上非遗文化。坚持古为今用、守正出新，促进非遗文化内容转化，将其融入人们的生产生活中，使其与节日庆典、礼仪规范、民风民俗相衔接，与文艺体育、旅游休闲、饮食医药、服装服饰相结合，推动非遗文化融入国民教育、道德建设、文化创造等之中。

四川数量众多、种类齐全的非物质文化遗产项目及其代表性传承人，通过"非遗+科技""非遗+旅游"等的跨界创新融合，以及其传播推广模式研究，探索与构建四川非遗保护传承发展的创新路径。

一是激发非遗传习中心、生态保护区和体验基地的活力。四川省各地根据自身特色，建设了大量非遗传习中心与非遗生态保护区，将一些优秀的国家级、省级非物质文化遗产项目进行集中的保护、活态的展示，为国家级、省级代表性传承人提供创作、研究、传承、展示的工作场所；同时为四川非遗的集中保护和传承提供稳定环境。

2019 年 7 月 16 日，在第七届非遗节动员部署会暨四川省非遗保护管理干部培训会上，四川省文化和旅游厅公布了 171 个第一批四川省非物质文化遗产项目体验基地。这是推进"非遗之旅"创新理念落地实施，促进文化和旅游深度融合发展的又一重要举措。体验基地遍布全省各地，涵盖了非遗十大类别，是四川特色非遗项目和传承实践、传承成果的典型代表，均具备较为深厚的文化氛围，可为游客提供非遗项目互动体验，增加游客对四川非遗技艺和特点的认知与感受，丰富游客的文化体验，增加旅游的文化价值。以非遗项目为核心，旅游线路和景区景点为依托，推进非遗元素与旅游线路、知名景区、旅游服务、旅游体验融合，促进文化和旅游深度融合，实现以文促旅、以旅彰文的目标。

二是推进非遗文科融合，搭建数字服务平台。深入探索"互联网＋公共文化服务"的有效模式，实现非遗文化服务、产品与市民实际需求的精准对接。将 4K/8K/HDR/IPS、3D/4D/全息、VR/AR/MR（增强现实/虚拟现实/混合现实）、AI（人工智能）、知识图谱、媒体融合以及可视化等为代表的新一代跨媒体智能化信息技术引入非遗保护领域，研究建立非遗领域的可虚拟感知的数字化信息资源系统、可定位追溯的文化脉络结构系统和可广泛传播的文化价值观念系统，为用户创造更多文化交融、愉悦感官、价值共享、新知及便利，向生活化、社会化服务发展，变简单、僵化、死板的保护、自需和物物交换为开发式保护、他需和出口贸易。同时，创新四川非遗保护方法和成果转化应用模式，提高四川非遗保护的效应和质量，形成完整的文化与科技集成的机制范式供非遗保护机构运用，推动开展四川非遗文产保护工作。

三是促进非遗文旅融合，塑造文化品牌名片。以四川丰富多变的非遗文化资源基础，结合四川旅游业发展的市场潜能，激发非遗文化的内在动能，扩宽非遗文化的生存空间。针对非遗资源多样性的特征，通过资源开发、体验式服务、功能性感知等探索，提供"菜单式""订单式"服务，开发四川"非遗+旅游"融合发展模式，建立适宜四川不同非遗特色的旅游发展途径。传承与实践相结合，形成四川非遗和旅游业融合的动力系统，打造四川非遗文化品牌名片，从供给端真正做到文化惠民。

2019年，借"文化和自然遗产日"的契机，四川省推出10个非遗旅游项目和旅游产品——"非遗之旅"路线，以非遗传习所、非遗体验区和非遗体验基地为载体，将非遗融入旅游线路和旅游产品，通过产品设计、线路策划，让非遗走进千家万户，进入游客的"菜单"，在借力旅游线路和知名景区丰富的游客资源宣传四川特色非遗保护项目的同时，非遗也为地方旅游品牌加分，形成的新优势提升了四川旅游的文化品位和旅游价值。

四是创新非遗文化传播推广。保护、推广与传播既是一个过程，又是一个立体的状态。四川各地深入自身挖掘非遗的文化内涵，从"赛、展、演、会、课"等多个角度，鼓励支持社会力量开展四川非遗题材文学、动漫、影视、音乐等领域的创作，打造一批具有时代特征、地域特色、深受人民群众喜爱的非遗精品佳作；创新宣传推广渠道，支持四川省各级文化部门发挥新媒体、自媒体和全媒体在以互联网为基础的数字媒介融合平台的传播优势，如自媒体、全媒体、智能媒体、用户画像、精准传播等多个传播与推广维度下的整合推广体系，让更多人能以新颖有趣的方式体验四川非遗文化的魅力，从而扩大四川非遗文化价值观念全面对外传播的影响力。从市场角度出发，明确四川非遗文化项目定位和受众需求分析，找准影响消费群体决策的众多因素，有针对性地面向精准受众进行宣传推广，促进四川非遗文化的市场转化；学习借鉴国内外具有影响力的非遗文化成功宣传经验，有效整合四川具有代表性和可复制性的非遗文化资源，支持社会力量集中打造一批四川非遗文化 IP，赋予四川非遗文化新的"生命力"，力争以最优费效比促进四川非遗文化行业和产业的共同发展，提升四川非遗文化的吸引力、知名度和美誉度。

五是加快产教融合，促进活态传承。"非遗传承"即以本区域的"非遗"项目为切入点，推动"非遗"项目融入专业建设中；开展"非遗"项目研究；利用"非遗"资源创作；将"非遗"代表性传承人引入师资队伍；开展"非遗"传承人群社会培训。"产教融合"即与优秀传统文化企业建立协同育人、协同创新机制，实现四川非遗创新发展平台的政、产、学、研、用协同发展。与此同时，增加通过学校培养非物质文化遗产后继人才的措施，以及对于代表性传承人、后继人才及相关从业者的研修、研习和培训，提高非遗相关人群的综合能力。

第三章
四川非遗文化保护与传承中的不足之处

四川省民族文化特色显著，文化遗产丰富，非遗资源绚丽多彩。四川省委第九届九次全会审议通过了《中共四川省委关于深化体制改革加快建设文化强省的决定》，把四川省建设成为文博强省、非遗强省是四川省发展战略目标之一，是建设具有四川文化特色的精神家园的重要着力点。非物质文化遗产资源是先辈们留下的宝贵精神财富，保护非物质文化遗产是建设四川文化强省的重要内容，其蕴含的意义十分重大。应站在文化强省战略的高度，重视和加强非遗保护与传承。非遗保护是建设和谐四川的重要条件。在某种意义上，优秀的非物质文化遗产所产生的凝聚力和亲和力，正成为维系四川省各民族各阶层生存和发展的重要纽带。但是由于当前经济、社会等各方面的原因，四川的非遗文化的保护与传承工作面临着环境、人才、资金、发展等的制约和不足。

一、非遗文化保护重视程度仍需进一步提高

（一）保护意识有所不足

四川省部分地方政府对于非物质文化遗产保护工作的自觉意识不强，忽视非遗保护的重要性和紧迫性，没有清楚认识到非遗在现代文明的冲击下正在不断加速消亡的现实，大多非遗的保护与传承工作还仅仅停留在文化系统的部门行为上。但现实中非遗项目涉及面十分宽广，文化部门因受职权所限，往往仅能在传统音乐、传统舞蹈、戏剧、曲艺等部分方面倾力而为，而对大多数其他非遗项目仅停留于一般程序性的保护层面。甚至存在部分传承单位和个人以为只要申请列入名录，项目就得到了保护；或者项目申报只是为了获得更大的利润，把名录当作荣誉，而未将其发展传承当作自己工作的重心。除此之外，非遗保护还没成为群众的自觉行动，不少群众对非遗了解不多，理解不深，保护意识不强。

（二）经费投入存在不足

现如今，四川省非遗保护工作经费主要依靠中央财政支持，省财政总投入额度远远难以适应保护工作的要求，还有许多地方甚至并没有将非遗保护经费纳入财政专项预算。由于投入不足，导致非遗保护的基础设施建设、设施设备配置、专业队伍培训以及对其抢救、保护、利用等工作受到较大的制约。

（三）非遗展示场馆未纳入免费开放范围

四川省目前有非遗博物馆、展示中心、传习所160余个，其中包含有一定数量的综合性的非遗展示馆,属于基本的公共文化服务场所,

担负着保障人民群众基本文化权益、满足人民群众基本文化需求的重要职能。但由于目前非遗展示场馆并没有被纳入国家免费开放的范围，非遗展示场馆缺少公开展示的运转保障资金，限制了非遗展示场馆的展陈效果和有效运行。

二、非遗文化保护人才队伍薄弱

文化发展核心在人才，但四川省目前非遗文化保护人才匮乏，这已成为制约四川非遗文化保护、传承与发展的关键因素，也是非遗文化保护抢救不力、创新利用不足、核心竞争不强的重要原因，主要体现在以下几个方面。

第一，人员素质亟待提高。非遗保护需要一定人员、经费的保障。但目前，四川省还存在有部分地区并未建立起非遗保护工作机构，甚至许多地方没有专职工作人员。现有非遗保护工作人员通常由文化部门工作人员直接兼任，甚至还有很多工作人员是一人兼多职或临时借用人员，他们难以潜心从事非遗保护工作，无法满足保护工作不断深入的需要。

第二，由于非遗工作的专业性较强，往往需要对非遗保护工作从业人员进行长期、系统的专项业务培训。而现有的工作人员对非遗保护工作缺乏相关的基础知识，业务培训短期内难见成效，达不到非遗抢救、保护的要求，导致各地特别是县级非遗资源调查、项目申报、抢救性记录等基础工作质量不高，甚至在个别地方还存在申报传承人是为个人服务的错误观念。在实际工作中，省内还存在普查手段落后、普查资料不全、普查不科学和准确性不高等诸多问题，使得一些非遗项目失去了保护的依据。

第三，非遗传承后继乏人。受现代文明和城镇化的影响，非遗生存环境发生急剧变化，大多数非遗项目赢利困难，在市场经济条件下难以生存，非遗保护形势严峻。很多非遗项目没有经常性、长期性的展示平台，参与人员越来越少，传承者和受众群体明显减少，生存空间逐渐萎缩。还有许多口传心授的民间艺术属独门绝技，代表性传承人年龄偏大，大多年过古稀，精力不济，收入微薄。而由于学艺艰难、收入低，传统文化很难对当代年轻人产生吸引力，使得非遗传承后继乏人。

三、非遗文化保护力度有待进一步提高

随着城镇化、工业化进程的加快，四川省非物质文化遗产保护形势严峻。

一是非遗文化保护机制亟须健全完善。四川地域辽阔，各地各级政府，尤其是广大农村地区与边远山区，普遍存在地方政府和人民群众非遗文化保护意识薄弱，非遗文化保护管理缺失及多头管理的问题。非遗文化保护工作往往涉及文化、住建、规划、农业、教育等多个部门，需要进行全面统筹管理，建立工作协调机制。但许多地方各级部门往往在涉及非遗保护的具体工作开展中以自我规则为主，忽视文化部门意见。例如在城市规划建设中，省内很多地区盲目清理或改变原有的地貌、植被、道路、街道、民居等环境要素，不断新建超高、超大体量建筑，致使大量以传统建筑街区为保护传承载体的非遗文化的历史价值和文化价值受到极大地削弱。

二是非物质文化遗产抢救、保护迫在眉睫。四川省许多地区，尤其是边远山区与农村地区，其非遗文化生存环境堪忧，非遗传承者和受众群体明显减少，不少依靠口传心授的非物质文化遗产正在消失，非遗生存空间逐渐萎缩。

三是非遗文化遗产传承动能不足。四川省绝大部分优秀非遗文化资源价值未能实现充分挖掘、整理和有效利用，非遗文化资源出现明显的闲置现象，长效化的非遗文化遗产活化展示传播平台较为缺乏，非遗文化主体的自主保护、传承的动力与能力不足。例如，各地在非遗项目、非遗传承人等的申报时，地方政府热情高涨，但申报成功后却不注重保护、利用和发展。又如四川非遗文化生产性保护与地方经济社会发展融合不足，对接度较差；非遗文化被盲目开发、过度开发，非遗名录项目泛化、低俗化、庸俗化等情况仍然存在。

四、非遗文化转化利用能力不强

伴随着社会的转型，生产及生活方式的转变，文化生态环境发生了很大的改变，同时由于对传统美术、传统技艺等非遗传统工艺的挖掘、整理和创新创意不足，导致四川省非遗产品与市场结合度较差，不能满足市场的差异化需求，许多非遗产品缺乏市场，传承人收入得不到保障；再加上年轻人无法靠非遗技艺谋生，很多人都不愿意学习、传承传统技艺，部分传统手工艺正面临断代的危机。目前，除了刺绣、竹编、唐卡等少数项目具有相当发展规模的行业或产业，其他多数保护项目仅以传承人个体小工厂、工作室、作坊、店铺为中心，难以产生较大经济和社会效益。这些传承个体以传统技艺项目居多，存在人员少、资金少、平台小等问题，极大地束缚了项目的传承、发展空间，使生产性保护的目的难以实现。

不仅如此，四川省非遗文化缺乏产业化的发展动能。四川省各地非遗文化产业存在特色不鲜明，同质化倾向明显，缺少规模大、影响力强的重点非遗文化产业项目带动引领。非遗文化与旅游、体育、科技、休闲等产业融合的广度和深度不够，非遗文化新产品、新业态、新模式不多，文化产品结构相对低端，文化融入产品附加值未能得到有效挖掘和提升，市场竞争力不强。

五、非遗文化的传播度欠缺

常言道，酒香不怕巷子深，但在互联网信息爆炸的时代，这一命题变成了"酒香也怕巷子深"。传承非遗文化既需要保护凝聚着前人智慧的古老技艺，更需要拓宽非遗的传播渠道。非遗传承应认真梳理我国非遗传播相关工作的现状，发现其中亟待解决的问题，进一步明确"传播"是更好地保护和传承非遗的应有之义。

（一）媒介传播潜力尚待挖掘

据《第 47 次中国互联网络发展状况统计报告》显示，截至 2020 年 12 月，我国网民规模为 9.89 亿，互联网普及率达 70.4%，其中手机网民规模达到了 9.89 亿，网民使用手机上网的比例达 99.7%。"提速降费"推动移动互联网流量大幅增长，随着以国内大循环为主体、国内国际双循环的发展格局加快形成，网络零售不断培育消费市场新动能，通过助力消费"质""量"双升级，推动消费"双循环"。与此同时，网络支付通过聚合供应链服务，辅助商户精准推送信息，助力我国中小企业数字化转型，推动数字经济发展；移动支付与普惠金融深度融合，通过普及化应用缩小我国东西部和城乡差距，促使数字红利普惠大众，提升金融服务可得到性。从 1994 年 Web1.0 时代开始，在移动设备增长、网速提升、带宽费用降低等大背景下，越来越多的 PC 业务和服务一直在朝移动端迁徙。

伴随着"互联网+"的不断渗透，计算不再只和计算机有关，它在某种程度上决定人类的生存及其生产生活的维持。数不胜数的智能设备和数十亿互联互通的智慧大脑连接在一起，在摩尔定律和数字化的共同推动下，无休止地探索着各种组合和各种可能的重组式创新机会，传播已经由传统的"线下、单向、广播"转换为"线上、互动、社群"。

由此可见，规模庞大的年轻人是互联网尤其是移动互联网渠道开展非遗传播的主要目标群体。

（二）非遗文化传播存在"跑马圈地"思维

非遗属于活态文化，非遗文化的保护和传承应是以人为主体的技艺和记忆传承，而非物质或作品的传承。但受社会发展、经济变化和人口流动的影响，非遗文化往往具有很强的地域性和流变性。但是，目前四川省乃至全国对非遗的保护和传播依然主要按照传统行政区域进行划分，使得非遗传播主体产生了"跑马圈地"的思维，将非遗资源看成是自身独享的文化资源，从而产生较明显的排他性，这就为非遗传播设置了人为障碍，无形中也让非遗传播重点局限在当地。从文化传播层面来看，非遗传播主体应该有意识地打破区域限制，跳出自身的狭小空间，加强跨区域传播，强化非遗资源整合，从而使非遗真正融入当下的文化大环境之中。

第四章
四川非遗文化整合与传承对策研究

　　四川非遗文化的保护，关键在于延续非遗的"生命活力"，在发展中促进传承。首先要明确非遗文化活态传承的战略核心，即发展定位，如何将各式各样丰富的非遗资源有效地整合，寻求四川非遗文化保护与传承的战略与途径。当今社会发展正在快速向智能生态的方向演化，如何在智能商业时代协同网络中的市场竞争中得以存活乃至苗壮成长，是四川非遗文化保护传承工作中必须认真考虑的关键，是重要的战略选择，直接决定了四川省非遗的未来。

一、"点·线·面"——四川非遗文化活态传承的新定位

四川省非物质文化遗产资源丰饶，饱含着四川人民历史、文化、社会、生活的方方面面，与老百姓息息相关。但在历史社会发展之中，由于不同原因，原本源于生活的非遗逐渐脱离了人们的生活本身，往往以保护的名义将非遗束之高阁，成为游离于生活之外的"表演"，这极大地局限了四川非遗的传承和发展。因此，需要让非遗回归社会、回归人民群众生活。非遗传承应通过开发文创产品、拓宽传播渠道、打造非遗品牌等方式，研究四川非遗文化整合与传承的新定位，寻求四川非遗文化可持续发展的新途径。

非遗文化的持续发展需要非遗在生态化的发展中完成对其的保护与传承。让非遗"活"起来，以"鲜活"的具象化的形象走进人民群众的生活，才真正实现了非遗文化活态传承。如今，非遗文化的发展离不开产业化的创新转换，更离不开智能商业生态协同网络的助力。多元角色的复杂在线协同对于传统供应链管理的超越，是平台和多元物种的组合，催生非遗产业化的新型生态，四川非遗文化的活态传承更是离不开其生态核心角色"点·线·面"的战略新定位。

二、点：四川非遗项目与文化参与者

"点"，即是零维度对象的最简单概念。首先，"点"指的是每一个四川非遗项目本身，例如川剧、蜀锦、蜀绣、绵竹年画、藏族唐卡、彝族火把节、羌绣等。在非遗文化的保护过程中，挖掘不同非遗项目的不同特色，有针对性地进行设计与建设，将其打造成四川人民群众

生活的一部分；使每个非遗项目"点"，发挥其自身长处与特点，凝聚成很强的向心性，形成文化的关注焦点；同时以其自由化、非规律性的形式，丰富非遗文化本身的形态。

其次，指的是非遗文化相关参与者，包括非遗传承人、非遗文化保护从业者以及非遗文化旅游体验用户等。非遗传承人作为非遗文化"活态"传承的重要载体，对于四川省非物质文化遗产的保护与发展具有十分重要的意义，保护住了传承人，也就是保护住了非遗文化；扶持了传承人，也就是传承了非遗文化。例如，四川省阿坝州茂县国家级非遗项目"羌笛的演奏及制作技艺"及其代表性传承人何王金，一直默默耕耘、无私奉献、坚守岗位，用精益求精的精神追求极致的完美。何王金从事羌族古老乐器羌笛制作技艺 31 年，积极履行非遗传承人的职责，认真开展羌笛演奏与制作技艺的教学、展演、文化交流等活动，创新羌笛演奏与制作技艺。国家对于何王金这样的非遗"工匠"的保护与扶持，就是对诸如"羌笛的演奏及制作技艺"这样的非遗项目的传承与发展。不仅如此，国家近年来大力发展文化与旅游，催生了大量文旅产业从业者和体验者。在非遗文化旅游产业中，每一位参与者都蕴含着推动产业发展的潜力与可能性，他们可以凭借自己敏锐的嗅觉与特色的观感，在非遗文化发展过程中发现项目好的"点"，把握时机，推动非遗文化在产业发展中实现持续性保护与传承。

三、线：四川非遗项目的平台与手段

由无数个点连接而成的线，是点运动的轨迹，具有很强的概括性和表现性。在非物质文化遗产的保护与传承中，"线"就是非遗文化项目的展示平台和传播手段。四川省各地分析本地情况，建设了大量非遗传习中心与非遗生态保护区，为各类非物质文化遗产项目提供了集中保护与传承的场地和环境，便于传承人创作与研究，以及非遗项目的"活态"展示。例如，四川省阿坝州茂县的"中国古羌城"，占地面积2.15平方千米，建筑面积25万平方米，工程动态投资约6个亿。其中，中国羌族博物馆、羌族非物质文化遗产传习中心、神庙、祭祀广场、演艺中心、金龟寨等一大批具有羌文化典型特征的亮点项目共同构成"古羌城"的中心发展区域，同时还将打造以全县的十个少数民族保护村落及九环沿线的民居风貌为中心的"古羌城"外围环境。古羌城的建设打破了地域习俗的界限，充分整合了羌族文化遗产资源，保持了羌民族建筑风貌、民风习俗、祭祀礼仪，展示了原生态羌族文化，是集文化传承保护、休闲体验、科普教育、游乐观光为一体的品牌独特的羌族文化浓缩展示地和人文景区。古羌城的建设目标是整合资源、集中打造、点线延伸，以"中国古羌城"项目为切入点和突破口，以点带面，由小及大，最终带动一个大区域发展的典范效应，全面推动茂县羌族文化传承和发展；丰富产业链，实现经济体高效运营并带动周边旅游经济发展的既定经济目标。

与此同时，"线"也是"面"运动的起点。在"面"搭建的台子上，真正提供服务的是"线"，它不仅代表着非遗文化的展示平台，更代表着非遗文化的保护手段与传播方式。

第一，现代科技辅助非遗数字化手段的升级。科技的不断发展促进现代科技辅助手段的快速更新，数字资源的存储、传播方式也正经历快速迭代。我省借助现代化科技辅助作用，升级全省非遗数字化的手段，进一步促进非遗文化的保护效率。但实际上，仅作为非遗文化保护和记录实现手段的非遗数字化在实践中也存在有"步于表面、流于形式"的潜在危机。一方面，技术手段的高速更替不断增大存储、共享平台的投入风险；另一方面，一味追求与新技术的结合会使得一些非遗数字化项目流于形式，并不能实现预期传播效果。四川省应明确自身所需，正确利用恰当的现代化科技手段，给予非遗的传播数据的标准配置，以便于让它在合适的地点、合适的场景之下，跟需要它的人在合适的时间相遇。

第二，非遗品牌名片的进一步打造。近年来，一大批拥有鲜明四川特色和文化底蕴的四川非遗，例如蜀绣、蜀锦、银花丝、竹编、成都漆艺等，把大熊猫作为"形象大使"，结合以大熊猫为原型的熊猫IP，创立了多个"非遗+熊猫"的品牌名片，打造独具特色的四川非遗文化品牌名片。这些品牌在传承发展四川非遗的同时也取得良好的社会效益和经济效益。如今四川非遗文化品牌在全国范围的影响力不断扩大，从被"供养"的神坛逐渐走进人民群众的生活。

"线"的平台和手段均是客户导向的。从供给端发掘消费者的文化需求，将非遗资源打造成为四川最为独特的文化品牌名片和具有浓郁非遗特色的文化IP，需要一整套全新的打法。在整合发挥"点"带来的机会的同时，要利用"面"的各种基础服务和能力，以较轻资产的方式快速发展。也就是说，一是充分利用"面"的网络效应；二是尽量利用"面"上的资源和能力，而不是自己花费巨大精力和成本重复建设。

四、面：四川非遗文化的整合与传承

线动成面，面实际上就是由无数条线组成的。无数点连成线，密集的线造又成了面，是"形象"的呈现。"面"的立身之本并非单一产品或服务的研发能力，也不是市面上的稀缺资源。

对于非遗文化的保护工作而言，"面"即是非遗文化的整合与传承，其核心价值是网络效应和协同机制。"面"的工作是利用"线"的平台和手段广泛联接"点"的各类项目资源，使之合作协同，同时建立各种机制，促使全局利益优化。通过"面"的整合，非遗文化能够自由地被创造并形成不同业务形态，非遗文化的价值更能经由偶然性的匹配大幅提升其效率，各方参与者均能够享受网络效应的好处。

以此为基础，"面"扩张融合会进一步产生"体"。"面"是"体"的最根本组成要素，在"面"的扩张过程中，如果有足够强大的基础，也许还会衍生出其他的"面"，进而形成一个日趋完善的"体"。

四川非遗文化的整合与传承，是一个相互依存、共同演化的"点·线·面"体系——"点"即是传承人、用户，"线"即是非遗项目，"面"即是平台，包括各类节庆、艺术展演、非遗传习中心等。该体系不仅要为相关人/物（非遗传承人、法人/组织/机构、非遗项目等）创造非遗身份，还要赋予非遗身份更加宽广的内涵和外延，须从时间维、空间维、效益维、品牌维、传播维等诸多领域进行整体思考，通过"降维攻击"融合所有非遗资源领域并形成一种基础治理能力，为机构/用户提供非遗文化活动传承与服务。该体系在以传承人为中心、自下而上的演进与重构中，每位传承人都可以自由决策，找到合适的生态位，从而由弱变强。传承人可通过传递基于非遗的创意、生产、流通、消费、业态等信息与价值，提升非遗的使用价值。与此同时，非遗的传承又激励、赋能传承人，形成各个参与主体/节点平等的自发生产与消费，反哺非遗业态、传播与消费，从而达到优胜劣汰的正向循环。

第五章
"一带一路"视域下非遗文化融合发展的
模式与路径研究

作为中华民族传统文化重要组成部分的非物质文化遗产,其创造性转化与发展对于加强中国的民族自信、文化自信,以及提高国家软实力具有重要意义。"一带一路"倡议自提出到如今,已经进入全面落实阶段,构建起了中国与其他国家之间"民心相通"的经贸之往来和文化沟通的友谊之路。"一带一路"倡议中的"文化包容的利益共同体"理念与联合国教科文组织实施保护非遗的相关举措异曲同工,为非遗的保护传承提供了新的多维融合发展的机遇与可能。因此,以"一带一路"的视角去探索和构建非遗活态传承生态体系,通过政策、产业、推广等多方面探索未来中国非遗文化产业发展路径的优化方向,价值和意义重大。

一、问题的提出及相关研究

"一带一路"倡议自 2013 年提出，已经进入全面落实阶段。"民心相通"作为"一带一路""五通"建设中的"一通"，表明了"一带一路"倡议既是经贸之路，又是沟通文化、友好往来的友谊之路。民相亲在于心相通，文化交流便是最有效、最受欢迎的桥梁和纽带。但经过 5 年的实践，中国已经认识到"民心相通"是难度相对较大、耗时较长、功夫较细的难点。

非遗是中华民族传统文化的重要组成部分，创造性转化、创新性发展非遗对加强中国的民族自信、文化自信，以及提高国家软实力具有重要意义。各地非遗门类广泛、内容丰富，形态差异较大，但过去相关部门对非遗发掘、保护、开发以及推广的意识与理念不尽相同且相对滞后，方式方法与手段又较多与时代脱节，导致对其整体开发与利用程度较低且可操作性较弱，并不断被边缘化，发展日趋式微。

"一带一路"倡议中的"文化包容的利益共同体"理念与联合国教科文组织实施保护非遗的相关举措异曲同工。可以说，"一带一路"沿线国家的非遗为"一带一路"建设提供文化支撑，"一带一路"建设为沿线非遗的保护传承提供了新机遇，两者之间互惠互助、互动互为。因此，以"一带一路"的视角去探索和实践能够体现和传播中华民族优秀传统文化的非遗优秀基因、智慧元素，通过"文化先行""文化互融"的方式促进各地与沿线各国的经济合作，并以非遗反哺"一带一路"发展，对各地乃至全国文化和旅游建设的价值和意义重大。

20 世纪 90 年代，联合国教科文组织宣布"人类口头与非物质文化遗产代表作"的决议后，非遗的重大影响已引起国家与国内外学界的高度重视。相对于我国，国外对非遗的研究及开发实践工作已颇为成熟：意大利将每年 5 月最后一周作为一年一度的文化遗产周；英国利用老宅发展观光产业开发等项目；韩国在制定《文化财保护法》时便极力将文化财（包含有形的和无形的）开发为商品等，极大地推动了非遗的共享传承。

2004 年 8 月，中国正式加入了联合国教科文组织于 2013 年 10 月通过的《保护非物质文化遗产国际公约》；2006 年 5 月，国务院公布了第一批《国家级非物质文化遗产名录》，随后各地也相继出台了围绕非遗保护的政策方针；2011 年颁布实施《中华人民共和国非物质文化遗产法》，标志着我国进入依法保护非遗的新阶段。但在如何保护的措施上，我国学界尚未达成共识。王文章认为非遗保护的重中之重是立法保护，科学管理机制的构建、全民保护意识的提升与加强宣传教育等，是非遗保护有序进行的根基。苑利、顾军认为，收藏与展示非遗成果、建立传统文化生态保护区、建立非遗资料库、数据库等是非遗保护的重要举措。林秋朔认为应"以开发促进保护"。

总而言之，目前国内外对非遗虽然已做了多角度的研究，但是主要还局限于对其的保护、文化意蕴和价值发现等理论研究。随着"一带一路"地深入推进，中外非遗文化交流日益频繁，为沿线各国非遗传承和保护带来了新机遇。

二、多维融合发展的机遇与模式构建

"一带一路"覆盖了较大的地理空间，沿线各国在主体文化、宗教信仰、语言文字、思维行为、产业政策等诸多领域皆存在着巨大差异，缺乏一个彼此尊重、相互包容的文化认知共同体系。

中国非遗在践行"一带一路"倡议过程中，要实现跨越式发展，应结合艺术学、新闻传播学、经济学、社会学、信息科学等对非遗进行多学科交叉研究并通过"文化自信""文旅融合""文科融合"等多维视域，构建"挖出来""带起来"与"推出去"的多维融合发展模式，在传承的基础上求新、求变乃至跨界融合，追求"1+1=∞"的效应。多维融合发展的逻辑如图 1 所示。

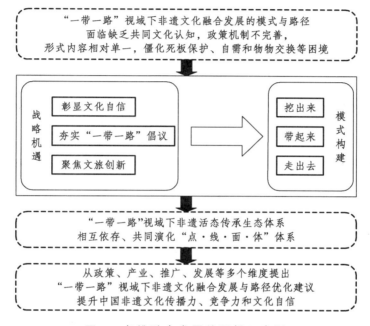

图 1　多维融合发展的逻辑示意图

（一）多维融合发展的机遇

1. 彰显文化自信，拓宽文化发展空间

中国非遗文化多维融合发展，有助于中国文化更好地走出去，向全世界展示中国的优秀文化、讲好中国故事、传播好中国声音、阐发中国精神、展现中国风貌、彰显并坚定文化自信。中国与"一带一路"沿线各国有明显的文化互补性、价值相通性，对文化交流项目路径的研究可使中国文化绕开与欧美文化的对抗，为中国对外文化交流开辟

空间，推动中国非遗的交融互鉴。

2. 夯实"一带一路"倡议，推动构建人类命运共同体

中国非遗文化多维融合发展，有助于进一步提升中国与沿线各国的文化双向交流，促进中国与沿线各国在文化信仰和价值理念上的"民心相通"，继而形成一种"多元+互通+交融"且能以共同的文化、相似的历史为内核的文化现象和价值观念，使其能够为未来人类的可持续发展提供持续的关注度和认同感。

3. 聚焦文旅创新，寻求协同发展

中国非遗文化多维融合发展，有助于中国用文化的理念发展旅游，用旅游的方式传承和传播中国文化，并使非遗成为沿线各国共享的文化产品，从而激发中国非遗文化活力与生命力，推动中国非遗生产性保护和衍生品创新工程，继而带动中国非遗文化区域经济、文化、旅游业和创新创业发展，提升中国非遗产业链融合发展的有效供给，增进沿线各国对中国非遗文化的认知与理解，联动旅游产业发展经济，打造"中国非遗文化旅游名片"。

（二）多维融合发展的方式

1. 挖出来：追根溯源

在长期的社会历史发展过程中，现代文明的冲击下，中国非遗已经面临着流失、断代与破坏的危机，挖掘、保护与传承必须提上日程。在"一带一路"命运共同体建设过程中，应进一步加大对中国非遗及其内涵的系统性挖掘、整理，对一系列古老的尤其是民族的中国非遗所承载的历史文化的育成体系与生存状况进行系统的梳理、总结和评述。对通过各种主体、各种方式与方法采集而来的文献资源进行全面细致的阅读、分析、鉴定与整合，以及对其进行挖掘、订正和补充。

与此同时，还应建立信息共享机制和档案，建立非遗文化的数据库、案例库、样本库等（如文本数据、图片数据、音频视频数据等），构建非遗文化资源统一揭示与服务第一手资料，优化非遗文化资源配置水平，从而打造中国非遗文化系统整理样板和示范。

2. 带起来：活态传承

关于非遗的保护与传承，文化和旅游部提出并强化了三个理念，即"非遗走进现代生活""在提高中保护"和"见人见物见生活"，在生活中融入非遗，非遗才能在生活中焕发生机。在践行"一带一路"倡议的过程中，中国非遗获得了体量庞大、开放共享的文化交流和贸易网络，可将其作为"带起来"的发力点，发挥非遗资源的集聚效应，整体提升非遗文化的有效利用和创造转化水平。应对"一带一路"沿线非遗文化活态传承的价值意蕴和全球化战略与发展的可能进行分析，结合实地调研的相关情况在已有的研究成果的基础上寻找误区与空白（如文旅融合、文科融合等），从理论层面向研究内容、深度等层面全方位拓展，使得非遗文化认知与体验的互联互通"双向交流"，从而使得非遗的管理模式和运作方式从僵化保护、自需与物物交换演进为开发式保护、他需及出口贸易，进而成为沿线共享的文化产品。

3. 走出去：全球传播

保护、推广与传播既是一个过程，又是一个立体的状态。在践行"一带一路"倡议过程中以及文科融合、媒介融合深度融合的大背景下，全球传播已远远超越仅靠媒体便能运作的概念，其发展更深层地涉及资源的融合与发展的跨界等问题。我们应充分挖掘中国非遗文化的潜力，找到非遗文化形态与现代推广及传播业态之间的关联点，积极探析非遗与旅游发展促进文化贸易、区域经济等相关领域的深度融合模式，并通过"文化先行""文化互融"的方式推动非遗文化资源利用转化向优质高效转变，进一步转变非遗文化的传播手段、经营模式及消费路径等，构建非遗"走出去"的全球传播机制，实现从个性推广到共性推广、由特殊推广到一般推广转变，从而不断建构起非遗文化资源的生发、生产与输出高地，为非遗的可持续发展提供重要内容和支撑，并以非遗反哺"一带一路"倡议发展，推动沿线非遗文化以整体的格局整合推广，实现共享传承与创新发展。

三、"一带一路"视域下非遗活态传承生态体系

中国非遗资源丰富，包含着历史文化的方方面面。可以说，非遗其实就是生活，与老百姓息息相关。但如今的非遗往往以保护之名将其束之高阁，成为游离于生活外的"表演"，这极大地局限了中国非遗的传承发展。在践行"一带一路"倡议的过程中，应把散落在城市各个角落的非遗资源（传承人、非遗文化项目、传习中心等）集合起来，通过开发非遗文创、打造非遗品牌、拓宽非遗传播等方式，让非遗回归社会、回归人民群众生活并学会"思考"，极有可能对非遗活态传承的生态体系产生重大的影响。

（一）非遗活态传承生态的新定位

在践行"一带一路"倡议的过程中，非遗活态传承应是一个相互依存、共同演化的"点·线·面·体"体系——"点"即传承人、用户；"线"即非遗文化项目；"面"即平台，包括各类节庆、艺术展演、非遗传习中心等；"体"则是由"面"扩张融合而生。该体系不仅要为相关人/物（非遗传承人、法人/组织/机构、非遗项目等）创造非遗身份，还要赋予非遗身份更加宽广的内涵和外延，须从时空维、技术维、周期维、效益维、传播维等诸多领域进行整体思考，通过"降维攻击"

融合所有非遗资源领域并形成一种基础治理能力，并分别从供给侧赋予机构/用户非遗创意、非遗生产、非遗流通、非遗消费及非遗业态等更多选择。该体系在以传承人为中心、自下而上的演进与重构中，每位传承人都可以自由决策，找到合适的生态位，从而由弱变强。传承人可基于非遗的创意、生产、流通、消费及业态等信息与价值，提升非遗的使用价值。同时，形成各个参与主体/节点平等的自发生产与消费，反哺"一带一路"的发展，从而形成优胜劣汰、正向循环与活态传承的生态体系。点·线·面·体：非遗活态传承生态的新定位如图2所示。

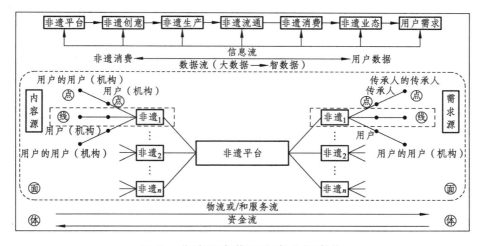

图 2　非遗活态传承生态的新定位

（二）解构与重构："一带一路"建设助力非遗生态体系

在践行"一带一路"倡议过程中，非遗活态传承最大的优势在于能够调动政府资源、传承人的积极性及更好地挖掘潜在消费人群。

从时空维度来看，既能持续呈现用户实践相关联的非遗信息，又能交叉验证与复现多角度、多层次、跨地域的非遗元素。例如，在首届"数字中国"建设峰会数字非遗板块中，公众只需佩戴 VR 眼镜，便可身临其境地置身于传承人的空间并与其一同学习烙画、漆画等非遗技艺。

从技术维度来看，既能通过 4K/8K/HDR/IP、VR/AR/MR（增强现实/虚拟现实/混合现实）等数字化技术实现非遗的全球化传播，又能通过 AI、知识图谱、媒介融合等跨媒体智能化技术实现非遗的智能化保护。例如，在首届"数字中国"建设峰会数字非遗板块中，公众只需使用手机扫描 AR 卡片、二维码等便可观看立体化的妈祖信俗、中国剪纸等非遗展品。

从周期维度来看，既能明确非遗的项目定位和深入用户洞察，又能动态配置优化非遗要素以带来更好的用户体验。例如，腾讯以故宫文化 IP 为核心，通过多重连接、情景分享与智能化算法等新一代信息技术，把过去古人的创作者和今天的创作者、把古代的用户和今天的用户串联在一起，从泛娱乐到新文创，从产业链到生态圈，不仅促进了非遗内容的有效分发与传播半径的不断拓宽，还实现了商业价值和文化价值的良性循环。

从效益维度来看，既能激发非遗内在动能，提升混合效益，又能创新业务模式，深挖 IP 价值，拓宽生存空间。例如，腾讯以故宫文化 IP 为核心，将故宫文化进行动漫文化创意，打造"胤禛美人图""皇帝的一天""清代皇帝服饰"等一系列 App，将故宫文化生动地展现在手机屏幕上，极具教育性和欣赏价值，同时还增加了互动体验和趣味性。

从传播维度来看，既能"良性进化"多元化传播，又能通过资源开发、功能性感知等探索，提供"菜单式""订单式""体验式"传播。例如，"锦绣中华——中国非物质文化遗产服饰秀"通过传统服饰文化与现代时尚产业相结合的方式举办了 10 余场精彩绝伦的非遗服饰秀。据悉，共有 23 家网络直播平台参与了联动直播，合计赢得了 6000

余万次的点击量及超过 1000 万的网友互动。

从品牌维度，既能传承与实践相结合，助力公共文化，又能形成文旅融合的动力系统，打造非遗文化品牌名片，从供给端真正做到文化惠民。例如，羌族传统刺绣工艺、羌族传统编织技艺等羌族非遗，其制成品在羌族人民生产生活中便是自带"流量"的公认品牌，若能在夯实现有市场的基础上大力开发其他市场对品牌的认同和信赖程度，便可保持品牌可持续发展的态势。

解构与重构："一带一路"建设助力非遗生态体系如图 3 所示。

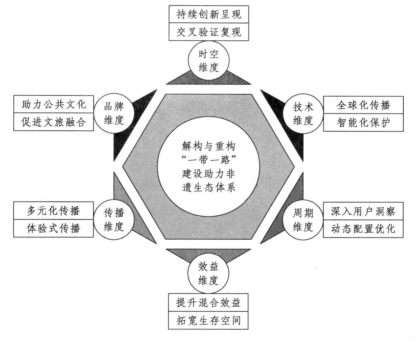

图 3 解构与重构："一带一路"建设助力非遗生态体系

四、路径优化建议

在践行"一带一路"倡议的过程中，为顺应世界多极化、经济全球化、社会信息化、文化多样化的发展，丰富和提升中国非遗文化的内涵和品质，实现中国非遗文化生产力的突破性解放和消费力的全新升级，更好、更快地体现与传播中华民族优秀传统文化，应积极探索中国非遗文化产业发展模式从资源依附到创新驱动、从粗放经营到集约发展、从单一展示到整合传播、从量的积累到质的嬗变的战略转换的内在诱因和机理，并在此基础上重点从政策、产业、推广及发展等多个维度探索未来中国非遗文化产业发展路径的优化方向。

（一）政策路径：从资源依附到创新驱动

不同时期，中国非遗文化的政策不尽相同。这些具有不同特点、理论依据、社会背景、政策体系、存在的问题及原因的政策，又潜移默化、循序渐进地渗透到社会的各个角落，深刻影响甚至改变着非遗文化未来的发展。因此，研究鼓励非遗文化发展的公共政策，有利于在兼顾不同国家、地区、民族、宗教等文化差异与风俗习惯的基础上，通过多元化、个性化、可视化等手段尝试突破文化壁垒，引发公众的"文化自觉""文化复兴""遗产变迁"等创造性活动。

"一带一路"建设背景下的非遗文化政策优化路径，应通过发布相关领域优惠扶持性政策法规等，通过开展专题研讨会、发表学术文章、组织开展学术活动等方式吸引公众关注非遗；应出台优秀传统文化企业建立协同育人、协同创新机制，实现中国非遗创新发展平台的政、产、学、研、用协同发展；应因地制宜，通过构建文化产业走廊等区域文化空间，使非遗从历史地理概念拓展延伸到社会、经济、文化等领域，为非遗文化与旅游业等产业的深度融合发展提供物理载体；应充分利用非遗文化的内在及本质，有针对性地对其展开相关分析，加强相似非遗区域联动并实现协同创新发展，从而使非遗在"政府+公众"共同参与的和谐共生中实现保护性开发和传承；应积极推动国内外互信体系建设，构建中国非遗文化产业输出保障机制，提高中国非遗文化产品输出的能力和水平，促进"一带一路"沿线各国非遗交融互鉴。

（二）产业路径：从粗放经营到集约发展

随着现代社会的发展和不同文化的碰撞，诸多非遗由于特殊的地理环境严重依托自然资源粗放式的简单的开发利用，仍向外界展示着僵硬的面孔，处于濒危灭绝境地，滋生了表现不一、程度不均但实质相同的"资源诅咒"现象及由此引发的"产业锁定"效应。中国特色社会主义进入新时代，要破解非遗文化产业可持续发展难题进而实现转型升级，就必须注入新的动能来推进"活态"传承，积极融入"一带一路"建设，从而走出传统模式和打破地域限制。

"一带一路"建设背景下的非遗文化产业优化路径，应发展非遗文化创意，即将可塑性强大的"原创性"非遗元素与文化创意的概念相结合，形成普及性和利于传播的"差异性""个性化"的非遗文化产品，以产业形式进行普世性和平等性的非遗文化推广，从而打造非遗创意产业发展新高地；应学习借鉴国内外具有影响力的非遗产业发展经验，有效整合具有代表性和可复制性的非遗文化资源，支持社会力量集中打造更多中国非遗文化 IP，扩大非遗产业主体，赋予中国非遗文化新的生命力；应以 IP 为核心，借助新一代跨媒体智能化技术，打破文化、科技、数字化的界限，打造非遗文化资源 IP 库，使其跨越内容生产的边界并从内容融合迈向产业生态融合，将 IP 价值开发最大化；应赋予用户非遗数字文化资源再创造的途径与手段，并可根据用户兴趣和消费力进行菜单式和订单式定制，从而激活非遗文化的商业价值和文化价值，承担起"一带一路"建设引导下延续文化命脉和文化生命的责任，助推沿线各国文化产业大发展。

（三）推广路径：从单一展示到整合传播

从传统媒体到新媒体再到智慧媒体，从数字化到网络化再到智慧化，从"相加"到"相融"，"一带一路"、非遗的相关资讯充斥着各大传播渠道，国际媒体合作融洽，然而沿线各国在彼此间经济发展、社会文化、基础设施及人文风俗等基础迥异，相对"低维"的传统媒介无法有效地管理和运作此类"高维"媒介的事务，导致"一带一路"、非遗理念的传播的广泛性、有效性还远远不够。

"一带一路"建设背景下的非遗文化推广优化路径，应在维护非遗品牌（产品、服务等）及专业化（生产者、经营者等）发展的同时，巩固现有市场成果并大力挖掘和开发消费者的潜在需求，进一步提升对品牌的认同感以及可持续发展的态势；应结合万物互联、万物皆媒、万众皆媒的背景积极创建文化科技深度融合的实验区，采用数字化等手段将非遗转换、再现、复原成可共享、可再生的数字形态，并利用自媒体、全媒体、智能媒体、短视频等新型渠道多元化传播；应加强重视传播信息本身的事实性和逻辑性，让非遗活动保持原有的文化背景、常态生活和生产情景，积极思索如何从关系维度和情感维度上拉近非遗与公众之间的距离，即从物质产品展示向智能与全息动态展示转化的体验传播；应深入探索"互联网+非遗"的有效模式，找准影响消费群体决策的众多因素，革除公众对非遗的陌生感和神秘感，并通过"市场下沉"逻辑、寓教于乐的方式提升公众的幸福指数，形成非遗"见人见物见生活"的良好环境，实现非遗文化服务、产品与用户实际需求的精细化对接；应扎实抓住县级融媒体中心建设的契机，将县域公共媒体资源整合起来、融合发展，按照"中央厨房"模式实现一次采集、多种生成、多元传播的要求，研究全媒体整合推广体系；应支持各级文化部门发挥新媒体、自媒体和全媒体在以互联网为基础的数字媒介融合平台的传播优势，赋能非遗传播，让更多人能以新颖有趣的方式体验中国非遗文化的魅力，扩大中国非遗文化价值观念全面对外传播的影响。

（四）发展路径：从量的积累到质的嬗变

提高非遗经济增长的质量和效益是中国非遗文化产业高质量发展的关键。而与发达国家相比，中国非遗保护与传承的水平仍较低，方式仍较粗放，面临着结构层次较低、特色不显著、结构不适应、传承人才匮乏等问题。由此可见，当前的建设更多是片面追求产品数量和经济效益，尚停留在量的积累阶段，真正的传统工艺则受到冲击，尽快提升至更高的质的嬗变层面已刻不容缓。

"一带一路"建设背景下的非遗文化发展优化路径，应在"工匠"已然成为对工艺技艺具有更高精神追求的外化符号、消费者头脑中已然形成"工匠=精品"的共识的环境下，精品化打造定制传承具有中国传统工匠精神的"符号"；应运用大数据技术对数字平台上的原始数据进行标引、采集、归集与聚类，探索建立以数据为纽带的生态链，分析监测沿线各国媒体和网民的关注焦点、变化趋势及情感倾向，归纳每种情绪的网民评论特征，从而定量化、常态化地为政府进展分析、态势研判、政策评价及潜力预测等决策服务；应以本区域的非遗项目为切入点，加强与专家、智库、高校的交流与合作，整体性考虑项目开发与周边经济、社会、文化事项的共生性；应抢救性保护非遗传承人，加快产教融合，推动非遗项目融入专业建设中，将非遗代表性传承人引入师资队伍，提高非遗相关人群的综合能力（文化素养、审美和设计创意等），促进创新创业与活态传承；应坚持理论结合实践，引导开展多维度、多视角与全方位研究，构建与完善重点指标体系，构建"一带一路"建设下的非遗智力支撑体系，并加强智库成果转化。

此外，还应探寻中国非遗文化交流的交叉地带，培育共性文化；加强中国非遗教育文化交流，促进沿线各国的教育合作。

"一带一路"建设是对古丝绸之路"丝路精神"的继承，在践行"一带一路"倡议过程中，若能以中国非遗的智慧为纽带，拓展与沿线各国在非遗文化的发掘、保护、研究、利用、交流和创新等领域的合作潜力和空间，便可进一步增进沿线各国对中国非遗文化的认知与理解，用非遗讲好中国故事，推动中国非遗文化以整体的格局整合传播，实现共享传承与创新发展，从而维护国家文化安全，增强文化自信。

第六章
"走出四川" —— 多维重构四川非遗文化活态传承与发展

现如今，非物质文化遗产的保护逐渐从过去的地方"局部性""独立作为"的传统观念走向了"整体性""多维度"的发展性传承新趋势。多维度的整体保护观更加强调非物质文化遗产存续的生态文化视角，注重文化遗产与自然生态、活用价值的开发和利用，也更加强调各利益相关方在非遗保护方面的作用，有利于四川省非遗文化的"活态传承""走出四川""走向世界"。

一、效益维度：文创+文科，深挖 IP 潜值

近年来，数字经济迅猛发展，数字创意扑面而来，从手机里音频、视频到电视、电影的制作；从场景模拟到环境沉浸；从语音的转换到音乐的下载，从信息的存储传输到大数据的采集分析，数字技术正改变着文化产业的生产和消费方式，更给予了文化创意产业日新月异的科技支撑与创意可能。

如今，四川省拥有 7 项联合国教科文组织非遗项目、153 项国家级非遗项目、611 项省级非遗项目以及若干地市县级非遗项目，众多非遗资源让四川成为中国非遗大省。四川非遗文化是四川人民祖祖辈辈在生产实践中总结出来的文化精华，展示的是四川地区的民族精神和风度。但随着现代社会经济文化诸多方面地不断发展和变迁，更有全球化浪潮带来的国内外不同文化的碰撞与冲击，四川非遗文化面临着生存危机，非遗保护需要走出传统模式的限制，以文化创意注入新的传承动能，以更好地保护非物质文化遗产。

所谓非遗的文化创意，即针对非遗文化，以创意概念创造出具有普及性和利于传播的产品，并以产业形式进行普世性和平等性的文化推广。当今世界，文化创意不仅是一个理念，更是有着巨大经济效益的产业现实。四川省丰富的非遗文化作为可塑性强大的"原创性"资源，能够提供文化创意产业以宝贵的内容创作的核心源泉。由非遗原创激发的"差异"和"个性"是文化创意产业的根基和生命，能够有效地促进其摆脱同质化现象。优良的非遗文化产品在如今"内容为王"的时代背景下，可以借助资本运作，打造出非遗创意产业发展新高地。

另一方面，非遗文化是一个非常宽泛的概念，表面上似乎并不能直接成为能进入市场流通的产品或商品。但文化里每一个宽泛的概念

背后都存在着一个鲜活的故事。在新文创时代，借力文创，把非遗文化中最美好的东西用当代年轻人最习惯的、最喜欢的方式，更好地诠释出来。换句话说，就是对不能天然地成为产品或商品的四川非遗文化资源经过一定形式的再创造，让其融入数字技术的血肉之中，成为具有丰厚知识产权的文化产品。如今，互联网的万物互联技术、数字化与新媒体技术的不断介入和发展，赋予了非遗文化资源以创意孵化和孕育出大量非遗数字文化产品再创造的途径和手段。亟须保护与传承的四川非遗文化，借用数字技术和文化创意的助益，根据人民群众的文化需求进行菜单式和订单式定制，实现资源的创造性地数字化开发。让非遗"活"起来，走进消费者的心中。

随着互联网基础设施的普及，万物互联技术把物体和物体、人和人、不同的世界联合在一起，在这个平台上有了更多的创意机会，可以去孵化和孕育出更多数字文化产品，表达文化精神，传播文化价值观，借用艺术表述手法展现、科学技术支持和产业模式运营，激活各类文化资源，让其成为人民群众喜闻乐见的文化产品，走进千家万户，同时在推广中培育人民群众的兴趣和消费力。

其中最著名的成功案例应属故宫博物院。以故宫文化 IP 为核心，将故宫文化转化为动漫文化创意，打造了《胤禛美人图》《皇帝的一天》《韩熙载夜宴图》《每日故宫》《故宫陶瓷馆》《清代皇帝服饰》《故宫展览》等一系列 APP，使故宫文化影响"接地气"地生动展现在手机屏幕上，在教育性和欣赏价值的基础上增加了互动体验和趣味性。这些文创产品都是依托故宫丰富藏品，通过数字化采集和交互，成为传播故宫文化的载体。把古代创作者和今天的创作者、把古代用户和今天的用户串联在一起，从泛娱乐到新文创，从产业链到生态圈，实现了商业价值和文化价值的良性循环。

丰富的非遗文化资源，独具特色的非遗历史和文化，赋予了四川得天独厚的优势，具备能够生产出极具特色的 IP 的强大实力。打造四川非遗文化 IP，关键在于合理有效地依托现代科技技术，深挖四川历史文化遗存，打破文化、科技、数字化的界限，充分激活四川历史文化资源，促使四川非遗文化资源跨越其内容生产的边界，从内容融合迈向产业生态的融合，实现 IP 价值开发的最大化。让文化创意科技表达，用数字化手段让文物资源"活"起来，在动态传承中进行保护，创造独属于四川的发展新模式。

二、品牌维度：打造非遗名片，促进文旅融合

（一）打造品牌，塑造 IP 影响力

当代社会，品牌的力量无时无刻不在影响着人们的生活。尤其对于具有一定商品属性的非遗项目而言，品牌可以在一定程度上反映非遗资源的当代价值。作为当代非遗保护实践成果重要体现的非遗品牌的传播效果，更能够反映大众对非遗的知晓度以及对非遗保护与传承的认可度。对于四川省来讲，需要着力将非物质文化遗产打造成为四川"文化名片"，扩大其传播效益，传递四川非遗文化的当代价值，构建品牌 IP 影响力。可以考虑以下形态：

1. 专业品牌：巩固跨越历史的信赖

就四川而言，传统民间工艺技术的非遗项目如"蜀绣""草编""蜀锦织造技艺"等，凝聚的是四川各地人民世代相承的智慧、经验而成的核心工艺技艺，其制成品是四川（尤其是非遗项目所在地）人民生产生活中的公认品牌，在羌族心中自带"流量"。此类品牌拥有"我有人无，人有我精"的专业性形象，但较为局限为特定市场对其的认同与信赖。

但其在其他市场的认可度仍极其有限，外加受外来文化的冲击，在四川本地也不可避免地面临品牌衰退期的危机。这些专业品牌需要在维护品牌所对应的产品、服务以及生产者、经营者专业化发展路径的同时，巩固现有市场，并增加其他目标市场消费者对品牌的认同和信赖程度，从而保持品牌可持续发展的态势。

2. 工匠品牌：抓住振兴传统的良机

国家大力弘扬"工匠精神"，实施"传统工艺振兴计划"，"工匠"一词已然成为对工艺技艺更高精神追求的外化符号。历经多年的舆论环境积累，消费者头脑中已形成"工匠=精品"的共识。因而，各地传承状况好、民间口碑佳的工艺品、日用品、食用品等迎来了"工匠品牌"打造的良机。

例如，《舌尖上的中国》第三季播出，"章丘铁锅"一夜成名。实际上，这事件并非偶然，背后是社会整体认知和消费习惯的支撑，是当代人对"手工锻造"这样的"工匠品质"的认同与信赖。

基于纯手工、好手艺建立和运营自有品牌，实质上就是一个将原本地方性、区域性的工匠精神"符号"传播推广开来的过程，精品化打造定制，最终实现品牌化发展之路。四川省的许多非遗项目具备"工匠品牌"孕育的特点与条件。一方面，非遗项目的品牌产品与特色传统工艺相关联，通常其工艺流程包含手工制作环节，如"蒸馏酒传统酿造技艺""自贡井盐深钻汲制技艺""羊皮鼓制作技艺"等；另一方面，非遗项目具有高于普通同类产品的质量和功效，能够让目标市场消费者得出"品牌即是品质的保证"的价值认同和消费体验，如"蜀绣""蜀锦""羌绣"等。

3. 时尚品牌：助力传承汇聚成潮流

非遗也时尚。一方面，四川非遗需要依靠更大范围的消费者了解非遗技艺的独特性，通过亲身体验、购买使用、确立认同、形成潮流等发展过程，最终形成以非遗资源为核心要素的时尚品牌；另一方面，四川部分诸如"彝族服饰""羌族服饰"等非遗项目，需要依靠多种形式的跨界合作，形成非遗元素与当代文化结合后的时尚卖点和流行趋势，进而吸引一批市场潮流行业与非遗从业者建立跨界合作关系，两者互动打造一批以非遗资源为主要创新要素的新兴时尚品牌，甚至以所研发的产品、子系列、子品牌以及所传递的概念进一步影响当代流行文化。

这类跨界是实体资源和业态之间的跨界。如今，大量处于成熟期前后的时尚品牌需要借助人文情感元素等手段，实现品牌形象的巩固与提升。而市场与非遗的跨界，不仅可以助力时尚品牌进一步提升自我价值，更是以"传承成为潮流"的方式让非遗得以更好的保护。

4. 公益品牌：结成社会力量保护链

保护活态存世的非物质文化遗产是当代人的责任。非遗保护需要全民参与，尤其需要吸纳更多社会力量，连结和带动全民参与主动性和积极性。如今，随着非遗保护的深入开展，与非遗传承、传播和转化相关的社会公益品牌不断涌现，规模和影响力不断扩大。例如，云锦织造技艺、金箔锻造技艺等一批非遗项目与星巴克、玛莎拉蒂等知名品牌合作的专业机构"稀捍行动"，其运营模式的基础就是对非遗资源的有效梳理与合理利用，采取借力国内外知名品牌实现非遗价值传播的方式，以市场角度扶持非遗项目。

在四川省非遗中存在一批只能在特定时间才能看到的项目，诸如"都江堰放水节""羌年""羌族瓦尔俄足节"和"自贡灯会"等节庆、游艺、传统祭祀等活动型项目，可以将其打造成为公益性目的为主的节庆文化品牌。这样不但有利于四川非遗项目借力价值传播、实现传统再造,也有利于凝聚社会保护力量、拓宽四川非遗传播推广的渠道。

5. 电商品牌：借网络市场传播文化

近年来,基于移动互联网,一批与非遗有着千丝万缕关联的电商、微商等线上品牌应运而生。他们常以手艺手作、工匠品质等作为品牌传播和平台营销的核心卖点,以非遗相关制成品、衍生品等为主要销售产品。社交电商以社交媒体内容推送、兴趣社群线上运营、线上线下互动等方式传播非遗价值,并以此增加和巩固平台目标消费人群、促进相关产品销售,促进起电商品牌的成长与发展。

对于一些四川非遗项目来说,由于地理限制,导致其文化与产品无法"走出大山、普达四川",更不用说"走出四川、闻名海外"了。例如藏族、羌族、彝族拥有大量可呈现物质载体的非物质文化遗产项目,如彝族服饰、藏族编织、羌族刷勒日统等传技艺,其所形成极具少数民族特色的文化品牌与产品,就可以借助网络电商平台进行有效的产品销售,以弥补其山高路远的地理限制。

总而言之,四川非遗项目的品牌打造,需要利用项目的商品性特质,增加吸引力和知名度,拓展认知范围和产品市场,帮助项目走进寻常百姓家、走向世界。因而,品牌化发展也是提高四川非遗传承水平、确保四川非遗生命力、激活四川非遗自身造血功能的重要保护措施。而促进四川非遗当代价值的传递、实现和增值,是品牌视角保护传承四川非遗的核心要义。

（二）文旅融合，非遗的活化与创新

文化是旅游的灵魂,旅游离不开文化。比如传统民俗和手工艺,在原住民看来并不会觉得它们是文化资源,但对旅游业来讲,这些都是值得被关注的资源,能够创造出"文化＋旅游""1＋1＞2"的效益。

因此，对于密不可分的文化与旅游二者来说，旅游业态和产品竞争力会很大程度上体现为文化的竞争，而文化软实力也特别需要借旅游这一路径促成推介和传播。只有把旅游与文化紧密结合起来，才能实现文化旅游的极大活力。

回顾中国旅游业的发展历程，不难发现，绝大多数游客直接参与体验的旅游产品，从最初的观光型产品到休闲型产品再到度假型产品，都可谓发展迅猛。新时代，随着我国社会生产力水平极大提高和社会供给能力显著增强，我国广大人民的基本物质需求逐步得到有效满足，推动精神文化需求从非主导性需求转化为主导性需求，"需求侧"升级为"对日益增长的美好生活的需要"。因此，游客对旅游产品文化内涵的体验、对休闲度假享受的需求以及对信息获取及购买效率的要求与日俱增，无法充分满足游客综合需求的旅游产品和旅游业态势必要从供给侧进行改革，构建具有"文科融合、业态整合、产品复合"特征的旅游业的文旅融合发展新方向。

对于四川非遗，需要将非遗产品、服务与文旅项目结合，打造属于四川特色的非遗文化旅游 IP，把非遗文化渗透进旅游的综合形态，从而可以帮助四川非遗更好地走出四川、走向世界。但由于四川各非遗项目之间形态差异较大，加之地域、政策、人才等因素的限制，许多地方非遗项目与旅游产业合力不好，文化旅游产品开发的力度不够大，限制了地方非遗文化旅游的发展，也在一定程度上制约了四川省整个文化旅游产业的繁荣。

实际上，非物质文化遗产所具备的不可替代的文化内涵，正好契合了人们对旅游个性化、体验化、情感化、休闲化以及审美化的体验追求，具有极大的旅游项目开发价值。开发时应切实考量地方现实与项目意义，"定制"符合实际的"非遗旅游产品"，才能真正实现良好的文旅融合。例如，羌族非遗的意义在于羌民族的文化传承，他们非遗项目体现的基本都是羌族聚集地人民生活的情趣及习俗。因此，在针对羌族非遗项目设计文化旅游项目时，丰富多彩独具特色的羌民族非物质文化遗产便成为其地方文化旅游业发展的资本和优势。独特的羌族非遗文化能为游客打造独具魅力的非遗旅游体验，如品咂酒羌餐、游碉楼羌寨、看推杆扭棍、跳羌族萨朗、购刺绣服饰、听羌笛口弦、聆羌戈大战等。这样的文旅产品对于非遗的保护、传承与创新，能够发挥良好的催化剂、粘合剂、润滑剂作用，有利于四川非遗的活化，让即将消逝的四川非遗重新获得生命，使四川非遗走进现代生活，"见人见物见生活"，成为"听得见的非遗、带的走的非遗、学得来的非遗"，焕发出鲜活的生命力。

三、传播维度：拓宽传播渠道，让主流变成潮流

传承非物质文化遗产既需要保护凝聚着先辈智慧的传统技艺，更需要不断拓宽非遗的传播渠道。传播能够提升大众对于非遗的价值评估和深厚情感，也能够提升整个社会对非遗传承人的认同与尊重，甚至还会为将来更广大的传承人群体培养后备军。从四川省非遗现状来看，最亟待解决的问题是如何须进一步明确非遗传播的意义和路径，实现以传播促保护，以传播促传承。

（一）非遗传播主体的扩大化：人人都是"广播站"

近年来，在国家的高度重视和支持下，我国非物质文化遗产的传播主体呈现日益扩大的趋势。从最初单纯依靠政府有关部门的组织推广，到民间传承人的自发宣传，再到学界、媒体界、商界的加入，非遗传播主体的基数在不断扩大。对于四川省来说，虽然近年非遗文化的传播主体也在社会进程中不断扩大，在一定程度上促进了四川非遗

的"广为人知"，但要更好地促进四川非遗保护传承的可持续性发展，非遗的传播推广主体仍需要进一步扩大。无论政府还是民间，都要不断强化"非物质文化遗产是民族共同财富""人人都是非遗文化的主人"的共识，由此促进社会各界在认识到四川非遗深厚的文化内涵后积极参与其中，帮助扩大四川非遗影响力。例如，政府可以通过发布相关支持性政策、法规或开展相关活动，学界可以通过开展专题研讨会、发表学术文章、组织学术活动等方式吸引公众关注四川非遗。除此之外，对于媒体界来说，除了传统媒体人，还可以争取自媒体人加入到四川非遗传播的队伍之中，不断扩大四川非遗的传播主体。

（二）非遗传播渠道的多元化与数字化

近年来，以互联网、物联网、大数据、人工智能等新技术为代表的数字经济发展迅猛，新一轮信息技术创新加速推动传统媒体与新型媒体群之间的聚合传播，促使物理空间平行的网络天地和数字世界正在形成，信息传播现象正呈现出日益显著的去中心化和碎片化趋势，成倍放大内容资源和信息消费。

数字化、科技化也是近年来非遗传播渠道的一大特点。非遗数字化是采用数字化的采集、储存、处理、展示、传播等技术，将非物质文化遗产转换、再现、复原成可共享、可再生的数字形态，并利用新媒体、短视频、直播等新型渠道进行多元化传播。运用现代数字技术将来自传统的非遗予以活态展现，通过多重连接和情景分享为受众营造身临其境之感，让非遗能够"听得见""带得走""学得来"，使之成为触手可及的生活方式。非遗的数字化保护不仅是要对其进行抢救性记录，更重要的是为其在互联网时代进行有效传播打下坚实基础。只有在数字化后非遗相关内容才可能打破时间和空间的限制，从而实现网络传播。同时，VR、AR 等新兴技术的出现也大大丰富了非遗的展示手法和传播方式。

例如，在首届"数字中国"建设峰会的数字非遗板块中，大众通过扫描 AR 卡片、AR 电子书就能在手机上观看立体化的妈祖信俗、中国剪纸等非遗展品；只需要戴上 VR 眼镜，便可置身于传承人工作室中一同学习烙画、漆画等非遗技艺。

因此，四川非遗也需要从单纯的数字化储存式的保护，转变对传统文化资源进行采集、梳理的数字化转换，将数字化基础工作扩大到数字化传播，同时增加人民群众对非遗文化的认识和参与性，将非遗活态化。大量四川的非遗传统技艺，诸如峨眉武术、成都漆艺、油纸伞制作技艺等，都可以考虑首先借用现代 AR 等新兴数字技术和独特的电影镜头语言对文化进行还原和展示，然后依托智能化算法机制以实现非遗内容的有效分发，再通过在社交平台制造话题、加强互动的方式加深大众对四川非遗的认知和了解，借助社交力量不断拓宽非遗传播路径。

（三）非遗传播过程的去"距离化"

在非遗数字化传播过程中，不仅要重视传播信息本身的事实性和逻辑性，更要思索如何从关系维度和情感维度上拉近与公众之间的距离，即从物质产品展示向过程动态展示转化的体验传播，如 AI、AR/VR、体感交互、可视化、小程序、全息投影等。为此，一要充分运用互联网共建、共享的特点，积极扩大非遗传播的影响力。二要利用新媒体和数字技术打造新颖的数字服务平台，让民众能及时、便捷地了解公共文化服务信息与内容，革除大众对非遗的陌生感和神秘感。只有"捧出"有温度、有质感的非遗，才能使人民群众的心灵与非遗发生情感共振，与非遗文化拉近距离，以接受度的提升创造消费潜力。除此之外，还可以有意识地促进传媒界与非遗界的专家们合作，使非遗传播更具系统性、逻辑性、针对性。

例如，国家文化部恭王府博物馆的品牌活动"锦绣中华 —— 中国非物质文化遗产服饰秀"巧妙地将现代时尚产业与传统服饰文化相结合，上演了精彩绝伦的非遗服饰秀。共计 23 家网络直播平台参与了联动直播，累计获得了广大网友近 5800 万次的点击观看量以及超 1000 万条的网友互动，在传播宣传方面取得了亮眼的成绩。

四、市场维度：拥抱资本，活化路径，展览品变消费品

全球经济一体化不断推进，古老的传统与文化迎头撞上现代世界的商业与市场，非遗文化不可避免地开始拥抱现代技术、互联网、品牌和资本，其保护与传承也逐渐孕育了全新的饱含"商业"痕迹的方式和途径。可以预见，市场化的良性运营可以成就非遗在未来发展的良好态势。

（一）"非遗"拉动千亿级市场

现如今，越来越多的非遗项目借助互联网与技术衍生创意设计，走出博物馆，从展览品变成消费品，告别手工作坊似的"自娱自乐"，朝着产业化、品牌化的模式过渡。

从高大上的收藏品、民俗展演到路边摊的工艺品，"非物质文化遗产"显然是一块金字招牌，彰显着"遗产"的稀缺性，成为各地企业和资本眼中的金矿，并试图用商业手段进行开发。保守估计，非遗市场化在传承与创新的摇摆、平衡间，非遗拉动的是一个千亿级市场。

（二）"非遗"商业化

据对四川省非物质文化遗产的普查结果来看，虽然我省有大量非

遗资源，但不是所有非遗项目都适合商业化，但从互联网角度看，70%以上有着很大的流量入口。随着现代化进程的加速，四川省的非物质文化遗产正遭受着猛烈的冲击。在很多年轻人眼中，非物质文化遗产的历史性对应的是"非常遗憾的过时"，文化性对应的是"土气"，就更谈不上对其的保护和传承了。

实际上非遗自诞生之日起，就在千百年的创造、生产和销售中，借助商业的力量流传至今。现阶段，随着"互联网+"的不断延伸，非遗文化拥有了新的表达途径和通道，不仅是实现对其的有效宣传，更将非物质文化遗产进行产品化变革以适应不断升级的消费环境，衍生出融入现代生活方式的产品，寻求具备市场基础的流量入口，通过资本的运作，实现非遗的商业变现。

例如，川剧、皮影、木偶戏等四川非遗项目，他们在历史上本来就是通过商演的方式"走市场"的。因此，在现代消费环境下，这样的非遗项目找到新的流量入口较其他项目显得相对容易。

又例如，2015 年，为纪念中国人民抗日战争暨世界反法西斯战争胜利 70 周年，大型现代川剧《还我河山》在中国西南片区巡演，通过现代舞台技术呈现传统戏剧的技艺，用现当代历史事件中的家国情仇与儿女故事引发观众共鸣，赢得观演群体的关注与喝彩，非遗文化借以传承。

不仅如此，传统手工艺生产的工艺品、生活器具、食品和药品，原本就是日常生活消费品，但由于其手工产能低，分布小、散、弱，难以与机器化生产相竞争，因此变得越来越稀少，越来越濒危。然而近年来，我国诸如《舌尖上的中国》《我在故宫修文物》《香巴拉深处》这样的纪录片，通过互联网进行传播，使"非遗+"成为商业变现的可能。又如，在《延禧攻略》一剧中，苏绣、苏扇、缂丝等非遗大量"出镜"，以匠心独具的服饰搭配体现出剧中每个人物角色不同的性格和命运,《延禧攻略》的热播进一步带动了人们对非遗的关注、保护与传承。

（三）场景销售，活化路径

开发新的场景和用途,可以成为非遗项目拓展市场的突破口。近年来不断涌现出的路径活化成功案例,为四川省非遗的市场拓展提供了借鉴意义。例如,具有160年历史的北京老字号内联升与动画电影《大鱼海棠》合作推出的"大鱼海棠"主题布鞋,线上开售不到一天就全部售罄。在这之前内联升还与迪士尼合作推出过迪士尼公主和米奇系列时尚布鞋,击中年轻女性和儿童的"萌点",一度成为热销单品。

除此之外,还有"非遗+众筹""非遗+教育""非遗+民宿""非遗+新零售"等新业态不断涌现,推陈出新,大量面临着品牌老化的非遗,正在寻找适合自己的姿势和方式,向年轻化、时尚化转型。其中不得不提的是"非遗+旅游"这一概念。传统手工技艺、民间音乐、舞蹈、民俗等非遗项目通过重新设定的场景满足日益增长的旅游消费的个性化、定制化,以"研学+社群"创新非遗传播和产品整合的途径。基于此,全国各地包括四川省催生了大量非遗小镇、非遗体验馆、非遗传习基地等非遗场景体验项目,挖掘非遗特点,结合地方实际,以吸引和留住游客。最具借鉴价值的场景打造应属由张艺谋、王潮歌、樊跃等人打造的"印象系列"山水实景演出项目,其将非遗元素成功融入旅游场景,引爆了国内旅游演艺的热情,获得了巨大的商业回报。

五、价值维度：非遗助力乡村振兴，推进"走出四川"

（一）盘活经济，四川非遗助推乡村振兴

2018年,国家文化和旅游部官网公布了两个关于"非遗扶贫"的

文件:《关于支持设立非遗扶贫就业工坊的通知》和《关于大力振兴贫困地区传统工艺助力精准扶贫的通知》。文件对"非遗+扶贫"工作做出具体部署,举措实、工作细,为非遗扶贫打出"组合拳",形成扶贫就业、产业发展和文化振兴的多赢格局。"非遗扶贫"并非简单地组织村民集体发展手工艺,更是社会各个层面的与时俱进和相向而行。各地各级政府制定研习培训计划,加强贫困地区非遗传承人群培养;组织专家团队,帮助贫困地区发展传统工艺产业;引进知名企业,帮助销售贫困地区的传统工艺产品。同时,提升广大非遗项目的从业者的自我主动意识,在保留核心制作技艺的同时,充分挖掘与发挥其审美、消费、实用、时尚等功能,提高产品品质,提升市场竞争力。

开展"非遗+扶贫",不管是从非遗传承发扬的角度,还是从扶贫效益的角度,都是文化底蕴深厚的贫困地区脱贫致富的新路径。四川省在实施精准扶贫的道路上,各级文旅部门充分利用非遗资源,通过建立合作社、"互联网+"、鼓励传承人创业等形式,引导群众脱贫攻坚,成效显著。

1. 带动就业,非遗引领脱贫前景

四川省各地纷纷结合地方实际情况,在保护与传承非遗项目的同时,帮助地方群众在参与中逐步脱贫。

在四川省绵阳市北川羌族自治县,羌族草编技艺传承人兼北川和谐旅游开发有限公司负责人黄强,从 2011 年就开始在北川乡镇及县城的禹羌传承培训学校培训草编技艺。当地村民学成后,与公司签订协议,利用田里的稻草秸秆等材料,加上公司提供的辅助物料,按订单生产草编产品,合作社提供技术指导,每月底由公司回收后加工成成品。当地留守妇女在不耽搁家务的同时,每月可稳定增收 1000 元左右。

如今,在北川羌族自治县文广新局的帮助下,黄强在各个乡镇的文化站已建成羌族草编传承及生产基地 20 余处，成立草编合作社 8 家，年销售额达 200 万元。不仅如此，羌族草编还走出北川，为凉山、攀枝花、雅安等地区的彝、藏、傈僳等少数民族群众开展草编技能培训。

2. 拓宽渠道，电商助力资源开发

四川基层，特别是民族地区，有脱贫的需求，更有丰厚的非遗资源，可以借助"互联网+"的新兴业态，进一步丰富非遗扶贫的方式。

四川省凉山州是全国深度贫困地区"三区三州"之一，但非遗资源丰富、民族特色鲜明，拥有以彝族服饰、彝绣、彝族羊毛擀毡、彝族银饰、彝族漆器等为代表的非遗传统工艺项目。2019 年 2 月 28 日，由国家文化和旅游部支持的唯品会驻四川凉山传统工艺工作站在西昌市揭牌。工作站采用"政府+唯品会+非遗扶贫工坊+贫困群众"的模式，由政府及相关部门加大政策支持和引导，由唯品会提供创意设计帮助和推广销售平台，再通过工作站下若干非遗扶贫工坊为贫困群众提供非遗技艺指导和产品订单，贫困群众可选取多种就业方式增收。

3. 全盘规划，推进脱贫奔小康

2018 年，四川省阿坝藏族羌族自治州壤塘县壤塘县委出台《关于促进壤塘县文化创新发展的决定》，将文化作为引领转型发展的旗帜，并制定《文化生态保护区总体规划（2018—2025）》，采取"政府扶持、传承人自主创办"的方式，鼓励、扶持传承人积极创办传习所。壤塘县共建立非遗传习所 26 个，项目涵盖觉囊唐卡、藏族石刻、藏香、藏医药、藏茶、藏式陶艺、觉囊雕刻、摩尼喜旋传统服饰、藏纸等非遗文化领域。得益于此，该县聚集了 1400 多人从事非遗文化生产性保护工作，许多被搁置、被遗忘的民间艺术重新回到农牧民群众身边，焕发出旺盛的生命力。

不仅如此，为解决传习所分布分散、发展规模小、产业结构单一、经济带动能力有限等问题，壤塘县投资 1 亿元建设非遗传习创业园，并启动了以中壤塘乡为核心、以南莫且湿地自然保护区和则曲河水利风景区为双翼的生态文化旅游产业园建设，计划用 3 年时间把中壤塘地区打造成 4A 级景区，促进"文化+旅游"和"文化+扶贫"融合发展，进一步将非遗文化优势转化为产业优势、经济优势。

与此同时，壤塘县每两年还定期举办民间手工艺技能大赛、壤巴拉节，开展壤巴拉锅庄、赛马会等文化活动，以此提升壤塘文化影响力和知名度。借助对口援建资源优势，壤塘县还积极谋划"浙壤文化交流""绵壤文化活动周"等活动，不断延长非遗文化发展半径，横向延伸文化产业链条。

（二）打造旅游经济强省，助力四川非遗"走出四川"

2013 年，为充分发挥旅游业对扩内需、调结构、促就业、惠民生和建设生态文明的重要引擎作用，加快推动四川省从旅游资源大省向旅游经济强省跨越，四川省人民政府下发了《关于加快建设旅游经济强省的意见》，将旅游业发展纳入我省经济和社会发展规划，提出引导旅游项目和旅游要素重组，打造多种类型的旅游产业集聚区的实施意见。2019 年，省委、省政府下发《关于大力发展文旅经济 加快建设文化强省旅游强省的意见》，提出加快建设文化强省旅游强省的发展目标：经过 5 年努力，把我省建设成为社会主义核心价值观广泛践行、文化事业繁荣发展、文旅产业深度融合的文化高地和世界重要旅游目的地。

2019 年颁布的四川 10 条"非遗之旅"以全省不同非遗项目为核心、以旅游线路为依托，以非遗传习所、非遗体验区和体验基地等为载体，通过产品设计、线路策划，推进非遗元素与旅游线路、知名景区、旅游服务和旅游体验融合，旨在促进非遗项目与旅游线路和景区景点融合，推动非遗保护设施与旅游服务融合，提升非遗技艺传承与旅游互动体验的融合，促进非遗资源更好地转化为旅游资源。项目包括藏羌环线非遗之旅、香格里拉非遗之旅、蜀道三国非遗之旅、古蜀名镇非遗之旅、川北巴山非遗之旅、茶马古道非遗之旅、川江沿线非遗之旅、青城峨眉非遗之旅、年画体验之旅和竹艺体验之旅。

其中，以"藏羌环线非遗之旅"依托"九寨沟环线"经典旅游线路为例，游客可以在欣赏美景的同时，深度体验藏羌年、羌绣、羌族羊皮鼓舞等羌民族非遗项目的独特魅力；通过"香格里拉非遗之旅"可以体验木雅藏戏、理塘锅庄、康定"四月八"跑马转山会等康巴非遗项目的神奇之处；在"蜀道三国非遗之旅"线路上，重点非遗项目数不胜数，包括金钱板、嘉陵江中游船工号子、广汉保保节、麻柳刺绣、阆中春节习俗等。此外，精心设置的"古蜀名镇非遗之旅""川北巴山非遗之旅""川江沿线非遗之旅""青城峨眉非遗之旅""年画体验之旅"和"竹艺体验之旅"等将全面为游客提供中华传统美学体验。

通过文化和旅游的融合发展，文化可以更加富有活力，旅游也会更加富有魅力。非遗与旅游的融合，一方面可借力旅游线路和知名景区丰富的游客资源，宣传四川特色非遗保护项目，另一方面也提升了四川旅游的文化品位和旅游价值。借力"非遗+旅游"的翅膀，四川非遗以其见证了四川各民族历程的厚度和深刻彰显着四川文化的特殊魅力，走出四川，闪耀全国乃至世界，这是四川非遗文化传承与发展的重要篇章和必经之道。

第七章
案例研究

本章通过案列分析对四川省国家级非物质文化遗产项目蜀绣进行研究，探讨媒体融合背景下非物质文化遗产蜀绣借助新媒介技术所孕育的崭新生命力，以及全媒体视域下的产业发展消费新趋势。

一、新媒介下蜀绣"关系传播"探析 —— 以蜀绣作为国礼承载关系为例

2013 年 3 月 25 日，媒体上出现了习近平的夫人彭丽媛在参观坦桑尼亚"妇女与发展基金会"时送出的国礼礼单，包含一款蜀绣"梅花双熊"。这款蜀绣背后有怎样的故事？作为礼物送给外宾蕴含什么样的意义？在以互联网为代表的新媒介上传播得如火如荼，只要在百度上输入"蜀绣国礼"四个字，瞬间显示出来的消息就有上千条。各大主流媒体、微博社区等纷纷报道，如四川新闻网"解密彭丽媛国礼蜀绣：《梅花双熊》出自成都"，扬子晚报网"彭丽媛赠非国礼蜀绣源自14 年前的画作《梅花双熊》"，中国网新闻中心"蜀绣成'国礼'蜀绣大师称制作大概需要 1 个月"，新浪博客"蜀绣成'国礼'价格再翻一倍"，泉州网"解密彭丽媛赠非国礼蜀绣：画家很好找，绣娘未定"等。蜀绣一下就在网络媒介上"火"了起来。

（一）新媒介及蜀绣"关系传播"

1. 新媒介传播即"关系传播"

1967 年，美国哥伦比亚广播电视网（CBS）技术研究所所长，NTSC 电视制式的发明者 P.戈尔德马克（P.Goldmark）首次使用了"新媒介"（New media）这个概念。1969 年，美国传播政策总统特别委员会的 E. 罗斯托（E.Rostow）在向时任总统尼克松提交的报告书中，多处使用了"新媒介"一词。由此，"新媒介"一词开始在美国社会上流行，并且这个趋势在不久以后扩展到了全世界。

近 20 年来，随着数字技术、移动通信技术、计算机技术、网络技术等新兴技术的广泛应用，媒介形态发生了巨大变化，基于报纸、杂

志、广播、电视等传统媒介形态的研究视角和研究效果，以互联网为代表的新媒介形态从根本上"改变了生产过程、体验、权力和文化的运作与结果"，深刻地影响着社会发展和人们的生活方式。

华中科技大学新闻与信息传播学院副教授、香港城市大学访问学者陈先红认为："对新媒介传播形态的界定，不能够仍然按照传统的线性思维，把它简单地归属于人际传播、小众传播、大众传播或者超人际传播的范畴，而应该从最本质的传播类型入手，在'信息传播'和'关系传播'之间，寻找新媒介传播的偏向……在新媒介传播中，传播被当作一个策略工具来帮助建立互动双方的关系……新媒介传播归属应该属于典型的'关系传播'。"这是传递关系信息的一种交往模式，其与关系传播理论的共同指向是交流者不需要解决人与人之间的差异问题，需要的是创建一个新的思维模式，寻求接受差异的方式，以差异为依据去认识关系中存在的同一性与差异性的永恒张力。正如彭丽媛送蜀绣作为国礼在新媒介上报道后反响热烈一事，某种意义上其实就是"关系传播"的体现，这也为新媒介蜀绣传播提供了一个新的方向或途径。

2. 蜀绣"关系传播"必要性分析

中国蜀绣又称川绣，源远流长，蜀绣之名早在汉代就已誉满天下。汉赋家扬雄在其《蜀都赋》中就道："锦布绣望，芒芒兮无幅。"悠久的历史、丰富的文化内涵及其针法技艺都对中国刺绣发展产生过重大影响，蜀绣作为国家非常重视的非物质文化遗产，与苏绣、湘绣、粤绣齐名，为中国四大名绣之一，并享有"蜀中之宝"的美誉。数千年的蜀绣工艺，历经风雨变幻，兴衰起落，随着新媒介传播时代的到来，蜀绣的文化内涵、艺术气质都需要现代化的新媒介传播途径更为直观生动地展现出来，通过采用一系列富有现代时尚气息的、科学完整的新媒介"关系传播"策略，与消费者建立密切的情感联系，从而使蜀绣这一承载着悠久历史文化的艺术经典焕发新的生机与活力。

其实，纵观蜀绣发展历史，蜀绣的传播形态一直是生动丰富的。早在西周青铜器上，考古学家就已发现了明显的辫子股绣印痕；魏晋南北朝时期出现了以人物、山川为对象的"绣画"；敦煌莫高窟发现了佛像绣像；北宋时期成都转运司奉旨绣军旗 500 面；西汉扬雄、蜀中才子司马相如、南宋章樵等文学家都曾作文称赞蜀绣；元末大夏政权的建立者明玉珍的龙袍，明代将领秦良玉的两件绣袍都展现了蜀绣华彩；1915 年，蜀绣在美国巴拿马太平洋万国博览会上获奖，清王朝嘉奖蜀绣"狮子滚绣球挂屏"，为蜀绣赢得很大的声誉；人民大会堂四川厅用蜀绣绣制的《万水千山》《芙蓉锦鲤》，令人遐想天府之国丰富的物产与迤逦的风光……这些形态各异的传播媒介与方式，使得蜀绣艺术在近三千年的历史中不断发展演绎、辉煌兴盛。

随着媒介技术的发展，当代社会正在步入一个传播意义上的新时代，即新媒介时代。新媒介以跨时间、跨地域、传播速度快、传播范围广、传播效率高、互动性强、传播生动直观等传播优势，已经越来越成为各种产业发展传播的主要途径。蜀绣要发展，更应该思考蜀绣的新媒介传播未来，能够实现比传统媒介更有效的传播，扩大不同区域的受众范围，更有效地感知人们对蜀绣的认识、了解和传播，提高人们对蜀绣的认同感、接受度。

彭丽媛把蜀绣作为国礼送出去以后，单这一事件，蜀绣在新媒介上的点击率、互动率就突破了以前，大众关注这款国礼蜀绣的作者是谁，关注这款国礼蜀绣所蕴含的意义，关注这款国礼蜀绣带来的两国之间未来的关系等，一系列思考无疑都成了蜀绣在新媒介上宣传、传播的契机，最后所有对这款国礼蜀绣的关注都会毫无疑问地回到大众对这个蜀绣产业的关注。不可否认，蜀绣作为国礼巩固两国良好关系这一事实在新媒介上的火爆，很大意义上为蜀绣形象的传播产生了重大作用。传播的本质是在传播主体与接受主体的互动之中建构起来的，传播者和接收者之间关系的现状直接影响着传播内容和传播行为的优劣。其实，传播本身就是社会关系的总和，当传播者和接收者之间的关系达到最饱和状态的时候，传播关系就会按照自身的意志来裁剪传播内容，传播也就产生了催眠效果。从另一个角度来说，就是当传播双方关系达到一定程度的时候，传播内容信息也就失去了意义，剩下的就是纯粹的传播关系。正如新媒介上曝光国礼礼单蜀绣以后，大众所关注并不是因为蜀绣本身，而是蜀绣所承担的承载两国友好关系的使命，这种"关系"才是蜀绣在新媒介上"火"起来的原因。事实也证明蜀绣国礼的新媒介传播如果加入"关系传播"的元素，那就有事半功倍的效果。

（二）蜀绣"关系传播"思考

1. 蜀绣社会"关系传播"

其实新媒介传播本应归属于"关系传播"。从社会层面上来说，新媒介传播方式从单向向双向转变，传播者和接收者都可以是信息的发布者，并且进行互动。这样为新媒介提供了发展关系的平台，比如在一个虚拟社区里，大众可以直接到自己感兴趣的地方去和自己志同道合者交流，传播机会与传统方法相比，可以无限放大。蜀绣的新媒介传播需要跨时间、跨地域、无限扩大的社交圈子，这些各种因为新媒介而建立起来的圈子使得在对蜀绣传播的时候更为个性化。个性地表达自己的观点，传播自己关注或想要知道的信息，并且随时可以把蜀绣中想要表达的元素或关于蜀绣的事情通过手机上网，在公交、出租车上看电视、听广播等移动性地表达出来，让全球更多人了解蜀绣的发展，缩小了传播蜀绣的时空距离。

2. 蜀绣文化"关系传播"

从文化层面上来说，蜀绣的魅力一直是令人心驰神往的，"绣棚花鸟逐时新，活色生香可夺真"。从古至今，蜀绣都拥有丰富的文化内涵和艺术审美价值，从蜀绣针法上来说，蜀绣拥有精湛的绝技，蜀绣以软缎和彩丝为主要原料，针法包括 12 大类共 122 种，用晕针、铺针、滚针、截针、掺针、盖针、切针、拉针、沙针、汕针等，讲究"针脚整齐，线片光亮，紧密柔和，车拧到家"。蜀绣画面设计也是极为考究，在蜀绣盛行时，当时一批有特色的画作如刘子兼的山水、赵鹤琴的花鸟、杨建安的荷花、张致安的虫鸟都纷纷入绣。古代名家画作如苏东坡的古木怪石、郑板桥的竹石等，从流行图案、山水花鸟、博古到民间传说八仙过海、凤穿牡丹无一不囊括在内，极大地丰富了蜀绣的文化内涵。彭丽媛送出去的国礼蜀绣就是"中国第一熊猫国画家"王申勇而作，绣的是两只小熊猫，原名为"娇子"，正如王申勇所说："熊猫不仅是四川成都的代表，也是中国的国宝，它们能作为中外友谊的桥梁，是件非常有意义的好事。"在新媒介上，从蜀绣的文化内涵和艺术审美欣赏价值出发，可以让蜀绣的传播速度实时化，新媒介的声音和视频、音频进行实时传播，从单一到交融。与传统媒体相比，蜀绣文化的新媒介传播内容方面更为丰富，集文字、图像、声音等为一体的优势可以使蜀绣在新媒介上呈现给大众的画面更清晰、更接近于真实。与此同时，新媒介的交融性还表现在终端上，一部手机就可以把通话、发短信、听广播、看电视、上网等多种媒体的功能集合为一身，对蜀绣文化的传播也是非常有利的。新媒介突破了地域化、国界化的局限，消解国家与国家、社群、产业之间的边界，消解信息传播者与接收者之间的边界，使蜀绣在更广阔的文化价值观关系网中得到传承。

3. 蜀绣人际"关系传播"

从人际层面上来说，在蜀绣传播中，一般传播者的名望越高，他在传播中所吸引的受传者就越多，因而其传播所影响的面也就更广。在信息爆炸的今天，每人每天都会收到各种各样的信息。如果这一信息来自该行业的成功人士、专家学者等，便能产生较好的效应。这也就启发了传播者，一旦接收者在专业上佩服传播者，在人格上爱戴传播者、亲近传播者，传播效果就会更佳。因此，善于把握和调节接收者情绪的高效传播艺术，吸引接收者的魅力，所传播的信息自然会受到大家的欢迎和接受。通过"名人效应"带动的"关系传播"就更有说服力。因此，以明星带动蜀绣传承，让明星的影响力延伸到蜀绣文化上，就会有更好、更直接的传播效果。

2009 年，素来被传媒冠为"舞台皇后"，以英姿飒爽为表演风格的年轻歌手李宇春成为蜀绣传播大使，成功演绎了歌曲和 MV ——《蜀绣》。李宇春表示，能够为拥有悠久历史积淀的蜀绣做点贡献是非常荣幸和骄傲的，希望借助自身的影响力使蜀绣文化得以推广，并发扬到世界上更多的地方。李宇春为蜀绣不遗余力的宣传、对中国传统技艺的支持，使更多的人认识、喜爱这一文化。在媒介技术发达的今天，新媒介为蜀绣人际传播提供了一种形成、发展和维系情感关系的工具。

二、全媒体视域下中国传统技艺消费产业化发展的供给侧改革研究 —— 以蜀绣为例

中国传统技艺是中华文化的重要组成部分，历史悠久，源远流长，是时代锤炼和文化传承的精华，凝聚了民族的性格、精神，创造了民族文化。但是，近现代以来，随着工业革命的发展，很多传统技艺都面临着失传，如果再不加以保护，这些优秀的传统技艺将会逐渐消亡。

在全媒体时代，中国的传统技艺在被保护和传承的同时更应该在消费产业化的高地上占领发展的先机，从供给侧改革着手谋求生存、发展和传承。因此，应该以传统技艺非物质文化遗产蜀绣为例，深入分析中国传统技艺消费产业化发展的供给侧改革。

蜀绣作为中国四大名绣之一，在 2006 年被正式列入第一批国家级非物质文化遗产名录。蜀绣拥有悠久的历史，精湛的技术，在中国传统技艺中别具一格。作为中国传统工艺的主要流派，蜀绣的技艺具有不可替代的历史价值、文化价值、艺术价值和精神价值。在全媒体融合时代，蜀绣的发展已经不再是单纯的行业发展态势，呈现出产业化发展的趋势，需要高端发展、价值升级、供给侧改革，更需要文化的传承。

（一）蜀绣产业发展现状：供给与需求的矛盾

历史上，蜀绣立足于蜀地，曾经有着"挥锦布绣"的蜀国繁荣纺织景象：三国时期，蜀绣作为纺织品成为重要的经济支柱；西晋时期，蜀绣同金、银、玉、珠并称为"蜀中之宝"；隋唐时期，蜀绣更是借助于丝绸之路西南起点成都的便利，传播到番邦诸国；到清朝中后期，蜀绣盛极一时，仅成都专营的刺绣作坊就 80 余家。

近现代以来，蜀绣企业和产品的发展呈现跌宕之势，因其产量低、价格高，在很长一段时间里，蜀绣的定位都只在奢侈消费品上，曲高和寡，相比于发展较快的苏绣、湘绣，其市场消费的潜力并没有得到充分的挖掘，虽然"叫好"，但是"不叫座"。客观地说，蜀绣生产和消费需求的严重不匹配，正是因为蜀绣产业长期对"供给侧"的疏忽。因此，蜀绣产业应该着力加强供给端的结构性改革，提高供给体系的质量和效率，增强经济持续发展生产动力，最终提高全要素生产率的有机整合水平。

长期以来，四川蜀绣产业呈现"两头小、中间大"的"橄榄球形"的状况。在生产的技艺和制造环节，绣娘的绣工水平无疑是精湛的，但是绣娘要绣出什么样的作品来供给市场，满足市场消费却成了难题。蜀绣产品走不出工艺品产业链，在实用绣品和高端定制上与苏绣、湘绣难以比拟，比起苏绣产品大量的实用性开发，蜀绣不管是质量还是效率都十分落后。蜀绣文化创意产业园和蜀绣文化产业发展示范区产业发展研究数据显示，截至2015年底，成都市的各类蜀绣创作、生产和经营企业也就40多家，销售网点只有100多个，在非物质文化遗产蜀绣之乡安靖集聚的蜀绣企业才28家，60%的蜀绣企业和作坊年产值在100万元以下，年产值在300万元以上的仅有3家，并且这些蜀绣企业发展大多是以家庭作坊为主，其产品开发和经营方式都呈现了品种单一、规模小、企业分布散的特点。近年来，蜀绣企业和作坊更是呈现一盘散沙的状况，有些蜀绣企业和作坊甚至逐渐退出市场舞台，蜀绣企业和作坊的进一步发展面临着重大的问题。但是，四大名绣中的苏绣和湘绣的发展却是蓬勃向上，根据中国绣品的外贸出口和国内消费相关调研报告统计，苏绣的市场占有率为83%，湘绣占12%，蜀绣和粤绣仅占5%。

另外，成都蜀绣工程技术研究中心相关研究数据显示，截至2015年底，长期从事蜀绣工作的绣娘仅1500余人，老的逐渐老去，年轻人不愿意以此为业，不愿意做蜀绣的传承人。一般情况下，要培养出一名合格的蜀绣的绣娘，需要5~7年的时间，但现在在蜀绣的人才培养上，是没有完整和系统的教材的，只能依靠老艺人的口授心传和绣娘、绣工们的体会和钻研。从蜀绣人才的现状来看，蜀绣的国家级大师仅有2人，省、市级大师有40余人，有高、中、初级职业技能资格证的绣工有500多人，剩下的就是经过专业培训的绣工，也不过一两千人。一方面，高层次人才短缺，导致供给端产品的设计和研发滞后，蜀绣绣品设计元素总是走不出除了熊猫就是芙蓉锦鲤的套路，产品体系更是走不出工艺品的产业链。在产业发展过程中，无论是营销渠道、自主品牌、服务环节，还是价值体现都比较薄弱，缺乏大品牌、现代化企业管理经验和营销理念；另一方面，蜀绣的需求在劳动力成本和原材料成本大幅度增加的前提下，可替代性产品越来越多，没有产品开发核心竞争力，也不可避免地受到现代文明、外来文化和经济市场的强烈冲击。

因此，开发蜀绣产品要打破原有蜀绣产品体系，多从深厚蜀文化品位、纵深感意境上打造适宜蜀绣产业发展的新兴产品和新业态。

（二）解读全媒体视域下蜀绣产业发展新消费趋势

1. 蜀绣产业发展新消费趋势

2006 年，蜀绣被列入第一批国家级的非物质文化遗产名录后，蜀绣的发展受到高度重视。近年来，蜀绣产品的知名度和美誉度都在消费者的心中显著提高。尽管如此，成都蜀绣产业的产值增长不快，新绣娘供给不足，符合现代消费文化和消费习俗的创意产品仍旧明显供给不足，消费动力也不足，尤其是和湘绣开发的 300 多个类别的日用品比起来更是相差甚远，蜀绣的消费增长空间还有待挖掘。在经济新常态下，蜀绣的消费趋势有待进一步深入研究，尤其对于蜀绣产业的整体发展，更需要从供给端了解现代产业发展的全新趋势：第一个趋势是蜀绣产业链的分解和组合之间的关系，蜀绣产业是文化保护和产业发展双驱动，只有实现蜀绣产业发展和经济联动发展，蜀绣才能带动文化、旅游、纺织等多行业经济价值的实现，引领新的消费增长点；第二个趋势是顾客价值的变化导致销售终端的个性化需求不断加大，形成了一个国际化的新型消费市场，传统的策略已经不足以应付新的消费观念。

2. 全媒体传播时代赋予蜀绣产业发展新动力

蜀绣产品开发，无论是作为非物质文化遗产，还是作为文化艺术的消费品，其市场消费潜力还远远没有被充分挖掘。从某种意义上来说，市场需求是蜀绣生存的土壤，非物质文化遗产不是"化石遗产"，"遗产"的使命是建立在消费需求上的传承"主体"和存活空间。在现实的情况下，蜀绣的消费能力和消费愿望都没有转化为生产力，成为大众的消费，在非物质文化遗产的体现，也是仅在于一种精神文化的作用。在国际市场上，蜀绣的发展更是苍白无力，如今在"一带一路"发展的契机下，成都作为古代南方丝绸之路的起点，蜀绣的发展更加需要国际市场的开拓，也需要传播格局和传播空间的拓展。

随着网络技术的发展，世界传播格局已经从以前的传统的单一的传播模式过渡到了复合的全媒体语境的传播方式。所谓全媒体，并不是以前的传统方式和手段的传播媒介的简单堆积，而是一种增值的传播效应的体现。客观地说，全媒体的传播模态对蜀绣国际发展的推广和应用具有重要助推力。一方面，从蜀绣发展的营运理念或者模式来说，蜀绣的拓展需要传承的主体。在全球化经济文化浪潮的冲击下，蜀绣的生存主体和传播空间如果还保留在原始的单一的原生性文化状态，就算是搬到了国际市场的传播舞台上，也不能和整合后的其他的多样的文化需求相融合，营运没有创新特色，在自然经济社会模式的小环境下产生的所谓天然特色，其文化生命力也是十分脆弱的。全媒体格局下的蜀绣拓展，正好整合了蜀绣天然特色，在世界传播格局中打造蜀绣的国际竞争力。另一方面，从蜀绣的传播形态来说，全媒体语境的表现形式凸显了丰富多彩的特色，可以从文、图、声、光、电来全方位、立体地展示蜀绣的内容，同时还可以通过文字、声像、网络、通信等传播手段来传播蜀绣文化，综合地表现蜀绣的各种形态。全媒体的传播模态是一个开放的系统，并不是单一的传播模式，可以想象，关于蜀绣的文字、图像、动画、声音、视频、图形等多种表现形式在不同的媒介上表现出来的时候，无论是传统媒体的纸媒、广播媒体、电视媒体还是新媒体的网络媒体、手机媒体，这种融合是全媒体语境下的视听盛宴。而蜀绣分解出来的多种表现方式和各种层次通过全媒体传播形态将会满足消费者需求的细分层次，使得消费者可以多渠道、多维度地在视觉、听觉、感知上获得满足，这种媒体体验和传播模态是蜀绣前所未有的拓展。

经济新常态下，消费大众个性化的市场需求早已经成为消费者新的消费热点和增长点，蜀绣产品只要把握了消费者个性化和多元化的需求，创造性累积将开辟更广阔的市场。

（三）引领蜀绣产业化发展的供给侧改革策略

1. 实现现代技术与传统艺术的一体化发展

客观地说，蜀绣的技艺本身就是一体的，无论是实用绣品还是装饰的绣品，在发展的过程中都有着极大的技术和艺术的包容性和兼容性。一方面，从技术上来说，蜀绣的针法是在吸收外来针法的过程中逐步成熟和完善的。现有的十二大类蜀绣针法是在多次与苏绣、湘绣等绣种的交流和融合中形成的，每一类针法又有了很多种绣法，蜀绣的技术是四大名绣中最丰富和多变的，用多样的组合形式来表现蜀绣艺术的精髓。另一方面，从艺术层面说，蜀绣绣品的形象表达诠释了蜀绣的艺术价值和文化价值，也实现了设计者和绣工表达蜀绣艺术的鲜活画意。

不管是从蜀绣的技术还是艺术来研究，蜀绣产业的发展都有着本质的社会属性，作为非物质文化遗产，在考察其意义和价值的时候，必须把蜀绣放置到产生它的人文生态和社会发展层面去整体考察，从整体上感知蜀绣存在的意义和价值。作为技术产品，蜀绣产品生命力在于价值的可用和实用，在于消费者的消费，产品的"活态"是美学审思和价值经济形态的呈现。从历史线性发展规律来看，技术的发展呈现由低级向高级发展的增长趋势，任何技术的内涵都是从低级技术到高级技术的逻辑增长，当技术达到更高一层的形态，其低级的形态就只能作为历史遗迹从而失去存在的独立价值和根据，新的技术不断替代老的技术已成为技术发展的规律。所以，蜀绣技术需要技法的完善和娴熟，同时也离不开艺术化的价值互渗，经典的技艺才能突破蜀绣传统发展藩篱，从而达到创造性的发展和积累，生成生长的活力，形成有效供给需求。

作为艺术形态，蜀绣的传承是一种活态的传承，是从集体的记忆、情感的需要和文化的认同层面诠释的活态传承，"活态"是价值和意义的体现，也是文化的认可。近年来，蜀绣产业的发展呈现断裂式模态，从社会的发展规律来说，蜀绣的发展已经面临着必须引进保护、养护和养活的文化生态生长机制，正如贡布里希·恩斯特·汉斯提出的艺术生态壁龛，要把蜀绣艺术形态的传承放在与之直接关系的文化环境中进行研究，才是特定的艺术形态的文化传承。因此，作为艺术形态的蜀绣其实是在技术化的环境条件和大众情感的需要中实现自身的价值。从意识形态上来说，只有社会拥有历史记忆，有着对蜀绣产品的情感的体验和对其文化传承的认同，蜀绣才会有真正的发展，才不会成为作为"化石"的遗产。

蜀绣的技艺一体化是娴熟技术和活态艺术的融合。技术源自人类的开端，是生产力水平的需求，满足人类的生存需求，随着技术的发展，也满足人类多样化的需求；艺术发端于人类文化的起源，"艺术是'又高级又通俗'，把最高级的内容传达给大众"的形态表现。在经济新常态下，蜀绣的发展离不开大众的内在消费需求和文化认同的深层发展机制，任何一门技艺在当今消费趋势下不能再发挥自身独有的文化功能和文化惯性，不能根据市场的变迁和环境的变化来适应社会，必然将在新的经济形态下被大众抛弃，从而消亡。

2. 从供给端拓展高端个性定制市场

市场因为需求的转变，供给更应该随之转变。在把握新消费趋势的基础上，要发掘蜀绣新的消费增长点，其关键就是蜀绣品牌价值的体现。研究表明，因为消费观念的变化，消费者是否愿意购买产品大多取决于对品牌的认同，尤其是艺术经济品，消费者的感知价值更是购买产品的重要影响因素。蜀绣，作为艺术经济品，其文化价值和实用价值都是模糊的，存在于消费者感知的价值观和感知水平上，情感偏爱者对艺术经济品价格就不太在意了，在意的是产品本身蕴含的艺术价值和文化价值。所以，感知价值与顾客自身的情感反应及其消费体验有关，顾客感知会进一步影响顾客的购买行为。一般情况下，消费者购买蜀绣，在消费心理上的定位，以及在新消费观念的引导下，炫耀性的消费心理（conspicuous consumption psychology）引导消费者感知产品价值，从而形成购买行为。这些新的消费观念和购买行为又引导着蜀绣的经济消费向价值模态体现上转化，触发了新的消费增长点，即个性化、高效化、网络化和价值化的行业结构调整和从点到面的蜀绣产业的转型和升级。

可见，消费者愿意支付更高的价格来购买蜀绣产品，其实是为了显示自己的社会地位和心理上的优越感。这些炫耀性的购买行为，恰好使消费者看重自己的身份地位，从而忽略了购买价格，或者对价格不敏感。总体而言，具有经济价值和文化内涵的蜀绣产品可以极大地调动消费者的购买欲望，把蜀绣产品的开发与产品本身内涵和外部延伸的价值、文化相关联，把蜀绣和城市发展、地区经济发展相结合，蜀绣的发展和价值模态才会充满活力。

3. 立足全媒体开发大众需求，提高蜀绣产品有效供给

蜀绣产业发展的供给侧改革，并不意味着和需求相对立，而是把生产要素的效率和质量的提高放置在一个平台。蜀绣产业发展的有效供给是政府—企业—市场共同发展的基本，是有效对资源市场进行配置的过程，分工、合作、互动，联通至生存供给、消费供给、投资供给，甚至到出口供给，才有可能满足各自的需求，因此，有效供给是生产力要素资源配置的优化。

第一，通过全媒体整合蜀绣产业发展，形成蜀绣产业新主体。任何产业的发展，供给和需求都是相互依存的，有效的需求决定供给主体的供给能力。在全媒体时代，要充分发挥市场在资源配置中的决定性作用，发挥政府、蜀绣企业、绣娘、蜀绣需求者在经济发展中的作用，在借鉴苏绣、湘绣发展的基础上，形成蜀绣产业发展的新主体，进一步拓展发展空间。

第二，培育蜀绣产业发展新动力。近年来，蜀绣产业发展停滞不前，其原因就是蜀绣发展后期动力不足。必须在蜀绣产业发展过程中全面改革，培育新的增长动力，通过全面创新形式，尤其是在蜀绣产品的生产端，通过设计图案、实用绣品开发、高端定制形成蜀绣产品新的增长点，通过提高全要素生产率来实现蜀绣产业的可持续发展。

第三，立足蜀绣产业，创新开发蜀绣产业的新技术和新业态。产业发展要尊重和顺应经济规律和市场规律，淘汰蜀绣产业发展中的僵尸企业，更要在市场的竞争中避免资源浪费和无效劳动，从互联网、新媒体等多渠道开发蜀绣产业发展的新技术和新业态。

第四，促进区域就业和创新创业。和苏绣"百万绣娘"规模相比，蜀绣产业的从业人员在数量上相形见拙。蜀绣作为非物质文化遗产，蜀绣产业的发展必须要与解决就业等社会问题关联，尤其是重视对农村妇女、下岗职工的再就业培训，对社会人员乃至大学生的创新创业

的引导。特别是在"互联网+"时代，蜀绣产业发展和互联网的有效结合，更是迫在眉睫。

　　由此可见，以蜀绣为代表的众多中国传统技艺在新消费趋势下，在"一带一路"发展的契机下，其发展表现出了从未有过的生机和活力。中国的传统技艺在全媒体视域下，其发展应冲破行业格局的藩篱，在"互联网+"时代和跨界融合的时代，实现价值升级和地方经济、城市名片、文化旅游的结合和联系，只有从传统技艺产业发展的供给侧改革入手，传统技艺的发展才会更接地气，符合时代发展的趋势。

下篇

第八章
四川省世界级与国家级非物质文化遗产
项目名录和中英文简介

本章通过对四川省世界级与国家级非物质文化遗产项目进行名录列表展示和中英文简介，普及四川非遗文化，让更多的四川人、中国人、国际友人了解四川非遗，了解四川文化。

一、世界级非物质文化遗产名录及中英文简介（7项）

（一）名录列表

一、联合国教科文组织非遗项目——人类非物质文化遗产代表作名录（6项）		
序号	项目名称	批准时间
1	格萨（斯）尔	2009年
2	中国桑蚕丝织技艺（蜀锦）	2009年
3	藏戏	2009年
4	中国雕版印刷技艺（德格雕版印刷技艺）	2009年
5	中国皮影戏	2011年
6	藏医药浴法	2018年
二、联合国教科文组织非遗项目——急需保护的非物质文化遗产名录（1项）		
7	羌年庆祝习俗	2009年

（二）四川省世界级非物质文化遗产项目中英文简介（7项）

List of Intangible Cultural Heritage of Sichuan Province （7）

1. 联合国教科文组织非遗项目——人类非物质文化遗产代表作名录（6项）

UNESCO Intangible Cultural Project — Representative List of Intangible Cultural Heritage of Humanity （6）

（1）格萨（斯）尔 *Gesar*

格萨（斯）尔，民间文学，2006年入选国家非物质文化遗产名录，2009年被列入联合国教科文组织人类非物质文化遗产代表作名录。格萨（斯）尔主要分布在西藏、青海、甘肃、四川、云南、内蒙古、新疆地区。其传承方式为派系传承、师徒传承，现有国家级传承人次仁占堆（西藏）等9人，目前已建立"果洛格萨尔口头传统研究基地""德格格萨尔口头传统研究基地"，进行进一步保护。西藏自治区还成立专门的抢救和整理机构，寻访说唱艺人，录制磁带，搜集藏文手抄本、木刻本，整理出版藏文本，汉译本，并翻译成英、日、法文出版。

格萨（斯）尔是世界上迄今发现的演唱篇幅最长的史诗，主要描写雄狮国王格萨尔率领岭国军队南征北战，救护生灵，晚年重返天国的故事。格萨（斯）尔集宗教信仰、本土知识、民间智慧、族群记忆、母语表达为一体。族群文化呈现多样性，是唐卡、藏戏、弹唱等传统民间艺术创作的灵感源泉，是多民族民间文化可持续发展的见证。20世纪50年代以来，受现代化进程影响，职业艺人群萎缩，老艺人相继辞世，"人亡歌息"局面呈现，面临消亡危险，受众群正在减少，亟待进一步抢救性保护。

As folk literature, *Gesar* was selected into the intangible cultural heritage of China in 2006 and UNESCO's Representative List of Intangible Cultural Heritage of Humanity in 2009. It prevails in the following provinces as Tibet, Qinghai, Gansu, Sichuan, Yunnan, Inner Mongolia and Xinjiang, which is mainly inherited within schools as well as between masters and apprentices. There exist altogether 9 national inheritors including Cirenzhangdui of Tibet. And two inheritance centers have been established. Tibet has set up a special rescue organization to seek Gesar performers, record tapes, collect Tibetan manuscripts/woodblock transcripts, and publish Tibetan/Chinese versions of *Gesa*r. Many contents of *Gesar* were translated into English, Japanese and French.

Gesar is the longest epic in the world. It mainly describes that *Gesar*, the lion king, led the army to fight up and down the country, rescued the living and returned to heaven in his later years. *Gesar* integrates religious belief, local knowledge, folk wisdom, ethnic memory and native language expression. Its ethnic diversity is the inspiration source of traditional folk art creation, such as Thangka, Tibetan Opera and traditional song. It also witnessed the sustainable development of multi-ethnic folk culture. Since the 1950s, influenced by the modernization process, the number of professional artists has shrunk, and the old artists have passed away one after another, which endangers the development of *Gesar*. Therefore, it is urgent to protect *Gesar*.

（2）中国桑蚕丝织技艺（蜀锦）

Chinese Silk Weaving Technique （Shu Brocade）

中国桑蚕丝织技艺（蜀锦），传统工艺，2006 年入选国家非物质文化遗产目录，2009 年被列入联合国教科文组织人类非物质文化遗产代表作名录，2018 入选文化和旅游部、工业和信息化部制定的第一批国家传统工艺振兴目录。其分布区域主要在四川省各地区。其传承方式为派系传承、师徒传承，现有国家级传承人叶永洲、刘晨曦、贺斌 3 名。

蜀锦有两千年的历史，具有古老的民族传统风格、浓郁的四川地方特色、厚重的历史文化底蕴。蜀锦与南京的云锦、苏州的宋锦、广西的壮锦一起，并称为中国的"四大名锦"。目前蜀锦面临的最大挑战是数码锦对手工蜀锦的冲击，即使是有经验的老艺人，一小时满负荷操作至多能织出二三厘米的蜀锦，因此成本高、价格也高，加上从业人员少、年龄普遍偏大，蜀锦正面临传承乏人的困境，因此蜀锦工艺急需保护。

As a traditional craft, the *Chinese Silk Weaving Technique （Shu Brocade）* was selected into the intangible cultural heritage of China in

2006 and UNESCO's Representative List of Intangible Cultural Heritage of Humanity in 2009. In 2018, it was included in the Revitalization List of the First Batch of Traditional Crafts, which was co-made by the Ministry of Culture and Tourism together with the Ministry of Industry and Information Technology. It prevails in Sichuan province. It is mainly inherited within schools, between masters and apprentices. There exist 3 national inheritors: Ye Yongzhou, Liu Chenxi and He Bin.

Sichuan Brocade has a history of 2000 years, with ancient traditional style, strong local characteristics, and profound historic and cultural heritage. It is a kind of colorful brocade with the characteristics of Han nationality and local style. It is known as China's "Four Famous Brocade" together with Nanjing brocade, Suzhou brocade and Guangxi brocade. At present, the biggest challenge for *Sichuan Brocade* is the impact of digital brocade. Even an experienced brocade weaver can weave up to two or three centimeters of brocade at full load in an hour, which means high cost and high price. At the same time, due to the shortage of brocade weaver and the aging of experienced waver, it is in urgent need of protection.

（3）藏戏 *Tibetan Opera*

藏戏，表演艺术，2006 年入选国家非物质文化遗产目录，2009 年被列入联合国教科文组织人类非物质文化遗产代表作名录。其分布区域主要在青海、甘肃、四川、云南省的藏语地区。现有国家级代表性传承人多杰太、塔洛、李先加等 15 人。

藏戏起源于 8 世纪藏族的宗教艺术，17 世纪从寺院宗教仪式中分离出来，逐渐形成以唱为主，唱、诵、舞、表、白和技等基本程式相结合的生活化的表演，是藏族宝贵的文化遗产，具备极高的研究价值。

但是，时代变革与经济社会的发展使藏戏逐渐陷入了与现代艺术和娱乐形式争夺观众和演出市场的竞争局面，面临资金缺乏、剧团生存艰难、艺术人才断档、传统表演技艺失传、理论研究薄弱等问题。藏戏发展面临重重危机，所以急需制定规划对这一古老的少数民族剧种加以保护。

As a performance art, *Tibetan Opera* was selected into the intangible cultural heritage of China in 2006 and UNESCO's Representative List of Intangible Cultural Heritage of Humanity in 2009. It prevails in Qinghai, Gansu, Sichuan and Yunnan. There exist 15 national representative inheritors as Duojietai, Taluo and Li Xianjia etc..

Tibetan opera originated from the religious art of Tibet in the 8th century. In the 17th century, it was separated from the religious ceremony of the temple, and gradually developed into a comprehensive performance with singing as the main part. And it combines singing, reciting, dancing and acting etc, being of great value. Therefore, because of the transformation of the times and development of economy and society, *Tibetan opera* has gradually fallen into the competition with modern art and entertainment forms for audience and performance market, emerging various problems like lack of funds, difficult survival of troupes, shortage of art talents, loss of traditional performance skills, and weak theoretical research, etc. *Tibetan Opera* is facing the crisis of extinction, and it is urgent to make plans to protect this ancient ethnic opera.

（4）中国雕版印刷技艺（德格雕版印刷技艺）

Chinese Woodblock Printing Techniques （Dege Woodblock Printing Techniques）

中国雕版印刷技艺（德格雕版印刷技艺），传统手工艺，2006年入选国家非物质文化遗产目录，2009年被列入联合国教科文组织人类非物质文化遗产代表作名录。其分布区域主要在四川省德格县，现有国家级代表性传承人彭措泽仁。

中国雕版印刷技艺（德格雕版印刷技艺）运用刀具在木板上雕刻文字或图案，再用墨、纸、绢等材料刷印、装订成书籍，迄今已有1300多年的历史，比活字印刷技艺早400多年。但目前由于制造的手工生产成本颇高，工艺复杂，藏墨生产工艺尚未恢复，加上活字版技术又被更先进的电脑照排所替代，中国雕版印刷技艺（德格雕版印刷技艺）的传承遇到了困难，亟待对此采取措施进行保护和传承。

As a traditional craft, *Chinese Woodblock Printing Techniques* was selected into the intangible cultural heritage of China in 2006 and UNESCO's Representative List of Intangible Cultural Heritage of Humanity in 2009. It prevails in Dege county, Sichuan Province, and now there exists 1 national representative inheritor: Pencuozeren.

Woodblock printers use knives to carve characters or patterns on wood boards and then uses ink to brush and print on materials such as paper or silk to bind books. So far, *Chinese Woodblock Printing* has a history of more than 1300 years, which is over 400 years earlier than movable-type printing. Due to the complexity of the process, the unrecoverable Tibetan ink production process and other problems, plus the movable type technology has been replaced by more advanced computer phototypesetting, the inheritance of *Chinese Woodblock Printing Techniques* has encountered difficulties. Therefore, effective measures should be taken urgently to protect it.

（5）中国皮影戏 *Chinese Shadow Play*

中国皮影戏，传统戏剧，又称"灯影戏"，2006 年入选国家非物质文化遗产目录，2011 年被列入联合国教科文组织人类非物质文化遗产代表作名录。其分布区域广阔，常见有四川皮影、湖北皮影、湖南皮影、北京皮影、唐山皮影等。其传承方式为派系传承、师徒传承，现有国家级代表性传承人王彪等 50 人。

皮影戏是一种以兽皮或纸板做成的人物剪影以表演故事的中国民间的古老的传统艺术。表演时，艺人们在白色幕布后面，一边操纵影人，一边用当地流行的曲调讲述故事，同时配以打击乐器和弦乐。各地皮影的音乐唱腔风格与韵律都吸收了各自地方戏曲、曲艺、民歌小调、音乐体系的精华。随着电影电视的出现，皮影戏的发展遭受了重大冲击，大量的皮影戏艺人为谋求生计而改行，这严重影响到了皮影艺术的传承，故亟待对此采取措施进行保护和传承。

As a folk drama, *Chinese Shadow Play* is also known as "Lantern Pay". It was selected into the intangible cultural heritage of China in 2006 and UNESCO's Representative List of Intangible Cultural Heritage of Humanity in 2011. It prevails in Sichuan, Hubei, Hunan, Beijing, Tangshan etc., which is inherited within schools, between masters and apprentices. At present, there exist 50 national inheritors as Wang Biao etc..

Shadow Play is an ancient traditional Chinese folk art. It is a kind of folk drama in which people are silhouetted with animal skin or cardboard to perform stories. During the performance, the artists, behind the white curtain, manipulate the silhouetted figures and tell stories with local popular tunes, accompanied by percussion instruments and strings. The singing styles and rhymes of all the shadow plays have absorbed the quintessence of their local operas, folk songs, tunes and local music system. With the emergence of film and television, the development of *Shadow Play* has suffered a significant impact. A large number of Shadow Play artists have changed their careers in order to seek survival, which has seriously affected the inheritance of shadow art. It is urgent to take measures to protect and inherit shadow play.

（6）藏医药浴法 *Bath Therapy with Tibetan Medicine*

藏医药浴法，预防疾病，藏语称"泷沐"，2018年被列入联合国教科文组织人类非物质文化遗产代表作名录。其分布区域主要在西藏和青海、四川、甘肃、云南等省的藏族聚集地，其传承方式为师徒传承。

藏医药浴是藏族人民以土、水、火、风、空"五源"生命观和隆、赤巴、培根"三因"健康观及疾病观为指导，通过沐浴天然温泉或药物煮熬的水汁或蒸汽，调节身心平衡，实现生命健康和疾病防治的传统知识和实践，为保障藏族民众的生命健康和防治疾病发挥着重要作用。由于历史原因，很多农牧区的老名医没有接受过正规教育，故需要建立继承人体系，为藏医提供行医和教学的资质认可。

Bath Therapy with Tibetan Medicine is also called "Long Mu" in the Tibetan language. It was selected into UNESCO's Representative List of Intangible Cultural Heritage of Humanity in 2018. It prevails in Tibet, Qinghai, Sichuan, Gansu and Yunnan, which is mainly inherited between masters and apprentices.

Bath Therapy with Tibetan Medicine is the combination of traditional knowledge and practice of Tibetan people, which is guided by the life concept of "five sources" of soil, water, fire, wind and air. The health concept of "three causes" of Helong, Chiba and Peigen also plays an important role in Bath Therapy. The balance of body and mind, health and disease prevention and control are achieved through bathing in natural springs or water boiled with Tibetan medicine. It is essential for the health and disease prevention of Tibetan people. Due to historical reasons, many famous doctors in rural and pastoral areas have not received a formal education, so it is necessary to establish an inheritance system to provide them with qualification recognition for medical practice and teaching.

2. 联合国教科文组织非遗项目 —— 急需保护的非物质文化遗产名录（1项）

UNESCO Intangible Cultural Project — List of Intangible Cultural Heritage in Need of Urgent Safeguarding （1）

（7）羌年 *New Year of Qiang People*

羌年，民俗，又称"日麦节"，2008 年入选国家非物质文化遗产名录，2009 年被列入联合国教科文组织急需保护的非物质文化遗产名录。其分布区域主要为四川省阿坝州茂县、汶川县、理县及北川羌族自治县广大羌族地区，其传承方式为亲族传承和师徒传承。现有国家级传承人肖永庆、王治升两名。

羌年是集历史、文化、宗教、美学、伦理学、哲学、建筑、民俗学、歌舞、饮食为一体的综合性民间节庆，是羌族早期农耕文化活动的产物，具有极高的历史价值、文化价值和旅游价值。每年农历十月初一，茂县羌族开展为期 3~5 天的羌年活动。羌年凝聚了古羌族对自然和祖先的崇拜、宗教情怀、集聚羌族文化品质和乡土风情，但因外来文化冲击，传承人年事已高，年轻人对传统文化的兴趣缺失，羌年的生存和发展面临危机，亟待进一步抢救性保护。

As a folk custom, *New Year of Qiang People* （also called *Rimai Festival*）, was selected in the intangible cultural heritage of China in

2008 and UNESCO's List of Intangible Cultural Heritage in Need of Urgent Safeguarding in 2009. It prevails in areas inhabited by Qiang people in Sichuan, such as Maoxian county, Wenchuan county and Lixian county etc., which is mainly inherited within the family as well as between masters and apprentices. At present, there exist 2 national inheritors: Xiao Yongqing and Wang Zhisheng.

As a comprehensive folk festival, *Rimai Festival* is the product of the early farming civilization of Qiang people, which has combined history, culture, religion, aesthetics, ethics, philosophy, architecture, folklore, dance and diet. It has special historical, cultural and tourism value. It falls on October 1st of the lunar calendar and usually lasts 3-5 days each year. *New Year of Qiang* embodies the ancient Qiang people's worship of nature and ancestors, religious feelings, cultural quality and local customs. However, due to the impact of foreign culture, the aging of inheritors and the devoid of interest of young people, the survival and development of New Year of Qiang is facing a crisis. Therefore, further rescue and protection are urgently needed.

二、国家级非物质文化遗产名录及中英文简介（153 项）

（一）名录列表

一、第一、二批国家级非遗名录（共 105 项）				
序号	编号	项目名称	申报地区或单位	保护单位
1	Ⅰ-27	格萨（斯）尔	四川省	甘孜藏族自治州文化馆
2	Ⅰ-75	彝族克智	四川省美姑县	美姑县文化馆
3	Ⅱ-16	巴山背二歌	四川省巴中市	巴中市文化馆

序号	编号	项目名称	申报地区或单位	保护单位
4	Ⅱ-24	川江号子	四川省	四川省艺术研究院
5	Ⅱ-27	川北薅草锣鼓	四川省青川县	青川县文化馆
6	Ⅱ-38	羌笛演奏及制作技艺	四川省茂县	茂县文化馆
7	Ⅱ-8	南坪曲子	四川省九寨沟县	九寨沟县文化馆
8	Ⅱ-102	制作号子（竹麻号子）	四川省邛崃市	邛崃市文化馆
9	Ⅱ-115	藏族民歌 （川西藏族山歌）	四川省甘孜 藏族自治州	甘孜藏族 自治州文化馆
10	Ⅱ-115	藏族民歌 （川西藏族山歌）	四川省阿坝藏族 羌族自治州	阿坝藏族羌族 自治州文化馆 （阿坝藏族羌族 自治州美术馆）
11	Ⅱ-115	藏族民歌 （川西藏族山歌）	四川省炉霍县	炉霍县文化馆
12	Ⅱ-115	藏族民歌（玛达咪山歌）	四川省九龙县	九龙县文化馆
13	Ⅱ-128	洞经音乐 （文昌洞经古乐）	四川省梓潼县	梓潼县文化馆
14	Ⅱ-136	口弦音乐	四川省布拖县	布拖县文化馆
15	Ⅱ-139	道教音乐 （成都道教音乐）	四川省成都市	成都市道教协会
16	Ⅲ-34	㑇舞	四川省九寨沟县	九寨沟县文化馆
17	Ⅲ-4	龙舞（泸州雨坛彩龙）	四川省泸县	泸县文化馆 （泸县美术馆）
18	Ⅲ-19	弦子舞（巴塘弦子舞）	四川省巴塘县	巴塘县文化馆
19	Ⅲ-33	卡斯达温舞	四川省黑水县	黑水县文化馆
20	Ⅲ-55	翻山铰子	四川省平昌县	平昌县文化馆
21	Ⅲ-62	羌族羊皮鼓舞	四川省汶川县	汶川县文化馆
22	Ⅲ-66	得荣学羌	四川省得荣县	得荣县文化馆
23	Ⅲ-67	甲搓	四川省盐源县	盐源县文化馆
24	Ⅲ-68	博巴森根	四川省理县	理县文化馆
25	Ⅳ-12	川剧	四川省	四川省艺术研究院

113

序号	编号	项目名称	申报地区或单位	保护单位
26	Ⅳ-77	灯戏（川北灯戏）	四川省南充市	南充市非物质文化遗产保护中心
27	Ⅳ-92	木偶戏（川北大木偶戏）	四川省	南充市非物质文化遗产保护中心
28	Ⅴ-75	四川扬琴	四川省曲艺团	四川省曲艺研究院
29	Ⅴ-75	四川扬琴	四川省音乐舞蹈研究所	四川省艺术研究所
30	Ⅴ-75	四川扬琴	成都艺术剧院	成都市非物质文化遗产保护中心（成都市非物质文化遗产艺术研究院）
31	Ⅴ-76	四川竹琴	四川省成都艺术剧院	成都市非物质文化遗产保护中心（成都市非物质文化遗产艺术研究院）
32	Ⅴ-77	四川清音	四川省成都艺术剧院	成都市非物质文化遗产保护中心（成都市非物质文化遗产艺术研究院）
33	Ⅴ-91	金钱板	四川省成都市	成都市非物质文化遗产保护中心（成都市非物质文化遗产艺术研究院）
34	Ⅵ-23	峨眉武术	四川省峨眉山市	峨眉山市体育总会
35	Ⅶ—11	绵竹木版年画	四川省德阳市	绵竹年画博物馆
36	Ⅶ—14	藏族唐卡（噶玛嘎孜画派）	四川省甘孜藏族自治州	甘孜藏族自治州文化馆
37	Ⅶ—21	蜀绣	四川省成都市	成都市非物质文化遗产保护中心（成都市非物质文化遗产艺术研究院）
38	Ⅶ—39	藏族格萨尔彩绘石刻	四川省色达县	色达县文化馆
39	Ⅶ-54	草编（沐川草龙）	四川省沐川县	沐川县文化馆

序号	编号	项目名称	申报地区或单位	保护单位
40	VII-56	石雕（白花石刻）	四川省广元市	广元市利州区文化馆
41	VII-56	石雕（安岳石刻）	四川省安岳县	安岳县文化馆
42	VII-64	藏文书法（德格藏文书法）	四川省德格县	德格县文化馆
43	VII-65	木版年画（夹江年画）	四川省夹江县	夹江县文化馆
44	VII-76	羌族刺绣	四川省汶川县	汶川县文化馆
45	VII-77	民间绣活（麻柳刺绣）	四川省广元市	广元市朝天区文化馆
46	VII-88	糖塑（成都糖画）	四川省成都市	成都市锦江区文化馆
47	VIII—16	蜀锦织造技艺	四川省成都市	成都蜀锦织绣有限责任公司
48	VIII—56	成都漆艺	四川省成都市	成都漆器工艺厂有限责任公司
49	VIII—58	泸州老窖酒酿制技艺	四川省泸州市	泸州老窖股份有限公司
50	VIII—64	自贡井盐深钻汲制技艺	四川省自贡市	四川久大盐业（集团）公司
51	VIII—64	自贡井盐深钻汲制技艺	四川省大英县	大英县文物管理所（大英县汉陶博物馆）
52	VIII—71	竹纸制作技艺	四川省夹江县	夹江县文化馆
53	VIII—80	德格印经院藏族雕版印刷技艺	四川省德格县	德格县文化馆
54	VIII-98	陶器烧制技艺（藏族黑陶烧制技艺）	四川省稻城县	稻城县文化馆
55	VIII-98	陶器烧制技艺（荥经砂器烧制技艺）	四川省荥经县	荥经县非物质文化遗产保护中心
56	VIII-101	毛纺织及擀制技艺（彝族毛纺织及擀制技艺）	四川省昭觉县	昭觉县彝族服饰文化研究中心
57	VIII-101	毛纺织及擀制技艺（藏族牛羊毛编织技艺）	四川省色达县	色达县文化馆

序号	编号	项目名称	申报地区或单位	保护单位
58	Ⅷ-120	藏族金属锻造技艺（藏族锻铜技艺）	四川省白玉县	白玉县文化馆
59	Ⅷ-121	成都银花丝制作技艺	四川省成都市青羊区	成都金银制品有限责任公司
60	Ⅷ-12	彝族漆器髹饰技艺	四川省喜德县	凉山彝族自治州民政民族工艺厂
61	Ⅷ-140	伞制作技艺（油纸伞制作技艺）	四川省泸州市江阳区	泸州市江阳区分水伞厂
62	Ⅷ-144	蒸馏酒传统酿造技艺（五粮液酒传统酿造技艺）	四川省宜宾市	四川省宜宾五粮液集团有限公司
63	Ⅷ-144	蒸馏酒传统酿造技艺（水井坊酒传统酿造技艺）	四川省成都市	水井坊股份有限公司
64	Ⅷ-144	蒸馏酒传统酿造技艺（剑南春酒传统酿造技艺）	四川省绵竹市	四川剑南春集团有限责任公司
65	Ⅷ-144	蒸馏酒传统酿造技艺（古蔺郎酒传统酿造技艺）	四川省古蔺县	四川省古蔺郎酒厂有限责任公司
66	Ⅷ-144	蒸馏酒传统酿造技艺（沱牌曲酒传统酿造技艺）	四川省射洪县	舍得酒业股份有限公司
67	Ⅷ-152	黑茶制作技艺（南路边茶制作技艺）	四川省雅安市	雅安市非物质文化遗产保护中心（雅安市茶马古道研究中心）
68	Ⅷ-155	豆瓣传统制作技艺（郫县豆瓣传统制作技艺）	四川省郫县	成都市郫都区食品工业协会
69	Ⅷ-156	豆豉酿制技艺（潼川豆豉酿制技艺）	四川省三台县	潼川农产品开发有限责任公司
70	Ⅷ-186	藏族碉楼营造技艺	四川省丹巴县	丹巴县文化馆
71	Ⅸ—9	藏医药（甘孜州南派藏医药）	四川省甘孜藏族自治州	甘孜藏族自治州藏医院

序号	编号	项目名称	申报地区或单位	保护单位
72	X—10	火把节（彝族火把节）	四川省凉山彝族自治州	凉山彝族自治州非物质文化遗产保护中心
73	X—18	羌族瓦尔俄足节	四川省阿坝藏族羌族自治州	茂县文化馆
74	X—30	都江堰放水节	四川省都江堰市	都江堰市文化馆
75	X-81	灯会（自贡灯会）	四川省自贡市	中国彩灯博物馆（自贡彩灯公园管理处）
76	X-82	羌年	四川省茂县	茂县文化馆
77	X-82	羌年	四川省汶川县	汶川县文化馆
78	X-82	羌年	四川省理县	理县文化馆
79	X-82	羌年	四川省北川羌族自治县	北川羌族自治县文化馆
80	X-87	抬阁（芯子、铁枝、飘色）（大坝高装）	四川省兴文县	兴文县文化馆
81	X-87	抬阁（芯子、铁枝、飘色）（青林口高抬戏）	四川省江油市	江油市文化馆
82	X-104	三汇彩亭会	四川省渠县	渠县文化馆
83	II-27	薅草锣鼓（川东土家族薅草锣鼓）	四川省宣汉县	宣汉县文化馆
84	II-30	多声部民歌（羌族多声部民歌）	四川省松潘县	松潘县文化馆
85	II-30	多声部民歌（硗碛多声部民歌）	四川省雅安市	宝兴县文化馆
86	III-4	龙舞（黄龙溪火龙灯舞）	四川省双流县	双流县文化馆
87	III-20	锅庄舞（甘孜锅庄）	四川省石渠县	石渠县文化馆
88	III-20	锅庄舞（甘孜锅庄）	四川省雅江县	雅江县文化馆
89	III-20	锅庄舞（甘孜锅庄）	四川省新龙县	新龙县文化馆
90	III-20	锅庄舞（甘孜锅庄）	四川省德格县	德格县文化馆
91	III-20	锅庄舞（马奈锅庄）	四川省金川县	金川县文化馆

序号	编号	项目名称	申报地区或单位	保护单位
92	Ⅳ-80	藏戏（德格格萨尔藏戏）	四川省德格县	德格县文化馆
93	Ⅳ-80	藏戏（巴塘藏戏）	四川省巴塘县	巴塘县文化馆
94	Ⅳ-80	藏戏（色达藏戏）	四川省色达县	色达县文化馆
95	Ⅳ-91	皮影戏（四川皮影戏）	四川省阆中市	四川川北皮影艺术团
96	Ⅳ-91	皮影戏（四川皮影戏）	四川省南部县	南部县文化馆
97	Ⅶ-46	竹刻（江安竹簧）	四川省江安县	江安县文化馆
98	Ⅶ-47	泥塑（徐氏泥彩塑）	四川省大英县	大英县文物管理所（大英县汉陶博物馆）
99	Ⅶ-51	竹编（渠县刘氏竹编）	四川省渠县	四川刘氏竹编工艺有限公司
100	Ⅶ-51	竹编（青神竹编）	四川省青神县	青神县文物保护中心
101	Ⅶ-51	竹编（瓷胎竹编）	四川省邛崃市	邛崃市文化馆
102	Ⅷ-26	扎染技艺（自贡扎染技艺）	四川省自贡市	自贡市扎染工艺有限公司
103	Ⅷ-40	银饰制作技艺（彝族银饰制作技艺）	四川省布拖县	布拖县文化馆
104	Ⅷ-81	制扇技艺（龚扇）	四川省自贡市	自贡市龚扇竹编工艺厂
105	Ⅸ—9	中药炮制技术（中药炮制技艺）	四川省成都市	成都中医药大学药学院
二、第三批国家级非遗名录（共计15项）				
106	I-91	禹的传说	四川省汶川县	汶川县文化馆
107	I-91	禹的传说	四川省北川羌族自治县	北川羌族自治县文化馆
108	I-122	羌戈大战	四川省汶川县	汶川县文化馆
109	Ⅲ-102	跳曹盖	四川省平武县	平武县文化馆
110	Ⅶ-97	棕编（新繁棕编）	四川省成都市新都区	成都市新都区文化馆

序号	编号	项目名称	申报地区或单位	保护单位
111	Ⅶ-106	藏族编织、挑花刺绣工艺	四川省阿坝藏族羌族自治州	阿坝藏族羌族自治州藏族传统编织挑花刺绣协会
112	Ⅹ-129	彝族年	四川省凉山彝族自治州	凉山彝族自治州非物质文化遗产保护中心
113	Ⅹ-139	婚俗（彝族传统婚俗）	四川省美姑县	美姑县文化馆
114	Ⅱ-115	藏族民歌（藏族赶马调）	四川省冕宁县	冕宁县文化馆
115	Ⅱ-136	口弦音乐	四川省北川羌族自治县	北川羌族自治县文化馆
116	Ⅱ-138	佛教音乐（觉囊梵音）	四川省壤塘县	壤塘县藏洼寺寺庙管理委员会
117	Ⅶ-94	盆景技艺（川派盆景技艺）	四川省盆景艺术家协会	四川省盆景协会
118	Ⅷ-25	蜡染技艺（苗族蜡染技艺）	四川省珙县	珙县文物管理所（珙县非物质文化遗产保护中心）
119	Ⅷ-186	碉楼营造技艺（羌族碉楼营造技艺）	四川省汶川县	汶川县文化馆
120	Ⅷ-186	碉楼营造技艺（羌族碉楼营造技艺）	四川省茂县	茂县文化馆
三、第四批国家级非遗名录（共计19项）				
121	Ⅰ-141	毕阿史拉则传说	四川省金阳县	金阳县文化馆
122	Ⅰ-152	玛牧	四川省喜德县	喜德县文化馆
123	Ⅱ-158	西岭山歌	四川省大邑县	大邑县文化馆
124	Ⅱ-163	毕摩音乐	四川省美姑县	美姑县文化馆
125	Ⅲ-122	古蔺花灯	四川省古蔺县	古蔺县文化馆
126	Ⅲ-123	登嘎甘伶（熊猫舞）	四川省九寨沟县	九寨沟县文化馆
127	Ⅶ-114	毕摩绘画	四川省美姑县	美姑县文化馆
128	Ⅹ-156	彝族服饰	四川省昭觉县	昭觉县文物管理所
129	Ⅱ-30	多声部民歌	四川省黑水县	黑水县文化馆

序号	编号	项目名称	申报地区或单位	保护单位
		（阿尔麦多声部民歌）		
130	Ⅱ-128	洞经音乐 （邛都洞经音乐）	四川省西昌市	西昌市邛都洞经古乐协会
131	Ⅲ-82	堆谐（甘孜踢踏）	四川省甘孜县	甘孜县文化馆
132	Ⅳ-92	木偶戏 （中型杖头木偶戏）	四川省资中县	四川省资中县木偶剧团
133	Ⅳ-157	阳戏（射箭提阳戏）	四川省广元市昭化区	广元市昭化区文化馆
134	Ⅶ-51	竹编（道明竹编）	四川省崇州市	崇州市文化馆
135	Ⅷ-110	地毯织造技艺（阆中丝毯织造技艺）	四川省阆中市	四川银河地毯有限公司
136	Ⅷ-154	酱油酿造技艺（先市酱油酿造技艺）	四川省合江县	合江县先市酿造食品有限公司
137	Ⅷ-100	传统棉纺织技艺（傈僳族火草织布技艺）	四川省德昌县	德昌县文化馆（县非物质文化遗产保护中心、县美术馆）
138	Ⅹ-85	民间信俗（康定转山会）	四川省康定市	康定市文化旅游和广播影视体育局
139	Ⅹ-90	祭祖习俗（凉山彝族尼木措毕祭祀）	四川省美姑县	美姑县文化馆
四、第五批国家级非遗名录（共计14项）				
140	Ⅳ-168	端公戏（旺苍端公戏）	四川省广元市	—
141	Ⅵ-83	藏棋	四川省阿坝藏族羌族自治州	—
142	Ⅵ-94	青城武术	四川省成都市都江堰市	—
143	Ⅵ-100	滑竿 （华蓥山滑竿抬幺妹）	四川省广安市	—
144	Ⅶ-123	藤编（怀远藤编）	四川省成都市崇州市	—
145	Ⅶ-130	彝族刺绣 （凉山彝族刺绣）	四川省凉山彝族自治州	—
146	Ⅷ-272	川菜烹饪技艺	四川省	—
147	Ⅷ-285	彝族传统建筑营造技艺（凉山彝族传统民居营造技艺）	四川省凉山彝族自治州	—

序号	编号	项目名称	申报地区或单位	保护单位
148	Ⅲ-4	龙舞（安仁板凳龙）	四川省达州市	—
149	Ⅶ-14	藏族唐卡（郎卡杰唐卡）	四川省甘孜藏族自治州	—
150	Ⅷ-61	酿造技艺（保宁醋传统酿造工艺）	四川省南充市	—
151	Ⅷ-115	工艺制鞋技艺（唐昌布鞋制作技艺）	四川省成都市郫都区	—
152	Ⅷ-148	绿茶制作技艺（蒙山茶传统制作技艺）	四川省雅安市	—
153	Ⅸ-2	中医诊疗法（李忠愚杵针疗法）	四川省	—

（二）项目中英文简介（153 项）

List of Intangible Cultural Heritage of Sichuan Province （153）

1. 格萨（斯）尔 *Gesar*（见四川省世界级非物质文化遗产项目中英文简介）

2. 彝族克智 *Kezhi Debate of Yi People*

彝族克智，民间文学，又叫"克使哈举"，2008 年入选第二批国家级非物质文化遗产名录。其分布区域主要在四川彝族聚集地。其传承方式为师徒传承，口耳相传，现有国家级传承人海来热几。

彝族克智是一种民间脍炙人口、广为传诵的固定格式的诗体文学。"克智"是彝语的音译，"克"是"口"，"智"是移动，"克智"说明具有口头性、灵活性、机动性，属于口头创作，是彝族具有历史价值、艺术价值的口头文学之一。多在逢年过节、婚丧喜事上进行"克智"表演，主客双方进行辩论。当今彝族群众之间的来往频繁，加之外来文化和现代传媒的影响，民众的文化生活丰富，"克智"论辩传统逐步削弱，年轻人对民族"草根文化"缺乏应有的情感，处于现代文明中心城市的彝族后代甚至不会自己的母语，"克智"论辩传统在消失，论辩高手越来越少，面临消亡危险，亟待进一步抢救性保护。

As folk literature, *Kezi Debate of Yi People* (also known as Keshihaju) was selected into the second batch of the intangible cultural heritage of China in 2008. It mainly prevails in areas inhabited by Yi people in Sichuan, which is mainly inherited between masters and apprentices through word of mouth. At present, there exists 1 national inheritor: Hailaireji.

Kezhi Debate of Yi People is a kind of popular and widely read poetic literature with fixed form. In the language of Yi people, Ke means "mouth" and Zhi means "mobile". It means the oral, flexible, and mobile characteristics of *Kezhi Debate of Yi People*. It has high historic and artistic value. On the occasions of festivals, weddings and funerals, *Kezhi Debate* will be performed. Nowadays, the debate tradition of "Kezhi" is gradually disappearing for many reasons, such as the frequent communication among the Yi people, the influence of foreign culture and modern media, the rich cultural life of people, the weakening of the debate tradition and young people's lack of emotion towards the national "grassroots culture". Because descendants of Yi People living in the city can't speak their mother tongue and debate experts are becoming less and less, this cultural heritage is facing the crisis of dying out. Therefore, it is urgent to protect it.

3. 巴山背二歌 *Labor Song of Bazhong City*

巴山背二歌，传统音乐，2006 年入选第一批国家级非物质文化遗产名录。其分布区域主要在四川东北部米仓山南麓巴中市辖区。其传承方式为口耳相传，现有国家级传承人陈治华。

巴山背二歌产生于地处山区、交通闭塞的巴中，庞大的背运队伍在漫长的背运途中，"背二哥"传唱"背二歌"，其表现形态多为一人领唱众人和或众人齐唱。巴山背二歌是巴山人精神文化的一种体现，是研究巴人历史的依据，是承载巴山风土人情、生活习俗的载体，具有独特的艺术价值。由于现代化进程的加剧，背运业由原来的长途背运演变为今天的短途背运，且从业人数越来越少，巴山背二歌正逐步失去生存和发展的空间，濒临危机，亟须保护。

As a traditional music, *Labor Song of Bazhong City* was selected into the first batch of intangible cultural heritage in 2006. It mainly prevails in the south foot of Micang Moutain in Bazhong City, which is mainly inherited through word of mouth. At present, there exists 1 national inheritor: Chen Zhihua.

The emergence of *Labor Song of Bazhong City* is originated inseparably from the fact that Bazhong is located in a mountainous area and the traffic is blocked. A huge group of people on the way of carrying goods sing the Labor Song in the form of one leading the song all others singing together. *Labor Song of Bazhong City* is a reflection of Bashan people's spiritual culture, the basis of studying the history of Bashan people and the symbol of local customs, which has unique artistic value. Due to the modernization process, the traditional transportation industry by manpower has evolved from the original long-distance transportation to short-distance, and the number of employees is becoming less and less. *Labor Song of Bazhong city* is gradually losing the space for survival and development. Therefore, it is in urgent need of protection.

4. 川江号子　*Boat Tracker Song of Sichuan Province*

川江号子，传统音乐，2006 年入选第一批国家级非物质文化遗产名录。其分布区域主要在金沙江、长江及其支流岷江、沱江、嘉陵江、乌江和大宁河等流域。其传承方式为口耳相传，现有国家级传承人曹光裕。

川江号子是川江船工们为统一动作和节奏，由号工领唱，众船工帮腔、合唱的一种"一领众和"式的民间歌唱形式。号子有十唱十不同，在行船中起着统一摇橹动作和调剂船工急缓情绪的作用，在三面临水、一面朝天的环境中，给贫苦的船工带来欢乐，具有"长江文化的活化石"之称。随着现代航运的普及，以人工为动力的船只在一些干流河湾和支流小河中运行，川江号子生存发展的基础开始动摇，加之传承断裂等因素，川江号子面临濒危困境，亟须抢救和保护。

As a traditional music, *Boat Tracker Song of Sichuan Province* was selected into the first batch of the intangible cultural heritage of China in 2006. It prevails in Jinsha River, Yangtze River and its tributaries: Minjiang River, Tuojiang River, Jialing River, Wujiang River and Daning river etc.. It is mainly inherited through word of mouth. At present, there exists 1 national inheritor: Cao Guangyu.

Boat Tracker Song is a kind of folk singing form which is led by one boatman and sang by all others together to unify the action and rhythm. There are ten different singing methods that play the role in unifying the action of rowing and pulling oars as well as adjusting the mood of a boatman. In face of choppy waters and difficult situation, *Boat Tracker Song* brings joy to the poor boatman. Therefore, it is known as "the living fossil of the Yangtze River culture". With the popularization of motor-driven iron ships, the boats powered by man are only running in some small rivers and tributaries. Its foundation of survival and development is beginning to shake. In addition, due to the difficulty of inheritance, it is facing a crisis of dying out. Therefore, it is in urgent need of rescue and protection.

5. 川北薅草锣鼓　*Weeding Song of Northern Sichuan*

川北薅草锣鼓，传统音乐，2006 年入选第一批国家级非物质文化遗产名录。其分布区域主要在四川省广元市四县三区境内。其传承方式为口耳相传，现有国家级传承人王绍兴。

薅草锣鼓是劳动人民将民间文化与音乐融入艰苦劳动中的聪明智慧的结晶，属于川北山区民间文化的重要组成部分。川北薅草锣鼓在田间作业中发挥了指挥劳动、活跃气氛、调节劳作者情绪的作用，音乐语汇中保留了大量古代体力劳动中的音乐文化信息，具有较高的学术研究价值。由于受现代生产方式的影响，传统的生产生活方式难以跟上时代发展的步伐，川北薅草锣鼓的生存空间正在日益缩小，老年歌手相继过世，年轻人多外出打工，劳动力大量外迁，歌手队伍青黄不接，亟须保护和传承。

As a traditional music, *Weeding Song of Northern Sichuan* was selected into the first batch of the intangible cultural heritage of China in 2006. It prevails in four counties and three districts of Guangyuan City, Sichuan Province, which is mainly inherited through word of mouth. There exists 1 national inheritor: Wang Shaoxing.

It is the wisdom crystallization of the working people and an important part of the folk culture in the mountainous areas of northern Sichuan. *Weeding Song* plays the role of directing labor, activating the atmosphere and regulating the mood of workers in the fieldwork. A large number of musical cultural information in ancient manual labor is preserved in its music vocabulary, which has high academic research value. Due to the influence of the modern production mode, the traditional production and lifestyle is difficult to keep up with the pace of the development of the times. Therefore, the living space of *Weeding song of Northern Sichuan* is shrinking day by day. Because of the death of old singers and the migration of young people to cities, the shortage of singers is deteriorating gradually. Therefore, it is in urgent need of protection and inheritance.

6. 羌笛演奏及制作技艺

Performance Skills and Craftsmanship of Qiang Flute

羌族羌笛演奏及制作技艺，民间音乐，2006年入选国家第一批非物质文化遗产名录。其分布区域主要在四川省茂县。其传承方式为派系传承，现有国家级传承人龚代仁。

羌笛吹奏主要采取鼓腮换气法，在吹奏中还有喉头颤音，手指的上下滑音等技巧，加之双管制作的律差，双簧共振的音响，其音质和旋律独具特色，具有较高的学术价值和社会价值。但因其演奏及制作技艺技巧多、难度大，现在愿意学习的人并不多，羌笛的制作和吹奏都面临失传，亟待进一步抢救性保护。

As folk music, *Performance Skills and Craftsmanship of Qiang Flute* was selected for the first batch of the intangible cultural heritage of China in 2006. It prevails in Maoxian County, Sichuan Province, which is mainly inherited within schools. At present, there exists 1 national inheritor: Gong Dairen.

Qiang Flute has unique tone quality and melody because of its special performance techniques, including cheek-bulging technique, laryngeal, portamento, and resonance sound. It has high academic value and social value. However, due to its large number of techniques and great difficulty of playing, the performance and craftsmanship are in the danger of dying out. Therefore, rescue and protection are in urgent need.

7. 南坪曲子 *Nanping Tune of Aba Prefecture*

南坪曲子，传统音乐，又称"南坪小调"，2008 年入选第二批国家级非物质文化遗产名录。其分布区域主要在川西北高原九寨沟县（原南坪县）一带。其传承方式为口耳相传，现有国家级传承人黄德成。

南坪曲子用当地的方言进行演唱，是流行于川西北高原九寨沟县一带汉族（含少数回族）民间自弹自唱的说唱艺术，是川西北最具有地方特色的民族民间文化的群体活动形式。虽然南坪曲子流传面广泛，但仅针对"花曲子"部分，而"背工曲子"则由于曲子长，歌词与旋律难于记忆，加之音域广，旋律跳动大，歌唱技巧难于掌握，目前能较为完整掌握其曲目和歌唱技巧的人已不足 3 人，如不及时加以抢救与保护，南坪曲子的呈现方式将不完整，独特魅力将会失去。

As traditional music, *Nanping Tune of Aba Prefecture* (also known as "Nanping Ditty") was selected into the second batch of the intangible cultural heritage of China in 2008. It prevails in Jiuzhaigou County (formerly Nanping County) of northwest Sichuan plateau, which is mainly inherited orally among people. At present, there exists 1 national inheritor: Huang Decheng.

Nanping tune, which is popular in Jiuzhaigou County, Northwest Sichuan Plateau, is a kind of folk art characterized by self-playing and self-singing. As folk tune and traditional folk art, it is the most distinctive group activity form in Northwest Sichuan. *Nanping Tune* is mainly divided into two kinds: Hua Tune and Beigong Tune. The former one is widely spread. While the latter one is in face of an inheritance dilemma due to many reasons such as its long tune, lyrics and melody, wide range, large melody beat, difficult singing skills etc.. At present, there are less than three people who can master its repertoire and singing skills completely. If we don't rescue and protect it in time, the expressing way of *Nanping tune* will be incomplete, its unique charm will be lost. Therefore, it is in urgent need of rescue and protection.

8. 制作号子（竹麻号子） *Labor Song of Qionglai City*

制作号子（竹麻号子），传统音乐，2008 年入选国家第二批非物质文化遗产名录。其分布区域主要在四川成都所辖邛崃境内平乐镇的金华村金鸡沟、金河村杨湾、同乐村的芦沟以及花楸村等地。其传承方式为口耳相传。

制作号子（竹麻号子）属于造纸工人在打竹麻时所唱的一种劳动号子，唱腔原始、质朴、粗放、高亢，是川西地区传统民间少数原汁原味演唱类的艺术传承，具有浓郁的川西地方特色和独特的艺术魅力。制作号子（竹麻号子）唱词所反映的内容主要包括当地的传统民风民俗和民间文艺，当地的社会经济状况以及人们的生产生活方式等。但由于相关文字资料记载十分缺乏，制作号子难以推广，目前能够完整演唱的仅有 3～5 人，随着老人的逝去，其传承面临濒危境地，亟须抢救性保护。

As traditional music, *Labor Song of Qionglai City* was selected into the second batch of the intangible cultural heritage of China in 2008. It prevails in Jinhua Village, Pingle Town, Qionglai County of Sichuan Province, which is mainly inherited through word of mouth.

Labor Song of Qionglai City belongs to a kind of labor song created by paper workers when producing paper with bamboo and hemp. Its singing style is primitive, simple, extensive and high pitched. Because of its strong local characteristics and unique artistic charm, it is an artistic inheritance of the traditional folk singing style in Western Sichuan. Its contents mainly include traditional folk customs, folk literature, art, social and economic conditions, local people's lifestyle, etc. However, there is a clear shortage of its written records and there are only 3-5 people who can sing it completely. It is in face of the great danger of extinction,which is in urgent need of rescue and protection.

9 ~ 11. 藏族民歌（川西藏族山歌）

Folk Songs of Tibetan People in Western Sichuan

藏族民歌（川西藏族山歌），传统音乐，在卫藏地区称为"拉鲁"，康巴地区称为"鲁"，安多地区称为"勒"，2008 年入选第二批国家级非物质文化遗产名录。其分布区域主要在西藏自治区及青海、四川及云南等省的藏族聚集区。其传承方式为口耳相传，现有国家级传承人降巴其扎。

川西藏族山歌是藏族人民在放牧、伐薪、田间劳动过程中为驱散疲劳、抒发感情而创作的歌曲，有山歌（牧歌）、劳动歌、爱情歌、风俗歌、诵经调等类型。由于川西藏族山歌的乐句中常出现密集音符组成多变音型的情况，其演唱难度颇大，一般人难以驾驭，因此长久以来，川西藏族山歌一直都是以自发方式在民间传承。但现代文明的冲击，改变了传统民族生活方式与习惯，导致这种民族音乐后继无人，处于高度濒危状态，亟须制定计划，全力保护。

As traditional music, *Folk Songs of Tibetan People in Western Sichuan* is also called "Lalu" in Weizang Tibetan area, "Lu" in Kangba area, and "Le" in Ando area. It was selected into the second batch of the intangible cultural heritage of China in 2008, mainly prevailing in areas inhabited by Tibetan people in Tibet, Qinghai, Sichuan and Yunan provinces. It is mainly inherited between masters and apprentices through word of mouth. At present, there exists 1 national inheritor:

Jiangbaqiza.

Folk Songs of Tibetan People in Western Sichuan is created by Tibetan people in the process of grazing, cutting firewood and field labor to dispel fatigue and express their feelings. The songs can be divided into folk songs (pastoral songs), labor songs, love songs, custom songs, chant etc. It is very difficult to sing *Folk Songs of Tibetan People in Western Sichuan*, because there are many dense notes which make up changeable tone patterns. For a long time, *Folk Songs of Tibetan People in Western Sichuan* has been passed down spontaneously among the people. However, modern civilization has made a huge impact on the traditional folk culture and people's living habits, which results in few inheritors to this kind of folk music. Therefore, its survival is in danger and it is urgent to make plans of protection.

12. 藏族民歌（玛达咪山歌） *Madami Folk Song of Tibetan People*

藏族民歌（玛达咪山歌），传统音乐，在卫藏地区称为"拉鲁"，康巴地区称为"鲁"，安多地区称为"勒"，2008 年入选第二批国家级非物质文化遗产名录。其分布区域主要在四川省甘孜州九龙县大河边片区的子耳乡、魁多乡、烟袋乡等地。其传承方式为口耳相传。

玛达咪山歌是一种形成发展于西番藏族生产劳动的别具特色的藏族民歌，至今已有上千年的历史。玛达咪山歌承载着西番藏族地区的风土人情和生活习性，生动体现了西番人的精神风貌，具有较高的民俗学和民族学研究价值。随着时代的发展，西番藏区相对封闭的农耕生产生活方式快速变迁，玛达咪山歌的生存面临危机，亟待抢救和保护。

As traditional music, *Madami Folk Songs of Tibetan People* is also called "Lalu" in Weizang Tibetan area, "Lu" in Kangba area, and "Le" in

Ando area. It was selected into the second batch of intangible cultural heritage of China in 2008, mainly prevailing in Zi'er Town, Kuido Town, Yandai Town in Jiulong County, Ganzi Prefecture, Sichuan Province. It is mainly inherited through word of mouth.

Madami Folk Song of Tibetan People was formed and developed in the production and labor of the Xifan Tibetan people, which has a history of more than a thousand years, owning special characteristics. *Madami Folk Song* carries the local customs and living habits of the areas where Xifan Tibetan people live, vividly embodies the spiritual style of Xifan Tibetan people, and has high folklore and ethnology value. With the modernization of society, the traditional production and lifestyle in Xifan Tibetan area is changing rapidly, and its survival is facing a crisis. Therefore, effective measures should be taken urgently to protect *Madami Folk Songs*.

13. 洞经音乐（文昌洞经古乐） *Dongjing Tunes*

洞经音乐（文昌洞经古乐），传统音乐，2008 年入选第二批国家级非物质文化遗产名录。其分布区域主要在四川省梓潼县七曲山文昌宫及县城周围的善堂、斋堂。其传承方式为口耳相传。

文昌洞经古乐又称"洞经音乐"，是祭祀文昌帝君时演奏的一种民间音乐。它最早起源于南宋乾道年间梓潼县七曲山作为文昌祖庭的大庙音乐，初时名为"檀炽钧音"，后因弹演《文昌大洞仙经》而改称"洞经古乐"。随着时间的推移，文昌洞经古乐逐渐走出寺庙，对其他民族音乐产生了较大影响，成为研究中国民俗文化、宗教文化不可多得的重要参考。目前，受现代文明的冲击，农耕文化习俗逐渐打破，与传统民间信仰联系在一起的文昌洞经古乐的生存空间不断压榨，传承发生严重危机。增加保护力度，最大限度地减缓这一民间古乐的衰亡速度已成当务之急。

As traditional music, *Dongjing Tunes* was selected into the second batch of the intangible cultural heritage of China in 2008. It prevails in Wenchang palace of Qiqu Mountain in Zitong County, Sichuan Province, as well as the charitable halls and chanting halls around the county. It is mainly inherited through word of mouth.

Dongjing Tunes, a piece of ancient folk music played when worshiping the emperor of Wenchang. It originated in Qiqu mountain of Zitong county in the Qiandao period of the Southern Song Dynasty. In the beginning, it was named "tanzhijun sound". Later, it was renamed "*Dongjing Tunes*" for the playing of "the great immortal Scripture of Wenchang". With the passage of time, *Dongjing Tunes* gradually walked out of the temple and into the life of common people, which had a great impact on other ethnic music. It is an important reference for the study of Chinese folk culture and religious culture. At present, under the influence of modern civilization, farming culture and customs are gradually broken, and the living space of *Dongjing Tunes*, which is associated with traditional folk beliefs, is shrinking. It has become an urgent task to strengthen protection and slow down the decline of this ancient folk music to the maximum extent.

14/115. 口弦音乐 *Buccal Reed of Yi People*

口弦音乐，传统乐器及音乐，又称为响篾、篾簧、口簧，2008 年由四川省布拖县申报入选第二批国家级非物质文化遗产名录、2011 年由四川省北川羌族自治县申报入选第三批国家级非物质文化遗产名录。其分布区域主要在四川省凉山彝族自治州布拖县以及北川羌族自治县等彝、羌族聚集区。其传承方式为口耳相传。

口弦音乐是彝族人民的喜爱之物，口弦也是布拖彝族男女最普遍携带的乐器。口弦音乐内容极其丰富，既可弹民歌，又可弹山曲；既可合弹，又可对弹；既可弹曲问答，又可弹曲斗骂。其曲调高雅，内容丰富，悦耳动听。但随着打工潮的冲击，彝族青壮年男女均外出打工，口弦音乐的原生态环境发生了巨大改变。加之地势遥远，由于无人购买口弦，彝族传统手工艺人不得不停止生产，转向其他行业谋生，导致口弦加工作坊几近灭绝，口弦音乐的传承面临危机，亟待抢救和保护。

As traditional musical instrument and music, *Buccal Reed of Yi People* is also called "Xiangmie" "Miehuang" "Kouhuang". In 2008, it was bid for the intangible cultural heritage by Bucuo county of Sichuan province and selected into the second batch of intangible cultural heritage of China. And then in 2011, it was bid again for intangible cultural heritage by Beichuan Qiang Autonomous County of Sichuan province and selected into the third batch of the intangible cultural heritage of China. It prevails in Butuo County, Liangshan Yi Autonomous Prefecture, Sichuan Province and Beichuan Qiang Autonomous County, etc., which is mainly inherited through word of mouth.

As a favorite of the Yi people in Butuo, *Buccal Reed* is the most popular musical instrument for both men and women there, which is a kind of music with extremely rich content. It can be used to play folk songs and labor songs, and can be played individually or together with other instruments. In a word, *Buccal Reed of Yi People* can express various contents and emotions, being also enjoyable to listen to. However, with more and more young Yi people going to work in the cities, he living environment of *Buccal Reed* has changed dramatically. Moreover, for the remoteness of Yi distract, there is few people who would like to buy the hand-made buccal reed instrument, which forces the folk craftsmen to stop production and turn to other industries in order to make the living. Thus the buccal reed workshops are almost extinct. Therefore, rescue and protection are urgently needed.

15. 道教音乐（成都道教音乐） *Taoist Music of Chengdu City*

道教音乐（成都道教音乐），传统音乐，又称"道场音乐"，2008年入选第二批国家级非物质文化遗产名录。其分布区域主要在四川成都辖区内道教名山、宫观和各区市县城镇、乡村中民间火居道坛。其传承方式为派系传承、师徒传承。

成都道教音乐历史悠久，其源头可追溯至一千八百多年以前东汉时出现的五斗米道斋醮科仪音乐。经过多年的传承，现已发展演变为融南北道教经韵之精华，汇名山道观古雅与民间道坛通俗之风，具有浓郁川西地方风格的传统道乐，其流派纷呈、形式多样、曲目丰富，在中国道教音乐中占据了突出的地位。由于社会发展进程中的诸多原因，20世纪50至70年代，四川成都辖区内的道教活动曾一度萧条甚至中断，如今虽有所恢复，但如果不加以重视及保护，成都道教音乐也将面临逐渐消失的境地。

As traditional music, *Taoist Music of Chengdu City* was selected into the second batch of the intangible cultural heritage of China in 2008. It prevails in the famous Taoist mountains, Taoist temples as well as counties and villages in Chengdu, Sichuan. It is mainly inherited in schools and between masters and apprentices.

Taoist Music of Chengdu City has a long history, and can be traced back to Taoist Ritual Music originated from the Eastern Han Dynasty over 1800 years ago. Through the inheritance of years, *Taoist Music of*

Chengdu City has combined the essence of North and South Taoism, with various schools, different forms and rich repertoire, owning prominent position and a great influence on Chinese Taoist music. However, due to various social reasons in modernization, Taoism activities in Chengdu were once depressed or interrupted from the 1950s to the 1970s. Though it has recovered somwhat at present, *Taoist Music of Chengdu City* will also disappear if protection measures are not taken.

16. 傩舞 *Auspicious Mask Dance*

傩舞，传统舞蹈，汉语俗称"十二相舞"，2006 年入选第一批国家级非物质文化遗产名录。其分布区域主要在四川省阿坝藏族羌族自治州九寨沟县的勿角、马家、草地、安乐、白河、郭元、双河、保华、罗依、永和等乡各山寨。其传承方式为师徒传承。

傩舞意为吉祥面具舞，是氐羌文化与藏文化的融合体，具有显著的祭祀性。"傩"，白马人方言，读音为 zhòu。白马人为纪念白马民族的首领杨戬而雕制面具和编排舞蹈，并戴面具跳舞，这种表现形式白马人称之为"傩舞"。由于傩舞面具所使用动物形象的丰富性和舞蹈套路动作的复杂性，学习"傩舞"十分不易，特别是能全面、完整地指挥领跳"傩舞"的人仅有几十个。与此同时，白马十二相面具雕刻艺人仅剩下几位老人，傩舞面临"绝代"危机，亟待抢救和保护。

As a traditional dance, *Auspicious Mask Dance* was selected into the first batch of the intangible cultural heritage of China in 2006. It prevails mainly in the villages of Jiuzhaigou County of Aba Tibetan and Qiang Autonomous Prefecture in Sichuan, such as Wujiao, Majia, Caodi, Anle, Baihe, Guoyuan, Shuanghe, Baohua, Luoyi, Yonghe etc.. It is mainly inherited between masters and apprentices.

Auspicious Mask Dance symbolizes good luck, thus got the name. It is a combination of Di Qiang culture and Tibetan culture, which is related to sacrifice. "伲" is the dialect of Baima People, with the pronunciation of Zhou. For the commemoration of their great leader in history, Yang Jian, Baima People carved masks and create their kind of dance called *Auspicious Mask dance*. And the various animal images used on the masks and sets of complex movements have made *Auspicious Mask Dance* difficult to learn, and only dozens of people can command the dance comprehensively and completely. What's more, there are only a few old artists who can carve the mask. Therefore, it is facing the crisis of extinction and in need of rescue and protection.

17. 龙舞（泸州雨坛彩龙） *Dragon Dance of Luxian County*

龙舞（泸州雨坛彩龙），传统舞蹈，也称"舞龙"，民间又叫"耍龙""耍龙灯"或"舞龙灯"，2006 年入选第一批国家级非物质文化遗产名录。其分布区域主要在四川泸州泸县雨坛镇。其传承方式为派系传承、师徒传承。现有国家级传承人罗德书。

泸州雨坛彩龙是四川省泸州市的传统龙舞，当地自古就有设坛耍龙以求风调雨顺、五谷丰登的习俗，雨坛乡亦因此得名，雨坛彩龙也在民间作为吉利祥和的象征，被誉为"东方活龙"。目前，虽然泸州雨坛彩龙传承人系统和流布区域都得到了较大的拓展，但与此同时也带来了更多的时代挑战，让泸州雨坛彩龙面临新的传承与发展危机，亟待保护。

As a traditional dance, *Dragon Dance of Luxian County*, also called "Playing Dragon" or "Playing Dragon Lantern", was selected into the first batch of the intangible cultural heritage of China in 2006. It prevails in Yutan County of Luzhou City, Sichuan Province, mainly inherited within schools as well as between masters and apprentices. At present, there exists 1 national inheritor: Luo Deshu.

Dragon Dance of Luxian County is a traditional dragon dance in Luzhou city. Since ancient times, there has been a custom of setting up an altar to play with the dragon in order to pray for a harvest. Yutan township is also named for this reason. The colored dragon is also a symbol of auspiciousness and peace among the people and is known as "Oriental living dragon". At present, although the inheritor system and distribution area of *Dragon Dance of Luxian County* have been greatly expanded, it also faces the challenge of the new era. Therefore, it is urgent to establish the protection and inheritance mechanism.

18. 弦子舞（巴塘弦子舞）

Xianzi Dance of Tibetan People in Batang County

弦子舞（巴塘弦子舞），传统舞蹈，弦子又称"谐""叶""巴叶"，2006 年入选第一批国家级非物质文化遗产名录。其分布区域主要在西藏东部及云南、四川、青海等藏族聚居区。其传承方式为派系传承、师徒传承。

巴塘弦子舞是一种优美抒情的藏族舞蹈，表演时由数名男性持拉弦乐器"毕旺"（胡琴）在队前演奏领舞，其余舞者则和他们一起边歌边舞。巴塘弦子舞是巴塘人民智慧的结晶，积淀着厚重的民族文化，拥有极高的学术价值和艺术价值。巴塘弦子拥有几千首曲目，是目前保存最完好的藏族音乐的"活化石"，对藏族歌舞艺术和藏族文化的研究具有十分重大的意义。但由于时代变化，年青一代对于传统文化的保护传承意识的缺失，渗透到藏族各种文学艺术中的巴塘弦子的音乐和唱词"后继乏人"，亟待抢救性保护。

As a traditional dance, *Xianzi Dance of Tibetan People in Batang County* is also called "Xie" "Ye" or "Baye". It was selected into the first batch of the intangible cultural heritage of China in 2006. It prevails in eastern Tibet and Tibetan gathering areas in provinces of Yunnan, Sichuan, Qinghai, which is mainly inherited within the school as well as between masters and apprentices.

Xianzi Dance of Tibetan People in Batang County is a kind of beautiful Tibetan dance. During the performance, several men played the sting instrument—Biwang (a traditional music instrument) in front of the team, while the rest of the dancers sing and dance with them. *Xianzi Dance i*s the crystallization of Batang people's wisdom, owning rich culture, high academic and artistic value. For its thousands of best preserved repertoires, *Batang Xianzi* is also regarded as the largest treasure of Tibetan folk music and "living fossil", and of great significance to the study of Tibetan song and dance art as well as Tibetan Culture. However, due to modernization, the young people lack the consciousness of protecting and inheriting this valuable heritage, which makes it lack inheritors. Therefore, it is urgent to rescue and protect.

19. 卡斯达温舞　*Armor Dance*

卡斯达温舞，传统舞蹈，汉语俗称"铠甲舞"，2006 年入选第一批国家级非物质文化遗产名录。其分布区域主要在四川省阿坝州黑水河流域。其传承方式为师徒传承。现有国家级传承人斯旦真。

卡斯达温舞是一种民间祭祀性歌舞活动。"卡斯达温"是黑水方言，"卡斯达"为"铠甲"之意，"温"或"贡"是"穿"的意思。古代黑水勇士出征前，亲朋们表演"卡斯达温"为他们祈求平安、祝福吉祥和祈祷胜利。但由于卡斯达温舞仅在四川省阿坝州黑水县的部分区域流传，目前能完整回忆和表演"卡斯达温"的民间艺人仅 10 余名，且均为 70 岁以上高龄，加之年轻人对传统民俗事象的关注日益减少，如不及时抢救或保护，这一传统文化艺术极可能会很快失传。

As a traditional dance, *Armor Dance* is known as "Kasdawen Dance" in Chinese language. It was selected into the first batch of the intangible cultural heritage of China in 2006. It prevails in Heishui River Basin in Aba Prefecture, Sichuan Province, which is mainly inherited between masters and apprentices. There exists 1 national inheritor： Sitanzhen.

Armor Dance is a kind of folk sacrificial singing and dancing activity. "Kasdawen" belongs to Heishui dialect. "Kasda" means "armor", and "Wen" or "Gong" have the meaning of "wear". In ancient times, before the warriors' expedition, their relatives and friends danced to pray for safety, good luck and victory. Nowadays, *Armor Dance* only enjoys popularity in some areas of Heishui County, Aba Prefecture, Sichuan Province, and there are no more than 20 folk artists in their 70s who can fully recall and perform the dance. Moreover, young people pay little attention to this art, *Armor Dance* is in face of extinction if proper measures are not taken to protect it in time.

20. 翻山铰子 *Small Cymbal Dance*

翻山铰子，传统舞蹈，2008 年入选第二批国家级非物质文化遗产名录。其分布区域主要在四川省平昌县一带。其传承方式为派系传承、师徒传承。现有国家级传承人吴华得。

翻山铰子是一种挥舞和击打铜质小镲"铰子"的男性舞蹈，铰子原是俗称"端公"的平昌巫师驱邪避毒时所使用的法器，至清代末年，翻山铰子在婚嫁、寿诞等各种喜事场合得到广泛应用，逐步形成现在的舞蹈样式。如今，翻山铰子在广大乡村中的展示平台日益减少，且仅剩 9 名 60 岁以上的代表性传承人，翻山铰子生存境况不佳，对它进行抢救保护已成为一项迫在眉睫的任务。

As a traditional dance, *Small Cymbal Dance* was selected into the second batch of the intangible cultural heritage of China in 2008. It prevails in Pingchang County of Sichuan Province, which is mainly inherited between masters and apprentices. There exists 1 national inheritor: Wu Huade.

Small Cymbal Dance is a kind of male dance in which the performers waving and striking small copper cymbals. The copper cymbals were originally magic instruments used by Pingchang witches to avoid evil spirits, commonly known as "Duangong". By the end of the Qing Dynasty, it was widely used in weddings, birthdays and other happy occasions. It gradually developed into the current dance style. Currently, due to the shrinking of displaying opportunities and the decrease of performers (only 9 inheritors in their 60s in the whole county), it has become an urgent task to protect it.

21. 羌族羊皮鼓舞 *Sheepskin Drum Dance of the Qiang People*

羌族羊皮鼓舞，传统舞蹈，2008 年入选第二批国家级非物质文化遗产名录。其分布区域主要四川省阿坝藏族羌族自治州汶川县的龙溪、雁门、绵篪等地，而以龙溪乡阿尔村的巴夺寨最为典型。现有国家级传承人朱金龙。

据文献记载，羊皮鼓舞原是羌族"释比"做法事时跳的一种宗教舞蹈，后逐渐演变为民间舞蹈。羊皮鼓舞作为释比祭祀舞，具有极强的宗教和民族特征，是羌族文化的外化表现。羊皮鼓舞具有娱神、娱人与自娱特征，具有历史、艺术、文化、健身和教育价值。但因羌族羊皮鼓舞的传承方式依附释比文化，局限性较大，传男不传女，传承难度大，技艺面临"断代"的危险，亟待进一步抢救性保护。

As a traditional dance, *Sheepskin Drum Dance of the Qiang*

People was selected into the second batch of the intangible cultural heritage of China in 2008. It mainly prevails in Longxi, Yanmen, Mianchi and other places in Wenchuan County, Aba Tibetan and Qiang Autonomous Prefecture, Sichuan Province. Among them, the Sheepskin Drum Dance in Longxi town is the most typical one. There exists 1 national inheritor: Zhu Jinlong.

According to the recording, *Sheepskin Drum Dance* was originally a religious dance and gradually evolved into a folk dance. As a Shibi sacrifice dance, with strong religious and national characteristics, the *Sheepskin Drum Dance* is an external manifestation of the Qiang culture. It has the characteristics of entertaining God, entertaining others and self-entertainment, combining historical, artistic, cultural, fitness and educational values. However, because the inheritance methods of the sheepskin dance rely on the Shibi culture, the inheritance is limited only to male, not female, it is difficult to pass on the dance. The skills are facing the danger of extinction. Therefore, further rescue and protection are urgently needed.

22. 得荣学羌　*Xueqiang Dance of Derong County*

得荣学羌，传统舞蹈，2008 年入选第二批国家级非物质文化遗产名录。其分布区域主要在四川省甘孜藏族自治州西南部得荣县子庚乡、子实村境内。其传承方式为派系传承、师徒传承。现有国家级传承人格玛次仁。

得荣学羌是一种自娱性的民间歌舞表演形式，它主要使用得荣方言表演，以得荣锅庄韵调为基本音乐，以得荣锅庄舞步为基本舞步。得荣学羌刚劲有力、古朴大方，脚下踏跺组合是其舞蹈动作的主要特点。学羌表演时，下步有力，踏脚清脆，舞者俯身变化踏点后，这一动作又转而表现出柔韧洒脱的特点，跺脚与踏脚动作相结合，形成学羌舞独特的韵味。目前，随着现代经济社会的发展，跳学羌的艺人日益减少，学羌舞面临传承乏人的状况，亟待抢救保护。

As a traditional dance, *Xueqiang Dance of Derong County* was selected into the second batch of the intangible cultural heritage of China in 2008. It prevails in Zigeng Town, Zishi village in Derong County, southwest of Ganzi Tibetan Autonomous Prefecture, Sichuan Province. It is mainly inherited within schools as well as between masters and apprentices. At present, there exists 1 national inheritor: Gemaciren.

Xueqiang Dance of Derong County is a form of folk song and dance for self entertainment. The dialect of Derong county is its main performing language. And the melody and dance step of *Guozhuang Dance of Derong County* are their basic music and dance step. Its dance steps are a combination of trampling and stamping. Therefore, it is famous for its simple and powerful dance steps. The steps are powerful and swift at the beginning, after the dancers bend over and change their steps, the movement turns to show the characteristics of flexibility and freedom. At present, with the development of the modern economy and society, the number of people learning *Xueqiang Dance* is decreasing. Therefore, it is urgent to protect *Xueqiang Dance*.

23. 甲搓　*Jiacuo Dance of Yanyuan County*

甲搓，传统舞蹈，又称甲措，2008 年入选第二批国家级非物质文化遗产名录。其分布区域主要在泸沽湖及其周围地区。其传承方式为派系传承、师徒传承。现有国家级传承人喇翁基。

甲搓是摩梭人在长期生产实践及生活习俗中形成的一种原始民间舞蹈，即打跳舞或锅庄舞，"甲"为美好之意，"搓"为舞的意思，甲搓即为美好的时辰而舞。这种舞节奏明快，舞步刚健粗犷。相传甲搓原有 72 种曲调和舞蹈，完整流传至今的仅有"搓德""了搓优""格姆搓""阿什撒尔搓""卧曹甲莫母"等十多种。随着时代的变迁，古老的原始民间舞蹈甲搓已处于濒危状态，传承乏人，亟待抢救保护。

As a traditional dance, *Jiacuo Dance of Yanyuan County* was selected into the second batch of the intangible cultural heritage of China in 2008. It prevails in Lugu Lake and its surrounding areas, which is mainly inherited within schools as well as between masters and apprentices. There exists 1 national inheritor: Lawengji.

Jiachuo Dance of Yanyuan County is a kind of primitive folk dance formed in their long-term production practice and living. "Jia" means beautiful, and "Cuo" means dance in their language, therefore "Jiacuo" means dancing for a good time. It has a swift rhythm and vigorous steps. It is said that there are 72 original tunes and dance steps. However, only more than ten kinds of tunes and dances have been completely handed down. With the changes of the times, *Jiachuo Dance*—the ancient primitive folk dance is in an endangered situation. Therefore, it is urgent to protect it.

24. 博巴森根 *Bobasenge Dance of Tibetan People*

博巴森根，传统舞蹈，2008 年入选第二批国家级非物质文化遗产名录。其分布区域主要在四川省理县嘉绒藏族地区。其传承方式为派系传承、师徒传承。

博巴森根是民间大型叙事性群众锅庄舞蹈，"博巴"藏语意为"藏人"，"森根"藏语意为"狮子"。该舞蹈产生于 19 世纪中期（清道光年间），是藏人为了歌颂其族人英雄的英勇事迹和纪念牺牲战友而创作的，表达了藏族人民强烈的民族情怀。博巴森根在沿用四土锅庄部分特点的基础上，在表演形式中创造了"钻""扭""解"等舞蹈形式，并独创了由领舞者叙事性演唱，众舞者倾听的表演形式，独具地方特色。近年来，由于传统生产方式变化，主要经济支柱的改变，人民生活习惯的演变等原因，博巴森根的传承出现了严重的危机，急需抢救保护。

As a traditional dance, *Bobasengen Dance of Tibetan People* was selected into the second batch of the intangible cultural heritage of China in 2008. It prevails in Jiarong Tibetan area, Lixian County, Sichuan Province. It is mainly inherited within schools as well as between masters and apprentices.

Bobasenge Dance of Tibetan People is a large-scale narrative folk dance. "Boba" means "Tibetans" and "sengen" means "lions" in Tibetan language. The dance originated in the middle of the 19th century (Daoguang period of the Qing Dynasty) . It was created to commemorate the heroic deeds as well as their dead co-soldiers, fully expressing the patriotic feelings of the Tibetan people. The dance adopts some characteristics of Situ Guozhuang dance, but it creates some dance forms such as "crawling", "twisting" and "untwisting", as well as a unique performance form of narrative singing by the leading dancers and listening by the dancers. In recent years, due to the change of traditional production mode and the evolution of people's living habits, the inheritance of *Bobasenge Dance* is facing a crisis. Therefore, rescue and protection are urgently needed.

25. 川剧 *Sichuan Opera*

川剧，传统戏剧，2006 年入选第一批国家级非物质文化遗产名录。其分布区域主要在四川省、重庆市及云南、贵州、湖北省的部分地区。

其传承方式为派系传承、师徒传承。现有国家级传承人肖德美、徐寿年、任庭芳、晓艇等 14 人。

川剧是中国西南部影响最大的地方剧种，剧目丰富，有传统剧目和创作剧目六千余种，具有巴蜀文化、艺术、历史、民俗等方面的价值，在中国戏曲史及巴蜀文化发展史上具有十分独特的地位。近年来，川剧同其他各种地方戏曲一样出现了生存危机，观众减少，演出市场萎缩，经费不足，传承发展举步维艰，抢救、保护川剧的任务正严肃地摆在人们面前。

As traditional drama, *Sichuan Opera* was selected into the first batch of the intangible cultural heritage of China in 2006. It prevails in Sichuan Province, Chongqing city and some areas of Yunnan, Guizhou and Hubei Province. It mainly inherited within schools as well as between masters and apprentices. There exist 14 nation inheritors: Xiao Demei, Xu Shounian, Ren Tingfang and Xiaoting etc..

Sichuan Opera is the most influential local opera in Southwest China with rich repertoires. There are more than 6000 traditional and creative repertoires. It has high research value in Bashu culture, art, history, folk custom etc. It also has a unique position in the history of Chinese opera and Bashu culture. In recent years, due to the decreasing of audience, the shrinking of market and lack of funds, its inheritance and development have experienced survival crisis. Therefore, it is an urgent task to protect and develop it.

26. 灯戏（北川灯戏） *Lantern Opera of Northern Sichuan*

灯戏（北川灯戏），传统戏剧，2006 年入选第一批国家级非物质文化遗产名录。其分布区域主要在四川省东北部地区。其传承方式为派系传承、师徒传承。现有国家级传承人汪洋、彭涓。

川北灯戏是在川北一带流行的历史悠久的民间歌舞小戏。川北灯戏又被称为"农民戏""喜乐神"，其剧目多取材于当地民间生活，反映了民间的人生理念和审美情趣，并为民众喜闻乐见。虽然建国后川北灯戏已在党和人民政府的扶持下得到了一定程度的保护，但随着社会现代化的发展，年轻一代对传统艺术的兴趣缺失，川北灯戏逐渐出现传承危机，急需抢救保护。

As traditional drama, *Lantern Opera of Northern Sichuan* was selected into the first batch of the intangible cultural heritage of China in 2006, which prevails in the northeastern Sichuan. It is mainly inherited within schools as well as between masters and apprentices. There exist 2 national inheritors: Wang Yang, Peng Juan.

Lantern Opera of Northern Sichuan is a popular folk drama with a long history in northern Sichuan. It also gets the name of "peasant drama" and "God of Jo", for it is based on local folk life, reflecting the common people's philosophy of life and aesthetic taste, so it gains great popularity among ordinary people. With the support of CPC and the government after the founding of the People's Republic of China, *Lantern Opera* has gained proper protections to some extent. However, in recent years, due to social development and modernization, young people lack interest in the traditional arts, which makes its inheritance facing the crisis. Therefore, rescue and protection are urgently needed.

27. 木偶戏（北川大木偶戏） *Beichuan Big-sized Puppet Show*

木偶戏（北川大木偶戏），传统戏剧，2006 年入选第一批国家级非物质文化遗产名录。其分布区域主要在四川省南充市。其传承方式为派系传承、师徒传承。现有国家级传承人李泗元。

川北大木偶如真人般大小，并可做出穿衣、点火、喝茶、叩首、舞刀等动作，表情丰富、动作灵活；表演时木偶多与"人偶"（幼童扮演的）同台，形成以假乱真、亦真亦假的艺术特色，蕴藏着各地、各民族人民的思想、道德和审美意识。如今，虽然北川大木偶戏除演出传统的戏曲节目外，还表演话剧、歌舞剧、连续剧，甚至出演广告等，但仍面临着与其他艺术形式之间的激烈竞争。特别是由于木偶制作人才和技艺演出人员的奇缺，川北大木偶戏这一文艺瑰宝面临"断代"危机，保护和传承迫在眉睫。

As traditional drama, *Beichuan Big-sized Puppet Show* was selected into the first batch of the intangible cultural heritage of China in 2006. It mainly prevails in Nanchong City, Sichuan Province, which mainly inherited within schools as well as between masters and apprentices. There exists 1 national inheritor: Li Siyuan.

The *Big-sized Puppet* is as tall as a real person, and it can do movements flexibly as putting on clothes, lighting fire, drinking tea, kowtowing and waving a sword based on the show. In most cases, the puppet performs together with the kids, making it difficult to distinguish their performances. And *Beichuan Big-sized Puppet Show* is characterized by its vividness and authenticity, containing the thoughts, morality and aesthetic of people from all over the country and all ethnic groups. Nowadays, in addition to traditional operas, it also performs drama, song and dance drama, series and even advertisements. But there are still facing fierce competitions between *Beichuan Big-sized Puppet Show* with other art forms. Especially the severe shortage of puppet-making talents and personnel performing, *Beichuan Big-sized Puppet Show* is in danger of extinction, and it is urgent to protect and inherit this art rarity.

28 ~ 30. 四川扬琴 *Dulcimer Opera of Sichuan Province*

四川扬琴，曲艺，又称"四川琴书"，2008 年入选第二批国家级非物质文化遗产名录。其分布区域主要在四川的川东、川西、川南一带。其传承方式为派系传承、师徒传承。现有国家级传承人刘时燕、徐述等 4 人。

四川扬琴因演唱时主要以扬琴为伴奏乐器而得名，有"坐地传情"之称。四川扬琴吸收了川剧和清音之长，通过唱和道白，将叙事、抒情与戏剧融为一体，有层次地表现戏剧情节。如今，四川扬琴艺术面临重重困难：人才匮乏、作品匮乏；扬琴的老艺人大多逝世或年事已高；专业人员和业余爱好者缺少展示平台，表演市场的萎缩。这些直接影响到这门艺术的生存和发展，四川扬琴面临濒危状况，亟待抢救性保护和传承。

As a traditional music, *Dulcimer Opera of Sichuan Province* is also known as "Sichuan Dulcimer Show". It was selected into the second batch of the intangible cultural heritage of China on 7th, June 2008. It prevails in Eastern Sichuan, Western Sichuan as well as Southern Sichuan, which is mainly inherited within schools as well as between masters and apprentices. There exist 4 national inheritors: Liu Shiyan, Xu Shu etc..

Dulcimer Opera of Sichuan Province got the name because its main musical instrument is the dulcimer during a performance. It absorbs the advantages of Sichuan Opera and Sichuan Tunes, and integrates narrative, emotional expression and drama to show its plots. Nowadays, due to the shortage of talents and works, the death of aged artists, the shrinking of markets and the lack of display platform for professionals and amateurs, its survival and development face many difficulties. And it is in need of urgent protection to inherit this art rarity.

31. 四川竹琴　*Zhuqin Opera of Sichuan Province*

四川竹琴，曲艺，原名"名琴"，2008 年入选第二批国家级非物质文化遗产名录，分布区域主要在四川汉族地区。其传承方式为派系传承、师徒传承。现有国家级传承人张永贵等 4 人。

四川竹琴是一种汉族的传统戏曲剧种，因其伴奏的乐器是竹制的渔鼓筒，故又称"渔鼓道琴""道筒"。过去，表演时表演者手持渔鼓、简板说唱故事，而如今四川竹琴具有了更丰富多变的演唱形式和表演风格。除传统的坐唱外，还有站唱、走唱，并借身体、四肢、面部表情等辅助形式进行表演，竹琴的艺术表现力有了较大的丰富。但是近二十年来，四川竹琴的发展陷于停滞，作品匮乏、人才青黄不接、观众流失、市场萎缩，四川竹琴正面临严峻的危机，亟须保护振兴。

As a traditional music, *Zhuqin Opera of Sichuan Province* is also known as "Minqin". It was selected into the second batch of the intangible cultural heritage of China on 7th, June 2008. It prevails in Han People gathering areas in Sichuan province. The main inheritance is within schools as well as between masters and apprentices. There exist 4 national inheritors, one of which is Zhang Yonggui.

Zhuqin Opera of Sichuan Province is traditional Chinese Opera of Han Nationality, and it is also called "Yugudaoqin" or "Daotong" for its accompanying instrument is Yugu (a percussion instrument made of bamboo). Traditionally, performers hold Yugu and bamboo percussion clappers to tell stories. But nowadays, *Zhuqin Opera of Sichuan Province* has adopted various singing and performing styles. Besides the traditional way of sitting singing, there are also standing singing and walking singing, and with the help of auxiliary forms such as body, limbs, facial expressions, etc., its artistic expression has been largely enriched. However, in the past two decades, the development of *Zhuqin Opera* has been stagnated, due to the scarce of works, the shortage of talents, the decreasing of audience and the shrinking of the market. *Zhuqin Opera of Sichuan Province* is now facing a severe crisis of extinction, and in urgent need of protection and revitalization.

32. 四川清音　*Sichuan Tunes*

四川清音，曲艺，原名"唱小曲"，又叫"唱月琴""唱琵琶"，2008年入选第二批国家级非物质文化遗产名录。其分布区域主要在四川省汉族地区。其传承方式为派系传承、师徒传承。现有国家级传承人程永玲、肖顺瑜等人。

源自明清时期的四川清音，用四川方言演唱，曲调丰富，唱腔优美。表演时由女演员一人坐着独唱，右手击竹鼓，左手击檀板，自击自唱。四川清音的代表作品有《昭君出塞》《尼姑下山》等。但是如今，四川清音艺术面临传承困难：一方面，老艺人大多过世或年事已高，继承人缺乏；另一方面，清音艺术的市场不断萎缩，缺少艺术的展示平台。这直接影响了这门艺术的生存和发展，致使其面临濒危状况，亟待保护与传承。

As a traditional drama, *Sichuan Tunes* is also called "*Singing Xiaoqu*", "*Singing Yueqin*" and "*Singing Pipa*". It was selected into the second batch of the intangible cultural heritage of China in 2008. It prevails in Han People gathering areas in Sichuan province. The main inheritance is within schools as well as between masters and apprentices. At present, there exist national inheritors: Cheng Yongling, Xiao Shunyu etc..

Originated in Ming and Qing Dynasties, *Sichuan Tunes* is sung in

Sichuan dialect, with the characteristics of rich tunes and beautiful melody. When performing, the actress sings alone, with a drum in her right hand and boards in her left hand. Both the drum and boards are made of bamboo. Its representative works include *Zhaojun Going Out of the fortress*, *Buddhist Nun Going Down the Mountain*, etc. However, currently, *Sichuan Tunes* faces many difficulties: on one hand, the aging and passing-by of aged artists result in the shortage of inheritors; on the other hand, there exist the shrinking of markets and the lack of display platforms. Therefore, its endangered situation is self-evident, demanding urgent protection.

33. 金钱板　*Allegro of Chengdu City*

金钱板，曲艺，2008 年入选第二批国家级非物质文化遗产名录，分布区域主要在巴蜀汉族地区。其传承方式为派系传承、师徒传承。现有国家级传承人张徐、邹忠新等 3 人。

金钱板发源于 300 多年前的成渝两地，表演时表演者手持长约一尺、宽约一寸的三块楠竹板，其中两块还嵌有铜钱或其他金属片，说唱时竹板互击，发出金属声音，故得名"金钱板"。但是现如今金钱板艺术面临人才、作品匮乏的困境：金钱板的老艺人大多过世或年事已高；传统曲目大多失传；专业人员和业余爱好者都缺少展示平台，市场萎缩。这直接影响了这门艺术的生存和发展，致使其面临濒危状况，亟待保护与传承。

As traditional drama, *Allegro of Chengdu City* was selected into the second batch of the intangible cultural heritage of China in 2008. It prevails in Han People gathering areas in Sichuan and Chongqing provinces. It is mainly inherited within schools as well as between masters and apprentice. There exist 3 national inheritors: Zhuang Xu,

Zou Zhongxin etc..

Allegro of Chengdu City originated in Chengdu and Chongqing more than 300 years ago. When performing, performers would hold three bamboo boards about one foot long and one inch wide, two of which are also embedded with copper coins or other metal pieces. The bamboo boards, which are used as props for performing, can make metal sounds because of striking, thus getting the name "Jinqianban". However, at present, due to lack of talents and works, the aging or passing by of aged performers, the loss of traditional repertoire, the shortage of displaying platform for amateurs and professional performers and the shrinking of market, its survival and development face many difficulties, demanding urgent protection.

34. 峨眉武术　*E-Mei Martial Arts*

峨眉武术，传统体育、游艺与杂技，2008年入选第二批国家级非物质文化遗产名录，分布区域主要在四川乃至西南地区。其传承方式为派系传承、师徒传承。现有国家级传承人王超。

作为中国传统武术流派之一，峨嵋武术的发祥地为中国名山——峨嵋山。据史料记载，峨眉武术起源于殷商时期，至南宋形成较为系统的理论体系，门派八十多个，拳种、拳路成百上千。峨眉武术讲究刚柔相济、内外兼修，动作似快而慢、快慢相间，似柔而刚、刚柔相济。在佛、道、儒文化相互融合的影响下，峨眉武术不断发展变化，逐渐成为中华武术三大流派之一。但受现代生活方式冲击，如今峨眉武术的完整传承面临多种困境，亟待加以保护。

As traditional sports, entertainment and acrobatics, *E-mei Martial Arts* was selected into the second batch of the intangible cultural heritage of China in 2008. It prevails in Sichuan and even southwest China, which is mainly inherited within schools as well as between masters and apprentices. There exists 1 national inheritor: Wang Chao.

E-mei Martial Arts is one of the schools of traditional Chinese martial arts. According to historical records, it originated from China's famous Mount Emei in Shang Dynasty, and formed a relatively systematic theoretical system till the Southern Song Dynasty. It now has more than 80 schools and hundreds of fist positions. *E-mei Martial Arts* emphasizes the combination of hardness and softness, internal and external cultivation, as well as fast and slow movements. Under the influence of the mutual fusion of Buddhism, Taoism and Confucianism, it has been developing and changing, and has gradually become one of the three major schools of Chinese martial arts. However, under the impact of modern lifestyle, the complete inheritance of *Emei Martial Arts* is facing many difficulties. Therefore, effective protection is urgently needed.

35. 绵竹木版年画

New Year Wood-block Painting of Mianzhu County

绵竹木版年画，传统美术，2006 年入选第一批国家级非物质文化遗产名录。其分布区域主要在四川省德阳市绵竹市城区剑南镇和北部的拱星镇、清道镇、新市镇、孝德镇等地。其传承方式为派系传承、师徒传承。现有国家级传承人李芳福、陈兴才。

绵竹木版年画始于宋代盛于明清，以木版刻印、手工彩绘为特色，图画内容以吉祥喜庆、民间传说、乡土生活等为主，构图丰富夸张、色彩鲜艳明快，具有鲜明的农耕文化特色。20 世纪 50 年代以后，绵竹木版年画多次遭受毁灭性打击，不少传承人被剥夺绘画的权利，大量古版年画亦遭破坏。虽然近 20 年间年画的制作与生产已有所恢复，但由于市场的萎缩，出现了传承人卖版子毁笔、不再从事年画制作的现象，绵竹木版年画亟待加以保护。

As traditional art, *New Year Wood-block Painting of Mianzhu County* was selected into the first batch of the intangible cultural heritage of China in 2006. It prevails in Jiannan Town, Gongxing Town, Qingdao Town, Xinshi Town and Xiaode Town in Mian Zhu County of Deyang City. It is mainly inherited within schools as well as between masters and apprentices. There exist 2 national inheritors: Li Fangfu and Chen Xingcai.

New Year Wood-block Painting of Mianzhu County originated in Song Dynasty and flourished in Ming and Qing Dynasties. It is characterized by woodblock printing and hand-made color painting. The contents of the pictures are mainly auspicious celebrations, folklores, local life, etc.. The composition of the pictures is rich and exaggerated, and its color rich and bright. It has distinct characteristics of agricultural culture. After the 1950s, *New Year wood-block Painting of Mianzhu County has been devastated many times*. A great number of inheritors were deprived of the right of the drawing, and many ancient woodblock New Year pictures were destroyed. Although the production of New Year woodblock pictures has been restored in the past 20 years, due to the shrinking market, many artists tend to give up drawing it. Therefore, urgent protection of *New Year Woodblock Painting* is needed.

36. 藏族唐卡（噶玛嘎孜画派） *Gemagazi Thangka*

藏族唐卡（噶玛嘎孜画派），传统美术，又译为"嘎玛嘎赤画派"，简称"噶智派"，2006 年入选第一批国家级非物质文化遗产名录。其分布区域主要在藏区东部，以四川省甘孜德格和西藏昌都及青海玉树为中心。传承方式为派系传承、师徒传承。现有国家级传承人颜登泽仁。

噶玛嘎孜画派属于藏族唐卡的三大流派之一，相传是由南喀扎西活佛在16世纪创建，以施色浓重、对比强烈为显著特点，画面富丽堂皇；同时为使装帧的布与画完美地融为一体，从装帧的选料、颜色与布局都十分讲究。因其传统天然颜料的制作方法和使用技法纷繁复杂，以及其考究的技艺和口耳相传的传承方式，导致其传承与维系难度较高。近年来，以价格低廉的现代合成颜料替代传统颜料对其产生巨大冲击，同时噶孜画派的传统绘画风格也在时代变化中发生着变化，使藏族唐卡面临着失传的危险，亟须保护和抢救。

As traditional art, *Gamagazi Thangka* is also known as "Gamagazi School" or "Karzhi School". It was selected into the first batch of the intangible cultural heritage of China in 2006. It prevails in the eastern Tibetan area, with Dege County in Sichuan Province, Changdu City in Tibet and Yushu Tibetan Autonomous Prefecture in Qinghai Province as its center. It is mainly inherited within schools as well as between masters and apprentices. At present, there exist 1 national inheritor: Yandengzeren.

Gemagazi Thangka belongs to one of the three major schools of Tangka in Tibet, which is said was founded in the 16th century by the living Buddha at that time–Nankazhaxi. It is characterized by rich colors, sharp contrast and gorgeous pictures. In order to make the cloth and the painting perfectly integrated, the selection of materials, color and layout of the binding are all very exquisite. And due to the complexity of the production and use of traditional natural pigments as well as the exquisite skills and oral inheritance, it is difficult to inherit and maintain

Gemagazi Thangka. Furthermore, in recent years, there is also a huge impact of replacing traditional pigments with low-cost modern synthetic pigments. At the same time, the traditional painting style of "Karzhi school" is also changing with the change of times. Thus, it is in a great danger of extinction, in need of urgent to rescue and protection.

37. 蜀绣 *Sichuan Embroidery*

蜀绣，又名"川绣"，传统美术，2006 年入选国家级第一批非物质文化遗产名录。其主要分布在四川、重庆等地区，现有国家级传承人孟德芝、郝淑萍等。

与苏绣、湘绣、粤绣齐名为中国四大名绣之一的蜀绣，是在丝绸或其他织物上采用蚕丝线绣出花纹图案的中国传统工艺。作为中国刺绣传承时间最长的绣种之一，蜀绣以其明丽清秀的色彩和精湛细腻的针法形成了自身的独特韵味，丰富程度居四大名绣之首。但由于其手工制作性质决定了蜀绣的每件作品在创作中都必须耗费工艺师大量的时间和精力，投入产出比偏低，加之传承手段的限制，致使蜀绣面临着后继乏人、技艺失传等问题，亟须保护。

As traditional art, *Sichuan Embroidery* is also known as "Shu Embroidery". It was selected into the first batch of the intangible cultural heritage of China in 2006. It prevails in Sichuan and Chongqing provinces. At present, there exist 2 national inheritors: Meng Dezhi and Hao Shuping etc..

Sichuan Embroidery, together with *Suzhou Embroidery*, *Hunan Embroidery* and *Guangdong Embroidery*, is regarded as one of the four famous embroideries in China. It is a traditional kind of craftsmanship of embroidering patterns by using silk thread. As one of the embroideries with the longest history, *Sichuan Embroidery* has developed its own unique charm with bright and beautiful colors and exquisite needling techniques, which ranks first among the four famous embroideries. However, it is time-consuming to make *Sichuan Embroidery* due to its handmade nature. Because of the low input-output ratio and the limitation of inheritance way, *Sichuan Embroidery* is faced with many problems such as lack of successors, loss of skills and techniques etc.. Therefore, it is in urgent need of protection.

38. 藏族格萨尔彩绘石刻

Gesar Colored Stone-carving of Tibetan People

藏族格萨尔彩绘石刻，传统美术，2006 年入选国家级第一批非物质文化遗产名录。其主要分布在四川省甘孜藏族自治州色达、石渠、丹巴三县境内，以色达县的格萨尔彩绘石刻最有代表性。格萨尔彩绘石刻技艺的传承方式以师徒或家族传承为主。

藏族格萨尔彩绘石刻属于格萨尔文化的一种遗存，但由于石刻长期露天放置，高原严寒的侵袭和强烈紫外线的照射对其造成较为严重的损坏。加之格萨尔彩绘对艺人素质要求较高，而目前的石刻艺人基本都是业余从事彩绘石刻的农牧民或寺庙僧人，有艺不精，学而不成；还有一些艺人甚至逐渐放弃手艺改从他业，导致格萨尔彩绘石刻技艺面临着传人青黄不接的局面，亟须扶持、保护。

As traditional art, *Gesar Colored Stone-carving of Tibetan People* was selected into the first batch of the intangible cultural heritage of China in 2006. It prevails in Seda, Shiqu County and Danba County of Ganzi Tibetan Autonomous Prefecture in Sichuan Province. It is mainly inherited within family members as well as between masters and apprentices.

Gesar Colored Stone-carving of Tibetan People is the remains of

Gesar culture. However, due to the long-term exposure to the open air, the cold and intense ultraviolet radiation, it was badly damaged. In addition, it is technically demanding. The reality is that most of the stone carving artists are amateurs such as farmers, herdsmen or temple monks. Some stone-carving craftsmen even change their professions. Lack of successors is one of the big problems. Therefore, it is urgent to protect *Stone-carving Techniques*.

39. 草编（沐川草龙）　*Straw-dragon Weaving Techniques*

草编（沐川草龙），又称"黄龙"，传统美术，2008 年入选国家级第二批非物质文化遗产名录。其主要分布在四川省乐山市沐川县一带，现有国家级传承人陈焕彬。

沐川草龙历史悠久，形制讲究。其编扎原料须为当年收割稻草中精选出的色泽金黄、秆身没有斑点的上品。其扎制工艺也非常复杂，制作过程涉及编、织、镶、绕、缠等十多种手法，技巧性强。沐川草龙对于龙头、龙身、龙尾的设计十分精巧，龙眼、龙须、龙角、龙鳞、龙爪等细节处理追求活灵活现，舞起来气势夺人，蔚为壮观，表达了人们对吉祥、安康、幸福生活的追求和向往。但由于沐川草龙的制作全凭手艺人的悟性与手感，对传承人的手艺技能和艺术品位都有较高的要求，其传承难度较大，需要及时进行抢救性保护。

As traditional art, *Straw-dragon Weaving Techniques* is also called "Yellow Dragon". It was selected into the second batch of the intangible cultural heritage of China in 2008. It prevails in Muchuan County, Leshan City, Sichuan Province. At present, there exists 1 national inheritor: Chen Huanbing.

Straw-dragon Weaving Techniques has a long history and exquisite shape. The raw materials are the gold, fine and spotless straw selected from the rice straw harvested in that year. Its weaving techniques are very complicated. The whole making process involves weaving, knitting, binding, winding etc.. The design of the dragon's head, body and tail are extremely exquisite. The details of the dragon's eye, whisker, horn, scale, and claw are vivid. The dragon dancing is magnificent, which expresses people's pursuit and yearning for an auspicious, healthy and happy life. However, because the production of straw-dragon totally depends on the craftsmen's understanding and experiences, which set high requirements on both the techniques and art taste of the craftsmen, making its inheritance great trouble. Therefore, it is urgent to protect this skill.

40. 石雕（白花石刻） *Stone-carving of Guangyuan City*

石雕（白花石刻），传统美术，2008 年入选国家级第二批非物质文化遗产名录，主要分布在四川省广元市，现有国家级传承人唐骏。

白花石刻，以大巴山白花石为原料，是自清代以来不断发展形成的一种极具特色的地方传统雕刻艺术。常取山水、人物、花鸟、走兽为题材，制品以烟盒、文具、花钵、花架、石屏等实用品居多，体现了艺人精湛的工艺水平和独特的艺术面貌。石刻艺人善于因材施艺，通过深雕、浅雕、镂空等各种雕刻技艺将石料的天然美感和精微的构思巧妙统一。但由于白花石非常稀有，深藏于大巴山深处，开采难度大，保护这一濒危的民间艺术瑰宝，迫在眉睫。

As traditional art, *Stone-carving of Guangyuan City* was selected into the second batch of the intangible cultural heritage of China in 2008. It prevails in Guangyuan City, Sichuan Province. At present, there is 1 national inheritor: Tang Jun.

Stone-carving of Guangyuan City is a kind of unique local traditional carving art that has been developed since Qing Dynasty. Its main raw materials are "white-flower" stones from Daba Mountain. Landscapes, figures, flowers, birds, and animals are often taken as the themes, and the most commonly seen products are cigarette boxes, stationery, flower pots, flower racks, stone screens, etc., which reflect their exquisite craftsmanship and unique artistic features. The stone-carving craftsmen are good at carving art works based on materials, skillfully unifying the natural beauty of stone and the subtleties of conception by using various carving techniques such as deep carving, shallow carving and hollowing out. However, "white-flower" stones are very rare and hidden in the deep Daba Mountain. Therefore, it is urgent to protect this endangered folk art treasure.

41. 石雕（安岳石刻） *Stone-carving of Anyue County*

石雕（安岳石刻），传统美术，2008 年入选国家级第二批非物质文化遗产名录，主要分布地区为四川省安岳县，现有国家级传承人石永恩。

安岳以摩崖造像闻名，当地的摩崖造像始于南北朝而盛于唐宋，以佛教造像为主，亦有道教造像，境内现有古代石刻遗存 500 余处、造像 10 万余尊，且分布呈现点多、线长、面宽的特点。安岳石刻有圆雕、塔雕、壁雕、碑刻等技艺形式，刻工精细，刀法娴熟，匠心独运，人物形象生动而富有情趣，展现了高超的工艺水平。但正是由于安岳石刻呈现的丰富文物和众多资源，使得亟需根据其现在的传承等级和实际及时保护。

As traditional art, *Stone-carving of Anyue County* was selected into the second batch of the intangible cultural heritage of China in 2008. It prevails in Anyue County, Sichuan Province. At present, there exists 1 national inheritor: Shi Yong'en.

Anyue is famous for its cliff statues. The local cliff statues began in the Northern and Southern Dynasties and flourished in the Tang and Song dynasties. They are mainly Buddhist statues and Taoist statues, with wide distributions in various places. Stone carvings of Anyue County have the skills of round carving, tower carving, wall carving and stele carving. They are exquisite in carving, skillful in technique, ingenious in craftsmanship and have vivid and interesting characters, which show a high level of craftsmanship. However, it is the abundance in a quantity of *Stone-carving of Anyue County* that makes it necessary to protect urgently according to the current inheritance level and the actual situation.

42. 藏文书法（德格藏文书法）

Tibetan Calligraphy of Dege County

藏文书法（德格藏文书法），藏语称为"德真"，传统美术，2008年入选国家级第二批非物质文化遗产名录，主要分布地区在藏区。

德格藏文书法是在藏区广为流行的一种传统藏文字书写艺术，至今已有700多年的发展历史。德格藏文书法线条遒劲，布局精巧，结构疏密得当，其楷书、行书、草书等不同书体均显出轻快而劲健、凝重而灵动、舒放而练达的风格特色。至今为止，仍有不少藏区学者在书写中仍采用德格书法谋篇布局的方法。但随着现代化的社会发展，越来越少的现代人能够仅凭借着兴趣、热爱和坚持将藏文书法传承下去，德格藏文书法面临着"后继无人"的传承困境，亟须采取有效措施进行保护。

As traditional art, *Tibetan Calligraphy of Dege County* is also called "Dezhen" in Tibetan language. It was selected into the second batch of intangible cultural heritage of China in 2008, prevailing in Tibetan area.

Tibetan Calligraphy of Dege County is a traditional Tibetan writing art that is widely popular in Tibetan areas. It has a history of more than 700 years, which is characterized by vigorous lines, exquisite layout and appropriate structure. Its regular script, running script, cursive script and other different styles are light and vigorous, dignified and flexible, relaxed and practical. So far, there are still many Tibetan scholars who still use the method of the layout of *Tibetan Calligraphy of Dege County*. However, with the development of modern society, fewer and fewer people would inherit *Tibetan calligraphy* just due to their interest, love and persistence in this kind of art, which makes the inheritance of *Tibetan calligraphy of Dege county* in great danger. Therefore, effective measures should be taken to protect it.

43. 木版年画（夹江年画）

New Year Wood-block Painting of Jiajiang County

木版年画（夹江年画），传统美术，2008 年入选国家级第二批非物质文化遗产名录，主要分布在四川省夹江县。

夹江年画是四川省夹江县特有的一种民间美术样式，与绵竹年画和梁平年画齐名，为四川三大年画之一。夹江年画作为川西南独具特色的农民画，在民间土生土长，经过长期的修改和提炼，集中体现了当地劳动人民的勤劳和智慧，包含着广大人民群众对于和平、安康生活的追求和向往。但在现代化的发展过程中，夹江年画因其地域的局限性导致市场不断萎缩，再加之年画制作手艺人的青黄不接，夹江年画出现传承危机，亟待采取具体而有效的保护措施。

As traditional art, *New Year Wood-block Painting of Jiajiang County* was selected into the second batch of the intangible cultural heritage of China in 2008. It mainly prevails in Jiaojiang County of Sichuan

Province.

New Year Wood-block Painting of Jiajiang County is a unique folk art style in Jiajiang County, Sichuan Province. It is as famous as *Mianzhu New Year Painting* and *Liangping New Year Painting*, which is regarded as one of the three major new year pictures in Sichuan Province. As a unique farmer's painting in Southwest Sichuan, it was born and bred among the folk. After long-term modification and refinement, it embodies the hard-working wisdom of the local working people, and contains the pursuit and yearning of the masses for peace and healthy life. However, the geographical limitation of *New Year Wood-block Painting of Jiajiang County* has resulted in the shrinking market. At the same time, there has been a growing shortage of craftsmen. Therefore, it is now facing the crisis of inheritance, demanding urgent protection.

44. 羌族刺绣　*Embroidery of Qiang People*

羌族刺绣，传统美术，2008 年入选国家级第二批非物质文化遗产名录，主要分布地区为四川等地羌民族聚居区，现有国家级传承人李兴秀、汪国芳。

羌族刺绣历史悠久，制品图案多呈几何形状，构图严谨，组织匀整，装饰性极强。图案多以花草蔬果、飞禽走兽为题材，也可表现人物，所绣内容无不精致秀丽，栩栩如生，充满吉祥寓意，反映出羌族民众对美好生活的憧憬。然而，如今的羌族刺绣面临发展的瓶颈与市场的挑战，不仅传承人数量不断减少，另外还有旅游业快速发展的影响，日渐减少其生存空间，其传承与保护迫在眉睫。

As traditional art, *Embroidery of Qiang People* was selected into the second batch of the intangible cultural heritage of China in 2008. It prevails in some gathering areas of Qiang People in Sichuan. At present, there exist 2 national inheritors: Li Xingxiu and Wang Guofang.

Embroidery of Qiang People has a long history. The patterns of the products are mostly geometric shapes. Its composition is rigorous, fabric well-organized, decoration strong. Mostly, it takes flowers, plants, fruits, birds, animals and characters as the theme. All the embroidery contents are exquisite, beautiful, lifelike and full of auspicious implication, reflecting the Qiang people's longing for a better life. However, nowadays there have emerged development obstacles and market challenges for *Embroidery of Qiang People*, due to the decreasing of inheritors and influence of tourism, growingly shrinking its living space. Therefore, inheritance and protection are badly needed.

45. 民间绣活（麻柳刺绣） *Embroidery of Guangyuan City*

民间绣活（麻柳刺绣），传统美术，俗称"扎花"，2008 年入选国家级第二批非物质文化遗产名录,主要分布地区为四川省广元市朝天区一带，现有国家级传承人张菊花。

麻柳刺绣与生活习俗关系密切，民间有"谁家女儿巧，要看针线好"的说法。麻柳刺绣色彩明艳，题材丰富，内容涉及花鸟兽虫、耕种收割、婚嫁礼仪等。麻柳刺绣构图巧妙，洋溢出浓郁的乡土气息，具有很强的装饰感，但现代生活方式的冲击下，世代传承的麻柳刺绣出现生存危机，再加上老艺人的离去，青年一代不愿学习此项技艺，民间绣活（麻柳刺绣）陷入逐渐消亡的困境，亟待采取有效措施进行保护与传承。

As traditional art, *Embroidery of Guangyuan City* is also called "Embroidering Flowers". It was selected into the second batch of the intangible cultural heritage of China in 2008. It prevails in Chaotian District, Guangyuan City, Sichuan Province. At present, there exists 1 national inheritor: Zhang Juhua.

Embroidery of Guangyuan City is closely related to life and customs. There is a saying among the people that "whose daughter is skillful, it depends on the needle and thread". It has bright colors and rich themes, involving flowers, birds, animals, insects, farming, harvesting, marriage etiquette and many other aspects. And its skillful composition makes its products full of rich local flavor, with strong decorative sense and distinctive characteristics. However, due to the impact of modern lifestyle, young people lack aspiration in the traditional skill. Together with the death of old embroidery craftsmen, the inheritance and protection of *Embroidery of Guangyuan City* are in urgent need.

46. 糖塑（成都糖画） *Sugar Painting of Chengdu City*

糖塑（成都糖画），传统美术，2008 年入选国家级第二批非物质文化遗产名录，主要分布地区在四川省成都市，现有国家级传承人樊德然。

成都糖画俗称"倒糖饼儿""糖粑粑儿""糖灯影儿"，是流行于四川省成都的一种兼具雕塑性和绘画性的民间艺术。成都糖画手工技艺独特，多以花鸟鱼虫、飞禽走兽及戏剧人物为题材，其成品既是甜美的糖食，又是可供观赏的艺术品，可谓"观之若画，食之有味"。成都糖画蕴含人们的祈福愿望和审美理想，常见于成都地区的城乡庙会、集市等群众文化活动场合。如今，由于年轻人对传统技艺的兴趣缺失，糖画传承难度不断加大，亟须采取具体措施进行保护。

As traditional art, *Sugar Painting of Chengdu City* was selected into the second batch of the intangible cultural heritage of China in 2008. It prevails in Chengdu City, Sichuan Province. At present, there exists 1 national inheritor: Fan Deran.

Sugar Painting of Chengdu City, commonly known as "pouring sugar cake", "sugar cake" and "sugar shadow play", is a kind of folk art combining sculpture and painting together in Chengdu. It is a unique folk handicraft, with flowers, birds, fish, insects, animals and dramatic figures as the theme. The finished products are not only sweet candy, but also works of art for viewing. *Sugar Painting of Chengdu City* embodies people's wish for blessing and aesthetic ideal. Therefore, sugar painting is commonly seen in the urban and rural temple fair, market and other mass cultural activities in Chengdu. However, nowadays, young people are lack of interest in traditional arts, which intensifies the difficulty of its inheritance. Therefore, specific and effective measures should be taken to protect *Sugar Painting of Chengdu City*.

47. 蜀锦织造技艺 *Sichuan Brocade Weaving Techniques*

蜀锦织造技艺，传统技艺，2006年入选国家级第一批非物质文化遗产名录，主要分布在成都地区，传承方式为派系传承、师徒传承，现有国家级传承人叶永洲、刘晨曦、贺斌3名。

作为成都标志之一的蜀锦织造技艺，将蜀锦与花楼织机融合，一直秉承古老的手工织锦传统，已在成都地区传承发展了两千多年。蜀锦大多图案繁华、织纹精细，配色典雅，独具一格，是一种具有民族特色和地方风格的多彩织锦。在某种程度上，正是蜀锦技艺的繁多导致其在传承中困难重重，采取切实措施确保蜀锦织造技艺的传承是当务之急。

As a traditional skill, *Sichuan Brocade Weaving Techniques* was selected into the first batch of the intangible cultural heritage of China in 2006. It prevails in Chengdu City of Sichuan Province. It is mainly inherited within schools, between masters and apprentices. At present, there exist 3 national inheritors: Ye Yongzhou, Liu Chenxi and He Bin.

As one of the symbols of Chengdu, *Sichuan Brocade Weaving Techniques* integrates Shu brocade with Hualou loom. It has been inherited and developed for more than 2000 years in Chengdu. Its prosperous pattern, fine weaving and elegant color matching make it colorful brocade with national characteristics and local style. In other words, it is its variety that hinders its inheritance, and it is urgent to take practical and effective measures to protect *Shu Brocade Weaving Techniques*. Hope the relevant parties will pay attention to it.

48. 成都漆艺 *Lacquerware Making Techniques of Chengdu City*

成都漆艺,传统技艺,2006年入选国家级第一批非物质文化遗产名录,现主要存于成都市青羊区,通过口传心授的方式传承,现有国家级传承人尹利萍、宋西平。

成都漆艺是我国最早的漆艺之一,工序繁多、制作细致、耗时长,尤以极富地域特色的修饰技艺闻名于世。近年来,在传统与现代的夹缝中,产品市场狭小,制作者后继乏人,许多传统技艺已开始变形和失传。成都漆艺正面临巨大的生存危机,必须尽快采取必要的保护措施。

As a traditional skill, *Lacquerware Making Techniques of Chengdu City* was selected into the first batch of the intangible cultural heritage of China in 2006. It prevails in Qingyang District of Chengdu City of Sichuan Provinces. And it is mainly inherited through word of mouth. At present, there exist 2 national inheritors: Yin Liping and Song Xiping.

Lacquerware Making Techniques of Chengdu City is one of the earliest Lacquer arts in China. It has the characteristic of complex making procedures, meticulous production and a wide range of making procedure, meticulous production and time-consuming. It is particularly famous for its decoration techniques. In recent years, due to the shrink of the market, the lack of successors and the loss of traditional skills, *Lacquerware Making Techniques of Chengdu City* is facing a huge survival crisis. Therefore, it is urgent to take necessary and effective measures to protect this ancient technique.

49. 泸州老窖酒酿制技艺

Liquor-distilling Techniques of Luzhoulaojiao

泸州老窖酒酿制技艺，传统技艺，2006 年入选国家级第一批非物质文化遗产名录，主要分布地区在四川省南部的泸州市，现有国家级传承人沈才洪、赖高淮、张良 3 人。

泸州老窖酒传统酿造技艺包括泥窖制作维护、大曲药制作鉴评、原酒酿造摘酒、原酒陈酿、勾兑尝评等多方面的技艺及相关法则。在我国酒类行业中享有"活文物"之称，现代技术难以替代。泸州老窖传统酿造技艺传承人的保护、管理和培养都很艰难，亟须采取具体措施进行保护。

As a traditional skill, *Liquor-distilling Techniques of Luzhoulaojiao* was selected into the first batch of the intangible cultural heritage of China in 2006. It prevails in Luzhou City in Southern Sichuan. At present, there exist 3 national inheritors: Shen Caihong, Lai Gaohuai and Zhangliang.

The traditional *Liquor-distilling Techniques of Luzhoulaojiao* include the production and maintenance of mud cellar, the identification of distiller's yeast, the distilling and selection of original wine, the storage of original wine, the evaluation to wine, the blending of taste and other related techniques. It is known as a "living cultural relic" in

China's liquor industry. Even the best developed modern technology is difficult to replace. It is very difficult to protect, manage and cultivate the inheritors of *Liquor-distilling Techniques of Luzhoulaojiao*. Therefore, it is urgent to take specific measures to protect them.

50～51. 自贡井盐深钻汲制技艺

Well Salt Making Technique of Zigong City

自贡井盐深钻汲制技艺，传统技艺，2006 年入选国家级第一批非物质文化遗产名录，主要分布地区在四川省自贡市与遂宁市大英县。

四川自贡"因盐设市"，被誉为中国盐都，井盐文化源远流长。享誉世界的大英县卓筒井创始于北宋庆历年间，历史上井盐业最繁荣时期曾有卓筒井 1711 口，年产盐四千多吨。自贡井盐深钻汲制技艺沿袭宋代汲制井盐流程，包括钻井、取卤、晒卤（滤卤）、煎盐等工艺。其传承千年的完整流程被视为世界钻探深井的活化石。如何在现代化快速发展进程中通过多种方式和渠道传承自贡井盐深钻汲制技艺，让其持续活在人们视线中，是亟须思考的。

As a traditional skill, *Well Salt Making Technique of Zigong City* was selected into the first batch of the intangible cultural heritage of China in 2006. It prevails in Zigong City and Daying County, Sichuan Province.

Zigong is known as China's salt capital, whose prosperity is due to salt making and salt selling. It has a long history of the well salt culture. The world-famous *Zhuotong Salt Well* in Daying county was founded in Northern Song Dynasty. During the most prosperous period of well salt industry in history, there were 1711 Zhuotong salt wells with an annual output of more than 4000 tons of salt. *Well Salt Making Technique of Zigong City* involves many processes including well drilling, brine extraction, brine drying, brine filtering and salt frying. The whole salt making process, which has been inherited for almost a thousand year, is regarded as a living fossil for deep well salt drilling. However, it is a problem that how to ensure the vigorous living of *Well Salt Making Technique of Zigong Cit* in the process of modernization, demanding consideration.

52. 竹纸制作技艺 *Bamboo Paper Making Techniques*

竹纸制作技艺，传统技艺，2006 年入选国家级第一批非物质文化遗产名录，主要分布在四川夹江，现有国家级传承人杨占尧。

夹江竹纸以手工舀纸术制作，从选料到成纸共有 15 个环节、72 道工序，以嫩竹为主料生产的夹江手工书画纸具有洁白柔软、浸润保墨、纤维细腻、绵韧平整等特点，与安徽宣纸齐名，曾被国画大师张大千先生誉为"国之二宝"。目前虽仍有人沿袭传统造纸技艺生产竹纸，但受原材料供给困难的影响，竹纸生产陷于窘境，加上造纸匠人大都年事已高，年轻人不愿学习，竹纸制作技艺传承乏人，亟待保护和抢救。

As a traditional skill, *Bamboo Paper Making Techniques* was selected into the first batch of the intangible cultural heritage of China in 2006. It mainly prevails in Jiajiang County, Sichuan Province. At present, there exists 1 national inheritor: Yang Zhanyao.

The bamboo paper is hand-made. There are in-total 15 stages and 72 procedures from material selection to end product. The bamboo paper is white, soft, ink-proof, smooth. It is as famous as Anhui Xuan paper, which was praised as "the second treasure of the country" by Mr. Zhang Daqian, a master of Chinese painting. At present, although some people still follow the traditional paper-making method to produce bamboo paper, the production of bamboo paper is in a dilemma due to the difficult supply of raw materials. In addition, most of the paper-making craftsmen are old and young people are not willing to learn it. Therefore, rescue and protection to it are urgently needed.

53. 德格印经院藏族雕版印刷技艺

Tibetan Woodblock Printing Techniques of Dege Scripture Printing Lamasery

德格印经院藏族雕版印刷技艺，传统技艺，2006 年入选国家级第一批非物质文化遗产名录，主要分布地区为四川省甘孜州德格县，现有国家级传承人彭措泽仁。

坐落于德格县城的德格印经院素有"藏文化大百科全书"之称，为藏族地区三大印经院之首。德格版的经书在藏族地区及国内外的藏学界广泛流传，十分有名。经书以红桦木为原料，经火熏、水煮、烘晒、刨光等工序后经可几百年不变形。但由于经书手工生产成本高、工艺复杂，外加藏墨生产工艺尚未恢复，德格印经技艺很难传承，亟须抢救性保护。

As a traditional skill, *Tibetan Woodblock Printing Techniques of Dege Scripture Printing Lamasery* was selected into the first batch of the intangible cultural heritage of China in 2006. It prevails in Dege County, Ganzi Prefecture, Sichuan Province. At present, there exists 1 national inheritor: Peng cuozeren.

Located in Dege County, *Dege Scripture Printing Lamasery* is known as the "Encyclopedia of Tibetan culture", which is the first of the three printing Lamaseries in Tibetan area. The Scriptures made by Dege Printing Lamasery is widely spread in Tibetan areas as well as in the Tibetan academic circles at home and abroad. With birch as raw material, it can be preserved for hundreds of years after being fumigated by fire, boiling, drying, and polishing. However, due to the high cost of manual production and the complexity of the process, it is difficult to inherit it. In addition, the production process of Tibetan ink has not yet been restored. Therefore, it is urgent to protect this skill.

54. 陶器烧制技艺（藏族黑陶烧制技艺）

Black Pottery Firing Techniques of Tibetan People

陶器烧制技艺（藏族黑陶烧制技艺），传统技艺，2008 年入选国家级第二批非物质文化遗产名录，主要分布于云南省香格里拉市尼西乡汤堆村、四川省稻城县赤土乡阿西村和青海省玉树地区囊谦县等藏民居住区。

藏族黑陶烧制技艺历史悠久，极具鲜明地方特色。其以当地泥土为原料，借助捏、捶、敲、打等手工技艺使之成型，再用碎瓷片装饰花纹，之后架起松柴点火烧制，将黄褐色的陶土烧制为黑色。陶器烧制技艺（藏族黑陶烧制技艺）工序烦琐，仅靠藏族的民间艺人孜孜不倦地用双手传承是远远不够的，亟须采取措施实施保护。

As a traditional skill, *Black Pottery Firing Techniques of Tibetan People* was selected into the second batch of the intangible cultural heritage of China in 2008. It prevails in the following places: Tangdui Village, Nixi Town, Shangri-La County, Yunnan Province; A'xi village, Chitu Township, Daocheng County, Sichuan Province: and Nangqian County, Yushu prefecture, Qinghai Province.

Black Pottery Firing Techniques of Tibetan People has a long history, which has distinctive local characteristics. Using the local clay as its raw material, black pottery craftsmen utilize pinching, hammering, beating and other hand-made techniques. And then the patterns are decorated with broken porcelain pieces. After that, the pine wood is set up and the yellow brown clay is burned into black. However, the process of black pottery firing is complicated, which is not enough to only rely on Tibetan folk artists to inherit and protect it. Therefore, it is urgent to protect this skill.

55. 陶器烧制技艺（荥经砂器烧制技艺）

Pottery Firing Techniques of Xingjing County

陶器烧制技艺（荥经砂器烧制技艺），传统技艺，2008 年入选国家级第二批非物质文化遗产名录，主要分布于四川省荥经县。

四川省荥经砂器是一种工艺性强、文化内涵丰厚的民间手工艺品。砂器在生产过程中，手工操作力度的轻重、图案的精粗、打磨的程度、上釉的优劣、焙烧的火候等，都直接关系到成品的质量。但由于市场需求量降低，需求量少，市场发展面临冲击，许多砂器匠人纷纷转行，陶器烧制技艺（荥经砂器烧制技艺）亟须采取措施实施保护。

As a traditional skill, *Pottery Firing Techniques of Xingjing County* was selected into the second batch of the intangible cultural heritage of China in 2008. It prevails in Xingjing County, Sichuan Province.

Pottery of Xingjing County is a kind of folk handicraft with strong craftsmanship and rich cultural connotation. In the production process, the degree of manual operation, the fineness and coarseness of patterns, the degree of grinding, the quality of glaze and the baking temperature are all decided by craftsmen, which are directly related to the quality of finished products. However, due to the decrease of the market demand, the market development is facing an impact. Many craftsmen have changed their careers. Therefore, the pottery firing techniques need to be protected.

56. 毛纺织及擀制技艺 （彝族毛纺织及擀制技艺）

Wool Spinning and Rolling Techniques of Yi People

毛纺织及擀制技艺（彝族毛纺织及擀制技艺），传统技艺，2008 年入选国家级第二批非物质文化遗产名录，主要分布于四川省西南部的凉山彝族自治州。

毛纺织擀制技艺是一种特殊的织造工艺，先将羊毛、骆驼毛等用热水浸湿，然后加以挤压，用棍棒碾轧和揉搓等方式使毛绒粘在一起，形成名为"毡"的无纺织型毛织品。由于彝族主要生活在海拔 2 500 米左右的凉山地区，这里盛产绵羊，彝族人在长期的生产生活中形成了以羊毛和羊皮制作瓦拉、毛裙、毡帽、毡袜等服饰的习俗。凉山彝族毛纺织和擀制技艺工序复杂，费工费时，目前从事这一技艺的工匠日益减少，需要积极开展相关的抢救保护工作。

As a traditional skill, *Wool Spinning and Rolling Techniques of Yi People* was selected into the second batch of the intangible cultural heritage of China in 2008. It prevails in Liangshan Yi Autonomous Prefecture in the southwest of Sichuan Province.

Wool Spinning and Rolling Techniques of Yi People is a special weaving technology. The making methods are as follows： firstly, soak wool and camel hair in hot water, then extrude them, and then use sticks to roll and knead the plush together to form a non-woven wool fabric called "Felt". Yi people mainly live in Liangshan area, which is about 2500 meters above sea level, and there are abundant sheep. Therefore, Yi people get used to making Wala (the special cloak of Yi people), skirt, felt hat, felt socks etc., which are all made from wool. And due to its complexity and time-consuming characteristic as well the decrease of skilled workers, rescue protection is urgently needed.

57. 毛纺织及擀制技艺 （藏族牛羊毛编织技艺）

Wool Spinning and Rolling Techniques of Tibetan People

毛纺织及擀制技艺（藏族牛羊毛编织技艺），传统技艺，2008 年入选国家级第二批非物质文化遗产名录，主要分布于四川省色达县，现有国家级传承人有冬措。

藏族牛羊毛编织技艺是草原特定生态环境的产物，从古至今千百年来，草原藏族牧民从日常生活用品到衣着和居住帐篷等，都离不开牛羊毛编织技艺，使其成为藏族牧民历史文化重要组成部分。藏族毛绒织品是以牦牛、绵羊、藏山羊等牛羊毛为原料，应用纺织、擀制工艺加工生产而成的，既保温防潮，又经久耐用，极具青藏高原特色。但是，藏族牛羊毛编织技艺工序复杂，费工费时，目前从事这一技艺的工匠日益减少，需要积极开展相关的抢救和保护工作。

As a traditional skill, *Wool Spinning and Rolling Techniques of Tibetan People* was selected into the second batch of the intangible cultural heritage of China in 2008. It prevails in Seda County, Sichuan Province. At present, there exists 1 national inheritor: Dongcuo.

Wool Spinning and Rolling Techniques of Tibetan People is the product of the specific ecological environment of the grassland. From ancient times to the present, the Tibetan herdsmen in the grassland cannot do without *Wool Spinning and Rolling Techniques* which becomes an important part of Tibetan herdsmen's history and culture. Tibetan cashmere fabric is usually made of yak, sheep, Tibetan goat and other cattle wool as raw materials and processed by spinning and rolling process. It is not only heat preservation and moisture-proof, but also durable, which has typical characteristics of Qinghai Tibet Plateau. And due to its complexity and time-consuming characteristic as well the decrease of skilled workers, it is in urgent need of rescue and protection.

58. 藏族金属锻造技艺（藏族锻铜技艺）

Copper-forging Techniques of Tibetan People

藏族金属锻造技艺（藏族锻铜技艺），传统技艺，2008 年入选国家级第二批非物质文化遗产名录,主要分布在四川省甘孜藏族自治州,以白玉县河坡、热加两乡较为集中，现有国家级传承人俄色呷玛。

藏族金属锻造技艺历史悠久，风格独特，工艺精湛，其传统产品与藏族人民的生产、生活和宗教信仰紧密联系在一起，具有鲜明的民族性和地域性。其所生产的产品种类很多，主要有佛像、各种法器、香炉等，而尤以藏族刀具最为著名，也最为常见。但藏族金属锻造技艺选料非常讲究，目前从事这一技艺的工匠日益减少，需要积极开展相关的抢救和保护工作。

As a traditional skill, *Copper-forging Techniques of Tibetan People* was selected into the second batch of the intangible cultural heritage of China in 2008. It prevails in Ganzi Tibetan Autonomous Region, Sichuan Province, especially Hepo Town and Rejia Town of Baiyu County. At present, there exists 1 national inheritor: Esejiama.

Copper-forging Techniques of Tibetan People has a long history, unique style and exquisite technology. Its traditional products are closely linked with Tibetan people's production, life and religious belief, and have distinct national and regional characteristics. There are many kinds of products, such as Buddha statues, various kinds of magic tools, incense burner, etc.. Among them, Tibetan knives are the most famous and common ones. It is very particular about material selection. However, at present, the number of craftsmen engaged in this career is decreasing day by day. Therefore, it is necessary to actively carry out relevant rescue and protection work.

59. 成都银花丝制作技艺

Silverware Making Techniques of Chengdu City

成都银花丝制作技艺，传统技艺，2008 年入选国家级第二批非物质文化遗产名录，主要分布在四川省成都市，现有国家级传承人道安。

成都银花丝以贵重金属银为主要材料，同时运用镶嵌、平填等多种不同的工艺手法，使其更显精致细腻，体现了中国传统造物文化对持久恒远的追求与中国人追求内敛与细致入微的品格。银花丝手工艺品以其精美的设计、严谨的构图和白银富丽堂皇的质地，散发出迷人的光泽和高雅美观的气质，成品具有很高的艺术和收藏价值。但如今这一宝贵传统工艺却由于种种原因面临着失传的困境，需要积极开展相关的抢救和保护工作。

As a traditional skill, *Silverware Making Techniques of Chengdu City* was selected into the second batch of the intangible cultural heritage of China in 2008. It prevails in Chengdu City, Sichuan Province. At present, there exists 1 national inheritor: Dao An.

As its name, the main material of *Chengdu Silverware* is a precious metal like silver. It is purely handmade, using inlay, flat filling and other different techniques to make its products more delicate, which reflects the Chinese traditional culture's pursuit of permanence and the Chinese people's introverted and meticulous characters. With its exquisite design, rigorous composition and magnificent texture of silver, the silver handicraft exudes charming luster as well as an elegant and beautiful temperament. The finished products have high artistic and collection value. However, at present, its inheritance and development are facing the danger of extinction due to various causes. Therefore, relevant rescue and protection work should be actively carried out.

60. 彝族漆器髹饰技艺

Lacquerware Decorating Techniques of Yi People

彝族漆器髹饰技艺，传统技艺，2008 年入选国家级第二批非物质文化遗产名录，主要分布在四川省凉山彝族自治州喜德县，现有国家级传承人吉伍巫且。

　　彝族漆器髹饰一般以黑漆为底色，在上面加绘黄色和红色的花纹组成各式图案，色彩对比鲜明，显示出独特的民族风格。但由于彝族漆器制作需要经过锯、刨、磨、粘等数十道工序，还需要在器形表面用精心绘制的漆绘图案进行纹饰，制作难度大、工期长，导致这一珍贵的少数民族民间手工艺在现代社会文明发展中逐渐走向衰亡，现已濒临灭绝，亟须抢救和保护。

As a traditional skill, *Lacquerware Decorating Techniques of Yi People* was selected into the second batch of the intangible cultural heritage of China in 2008. It prevails in Xide County, Liangshan Yi Autonomous Prefecture, Sichuan Province. At present, there exists 1 national inheritor: Jiwuwuqie.

Lacquerware of Yi People generally takes black paint as its background color, and yellow and red patterns are added to form various patterns. Different colors form a sharp contrast, showing a unique national style. However, because the production of lacquerware needs dozens of processes with great difficulty and a long construction period, including sawing, planing, grinding, gluing etc. What's more, there still need well-designed decorating patterns on the surface, which results in the gradual decline of these techniques. To some extent, *Lacquerware Decorating Techniques of Yi people* is on the verge of extinction, urgently demanding the proper rescue and protection.

　　61. 伞制作技艺（油纸伞制作技艺）

Oil-paper Umbrella Making Techniques

伞制作技艺（油纸伞制作技艺），传统技艺，2008 年入选国家级第二批非物质文化遗产名录，主要分布地区为四川省泸州市，现有国家级传承人毕六福。

泸州油纸伞制作技艺是以传统手工方式制造的桐油纸伞，选料精细，上油厚。纸伞制作技艺流程复杂，制作要经过锯托、穿绞、网边、糊纸、扎工、幌油、箍烤等 90 多道工序。制成的纸伞质量优良，反复撑收 3000 余次不坏，清水浸泡 24 小时不脱骨，顶五级风行走不变形，深受用户和民间收藏者的欢迎。但油纸伞从业者，普遍存在保护传承意识淡薄、工艺制作粗糙、经营模式单一、包装与推广落后等问题；外部问题主要针对政府与市场方面，普遍存在与现代社会环境不适应、市场狭小、政府重视度不高等问题。油纸伞制作技艺传承面临着很多困境，亟须采取措施进行保护。

As a traditional skill, *Oil-paper Umbrella Making Techniques* was selected into the second batch of the intangible cultural heritage of China in 2008. It prevails in Luzhou City, Sichuan Province. At present, there exists 1 national inheritor: Bi Liufu.

Oil-paper umbrella is handmade by using traditional making techniques, which has the characteristics of a fine selection of materials and heavy oiling. Its production process is complex. In total, there are more than 90 production procedures. The quality of the products is excellent. It is still in good condition even if after opening more than 3000 times and soaking in water for 24 hours. Therefore, it has gain popularity among users and collectors. Oil-paper umbrella craftsmen generally have weak awareness of protection and inheritance. It also faces many shortcomings such as rough production, a single business model, backward packaging, weak promotion, and other problems. External problems mainly focus on the government and the market, and there are widespread social environment changes, narrow market, and low government attention. Its inheritance is facing many difficulties. Therefore, it is urgent to take measures to protect it.

62. 蒸馏酒传统酿造技艺（五粮液酒传统酿造技艺）

Liquor-distilling Techniques of Wuliangye

蒸馏酒传统酿造技艺（五粮液酒传统酿造技艺），传统技艺，2008年入选国家级第二批非物质文化遗产名录，主要分布在四川省宜宾市，现有国家级传承人陈林。

五粮液酒酿造工艺诞生于拥有悠久酿酒业历史的四川省宜宾市，以高粱、大米、糯米、小麦、玉米五种粮食合理配比的"陈氏秘方"为核心，整个生产过程由制曲、酿源、勾兑等三大工艺流程一百多道工序组成。特殊而复杂的五粮液酒传统酿造技艺集中了众多传统酿酒工艺的精华，具有其不可替代的价值，是我国酒文化的重要组成部分。但由于现代工业化生产方式重塑了人们的生活环境和日常习惯，五粮液公司面临着不同的国际国内环境复杂、严峻的形势，这对五粮液酒传统酿造技艺形成巨大冲击，其传承面临着很多困难，亟须采取措施进行保护。

As a traditional skill, *Liquor-distilling Techniques of Wuliangye* was selected into the second batch of the intangible cultural heritage of China in 2008. It prevails in Yibin City, Sichuan Province. At present, there exists 1 national inheritor: Chen Lin.

Liquor-distilling Techniques of Wuliangye was born in Yibin City, a city with a long history of liquor making. The core of the production process is Chen's secret recipe with a reasonable proportion of sorghum, rice, glutinous rice, wheat and corn. The whole production process consists of more than 100 procedures including distiller's yeast making, distilling original liquor and blending. The special and complex traditional techniques have concentrated the essence of many traditional folk distilling techniques, having irreplaceable value and being an important part of our liquor culture. However, since the modern industrial production mode has reshaped people's living environment and daily habits nowadays, Wuliangye Company is faced with the different international and domestic environment as well as complex and severe situation, which has a huge impact on the traditional *Liquor-distilling Techniques of Wuliangye*. The skill becomes difficult to inherit, and therefore, it is essential to take effective protection measures.

63. 蒸馏酒传统酿造技艺（水井坊酒传统酿造技艺）

Liquor-distilling Techniques of Shuijingfang

蒸馏酒传统酿造技艺（水井坊酒传统酿造技艺），传统技艺，2008年入选国家级第二批非物质文化遗产名录，主要分布在四川省成都市，现有国家级传承人赖登煜。

水井坊酒传统酿造技艺于明清时期起源于成都东门府河、南河两江汇合处的水井街酒坊。配料上，其完美融合了单粮酒和多粮酒的特点，以上等小麦为主要原料，添加高粱焙制而成；其发酵蒸馏采用原窖分层堆糟法；以勾兑调味方法使多年贮存的原酒最终形成"浓而不艳，雅而不淡"的浓香型淡雅风格。但由于水井坊酒传统酿造技艺的生产依赖特殊的地理环境和气候条件，其复杂的酿制技艺传承困难度极大，亟须采取措施进行保护。

As a traditional skill, *Liquor-distilling Techniques of Shuijingfang* was selected into the second batch of the intangible cultural heritage of China in 2008. It prevails in Chengdu City, Sichuan Province. At present, there exists 1 national inheritor: Lai Dengyi.

The traditional Liquor-distilling Techniques of Shuijingfang originated from Shuijing Distillery at the junction of Fuhe river and Nanhe river in eastern Chengdu during Ming and Qing Dynasties. In terms of ingredients, it perfectly integrates the characteristics of single grain liquor and multi grain liquor, mainly made of wheat and sorghum. Fermentation distillation adopts the method of stacking grains in the original cellar layer by layer. The long-stored original liquor is used for blending, which makes *Shuijingfang liquor* have both strong but not heavy and light but long-lasting taste. However, its unique production process set high requirement on the geographical situation and weather condition, making it extremely difficult to inherit the complex *Liquor-distilling Techniques of Shuijingfang*. Therefore, effective protection measures need to be taken.

64. 蒸馏酒传统酿造技艺（剑南春酒传统酿造技艺）

Liquor-distilling Techniques of Jiannanchun

蒸馏酒传统酿造技艺（剑南春酒传统酿造技艺），传统技艺，2008年入选国家级第二批非物质文化遗产名录，主要分布在四川省绵竹市。

剑南春酒产于四川省绵竹市，酒芳香浓郁、纯正典雅、醇厚绵柔、甘洌净爽、余味悠长，酒体丰满圆润，传统酿造技艺繁复，被视为中国浓香型白酒的重要代表。但剑南春独特的生产工艺对地理环境和气候条件要求较高，加之老酒只能用陶坛贮存，传承难度极大，亟须采取措施进行保护。

As a traditional skill, *Liquor-distilling Techniques of Jiannanchun* was selected into the second batch of the intangible cultural heritage of China in 2008. It prevails in Mianzhu City, Sichuan Province.

Jiannanchun was born in Mianzhu City, Sichuan Province. It is regarded as an important representative of Luzhou-flavor liquor in China because of its strong aroma, pure, elegant and mellow taste, sweet, clean and long-lasting aftertaste, as well as complex skill. However, its unique production process set high requirement on the geographical situation and weather condition, and also there is a strict request to the storage earthen pot, making it extremely difficult to inherit the complex *Liquor-distilling Techniques of Jiannanchun*. Therefore, effective protection measures need to be taken.

65. 蒸馏酒传统酿造技艺（古蔺郎酒传统酿造技艺）

Liquor-distilling Techniques of Gulinlang

蒸馏酒传统酿造技艺（古蔺郎酒传统酿造技艺），传统技艺，2008年入选国家级第二批非物质文化遗产名录，主要分布在四川省古蔺县，主要传承方式是在当地酿酒工匠中以口传心授的方式世代相传，现有国家级传承人杨大金。

古蔺郎酒传统酿造技艺是古蔺郎酒厂传承百年的传统技艺，其中延续百余年的五月端午手工制曲、九月重阳投粮、高温生产、以洞藏方式促使新酿酒老熟陈化等技艺独具特点，在中国川南、黔北酿酒文化发展中具有很高的历史文化价值。古蔺郎酒传统酿造技艺善于培植独特的微生物菌群，显示出高超的传统技艺手段，为酱香型白酒的酿造提供了有益的借鉴。但是古蔺郎酒制作程序多，且需要特殊的水，使其独特的酿制技艺传承难度大，亟须采取措施进行保护。

As a traditional skill, *Liquor-distilling Techniques of Gulinlang* was selected into the second batch of the intangible cultural heritage of China in 2008. It prevails in Gulin County, Sichuan Province, which is mainly inherited through word of mouth. At present, there exists 1 national inheritor: Yang Dajing.

Liquor-distilling Techniques of Gulinlang is a typical technique with more than 100 year's history. Some liquor distilling techniques, such as making distiller's yeast during Dragon Boat Festival, feeding grain during Double Ninth Festival, high-temperature production, and promoting the aging of new wine by cave storage, are of great historical value in the development of liquor making culture in southern Sichuan and Northern Guizhou. Cultivating unique microbial flora is its unique peculiarity, showing excellent traditional scientific and technological means, which provides a useful reference for the distilling of Maotai-flavor liquor. However, its unique production process set high requirement on the water, and also there are a large number of complicated procedures, making it extremely difficult to inherit the complex *Liquor-distilling Techniques of Gulinlang*. Therefore, effective protection measures need to be taken.

66. 蒸馏酒传统酿造技艺（沱牌曲酒传统酿造技艺）

Liquor-distilling Techniques of Tuopaiqujiu

蒸馏酒传统酿造技艺（沱牌曲酒传统酿造技艺），传统技艺，2008年入选国家级第二批非物质文化遗产名录，主要分布在四川省射洪县，主要传承方式是口耳相授，现有国家级传承人李家顺。

沱牌曲酒传统酿制技艺历史悠久，是中国传统蒸馏白酒酿造技艺的典型代表，在我国酿酒历史及传统生物发酵工业等研究方面具有较高的学术价值。沱牌曲酒酿造技艺从原辅料选择到酿制储存，各环节均靠酿酒技师"看、闻、摸、捏、尝"来判断生产情况，实施操作。但是沱牌曲酒生产工艺需要特殊的酿造条件，且制作程序多，导致其独特的酿制技艺传承难度大，亟须采取措施进行保护。

As a traditional skill, *Liquor-distilling Techniques of Tuopaiqujiu* was selected into the second batch of the intangible cultural heritage of China in 2008. It prevails in Shehong County, Sichuan Province. It is mainly inherited through word of mouth. At present, there exists 1 national inheritor: Li jiashun.

Liquor-distilling Techniques of Tuopaiqujiu has a long history, which is a typical representative of traditional liquor-distilling techniques. It has high academic value in the research of China's liquor-distilling history and the traditional biological fermentation industry. From the selection of raw materials to liquor-distilling, all the procedures rely on the judgment of the liquor makers who adopt the methods of "seeing, smelling, touching pinching and tasting". However, its unique complex production process set high requirement on the making conditions, making it extremely difficult to inherit the complex *Liquor-distilling Techniques of Tuopaiqujiu*. Therefore, effective protection measures need to be taken.

67. 黑茶制作技艺（南路边茶制作技艺）

Dark Tea Making Techniques of Ya'an City

黑茶制作技艺（南路边茶制作技艺），传统技艺，2008 年入选国家级第二批非物质文化遗产名录，主要分布在四川省雅安市，现有国家级传承人甘玉祥。

南路边茶品质优良，汤色褐红明亮，滋味醇和悠长，加入酥油、盐、核桃仁末等搅拌而成的酥油茶，更是每个藏族同胞必不可少的饮品，形成南路边茶独有的特色。但随着社会经济的发展，受信息、交通、供求等因素影响，黑茶市场竞争激烈，价格差异加大，企业间的恶性竞争导致产品质量下降，影响了黑茶的声誉。整顿、规范黑茶市场，保护、弘扬黑茶制作技艺已成为目前刻不容缓的工作。

As a traditional skill, *Dark Tea Making Techniques of Ya'an City* was selected into the second batch of the intangible cultural heritage of China in 2008. It prevails in Ya'an City, Sichuan Province. At present, there exists 1 national inheritor: Gan Yuxiang.

The dark tea has an excellent quality, bright brown color, lasting mellow taste. The dark tea mixed with butter, salt and walnut kernels is a necessary drink for Tibetan people. However, with the development of the social economy, the dark tea is influenced by information, transportation, supply and demand as well as other factors. The cutthroat competition leads to a great difference of price and the decrease of quality which affect its reputation. Therefore, it is urgent to rectify and standardize the dark tea market, protect and promote the dark tea-making skills.

68. 豆瓣传统制作技艺 （郫县豆瓣传统制作技艺）

Horsebean Paste Making Techniques of Pixian

豆瓣传统制作技艺（郫县豆瓣传统制作技艺），传统技艺，2008年入选国家级第二批非物质文化遗产名录，主要分布在四川省成都市郫县（现更名郫都区），现有国家级传承人雷定成。

郫县豆瓣富有营养价值，是重要的川菜烹饪佐料，在川菜文化中占有重要的一席之地，被誉为"川菜之魂"。郫县豆瓣传统制作技艺，因其"晴天晒，雨天盖，白天翻，夜晚露"的十二字真诀，十分复杂烦琐。但随着市场需求的增长，郫县豆瓣的机械化、工业化生产不断膨胀，传统生产工艺受到挤压，逐渐萎缩。再加之传承人稀少，致使传统生产工艺几近失传。因此郫县豆瓣传统制作技艺的传承迫在眉睫，亟须采取措施进行保护。

As a traditional skill, *Horsebean Paste Making Techniques of Pixian* was selected into the second batch of the intangible cultural heritage of China in 2008. It prevails in Pixian County, Sichuan Province （Now it changed its name into Pidu District of Chengdu City）. At present, there exists 1 national inheritor: Lei Dingcheng.

Rich in nutritional value, *Pixian Horsebean Paste* is an important seasoning of Sichuan cuisine, playing an important role in its culture. And the traditional making technologies of horsebean paste is very complicated and cumborsorme due to the following pithy formula: exposing to the sun, covering in rainy days, stirring during daytime and uncovering at night. However, with the increase of market demand, the expansion of mechanization and industrial production of horsebean paste, the traditional making technologies have been squeezed and gradually shrunk. In addition, there are few inheritors of *Horsebean Paste Making Techniques of Pixian*. Therefore, effective protection measures need to be taken.

69. 豆豉酿制技艺（潼川豆豉酿制技艺）

Tongchuan Tempeh Making Techniques

豆豉酿制技艺（潼川豆豉酿制技艺），传统技艺，2008 年入选国家级第二批非物质文化遗产名录，主要分布在四川省三台县。

作为最具盛名的汉族传统调味品之一，潼川豆豉至今已有 300 多年的生产历史。潼川豆豉是目前我国唯一采用手工毛霉制曲生产豆豉的传统工艺，酿制技艺严格，制作考究，具有纯手工酿制，窖藏周期长等特色。但由于 2018 年爆发的 7·11 特大洪水，潼川豆豉的生产基地遭到严重破坏，严重影响了此项技艺的传承与发展，亟须采取措施进行保护。

As a traditional skill, *Tongchuan Tempeh Making Techniques* was selected into the second batch of the intangible cultural heritage of China in 2008. It prevails in Shantai County, Sichuan Province.

As one of the most famous traditional condiments of Han nationality, *Tongchuan Tempeh* has a history of more than 300 years. It is the only traditional making techniques of Tempeh with Mucor in China, owning special characteristics of strict producing procedures, exquisite production, pure manual producing and long cellar time. However, due to the 7.11 flood in 2018, the production base of *Tongchuan Tempeh* was damaged, which hindered the inheritance and development of *Tongchuan Tempeh Making Techniques*. Therefore, effective protection measures need to be taken.

70. 藏族碉楼营造技艺

Watchtower Building Techniques of Tibetan People

藏族碉楼营造技艺，传统技艺，2008 年入选国家级第二批非物质文化遗产名录，主要分布在四川省丹巴县。

藏族碉楼建筑材质以石块为主，木料为辅，石砌高墙，易守难攻，是嘉绒藏族先民的建筑艺术杰作，兼具居住和防御功能。其中尤以丹巴古碉堡楼群最具代表性。但随着社会的发展，原来相对封闭的农耕文明不断受到现代文明的冲击，丹巴能熟练掌握砌石碉楼营造技艺的匠人已经不多，古老的藏族碉楼营造技艺濒临失传，亟待抢救和保护。

As a traditional skill, *Watchtower Building Techniques of Tibetan People* is selected into the second batch of the intangible cultural heritage of China. It prevails in Danba County of Sichuan Province.

Watchtowers of Tibetan people are mainly made of stones and supplemented by wood. The stone wall is easy to defend and difficult to attack. As an architectural masterpiece of Jiarong Tibetan ancestors, the watchtower combines the function of residence and defence. Among them, the most representative one is the ancient watchtower in Danba county. However, with the development of society, the original relatively closed farming civilization has been constantly impacted by modern civilization. The number of skilled workers is shrinking rapidly, which endangers the existence and development of watchtower skills. Therefore, it is urgent to rescue and protect *Watchtower Building Techniques of Tibetan People.*

71. 藏医药（甘孜州南派藏医药）

Tibetan Medicine of Gangzi Prefecture

藏医药（甘孜州南派藏医药），传统医药，2006 年入选国家级第一批非物质文化遗产名录。主要分布包括四川甘孜、云南迪庆、西藏昌都及青海玉树在内的地区，现有国家级传承人格桑尼玛、唐卡·昂翁降措。

藏医药分为南北两派，以康巴为中心的藏医药称为南派藏医药。南派藏医药特色突出，是继中医药之后第二大传统医药，位居四大民族医药（藏、蒙、维、傣）之首。随着社会不断发展，人们越来越认识到藏医药对健康保健的重要作用。现代科学更进一步证实了藏医药学对人类健康保健、疾病预防的科学价值。但是，由于藏药制药及藏药植物栽培等学科高级人才缺乏，严重限制了甘孜州南派藏医药的发展，亟须采取措施保护。

As a traditional medicine, *Tibetan Medicine of Gangzi Prefecture* was selected into the first batch of the intangible cultural heritage of China in 2006. It prevails in Kangba Tibetan areas in Sichuan, Yunnan, Qinghai and Tibet. At present, there exist 2 national inheritors: Gesang nima and Tangka. Angwengjiangcuo.

There are two schools of Tibetan medicine: the southern and

northern one, and the Tibetan medicine centered Kangba area is called the southern Tibetan medicine. With outstanding characteristics, southern Tibetan medicine is the second largest traditional medicine after Chinese medicine, ranking first among the four ethnic medicines (Tibetan, Mongolian, Uygur and Dai). As society develops constantly, its importance in health care has been noticed increasingly, and its scientific value has even been further confirmed in human health care and disease prevention. However, due to the lack of high-tech talents in its pharmacy and plant cultivation, which has become the biggest limiting factor for the development of *Tibetan Medicine of Gangzi Prefecture*. Therefore, effective protection measures need to be taken.

72. 火把节（彝族火把节）　*Torch Festival of Yi People*

火把节（彝族火把节），民俗，2006 年入选国家级第一批非物质文化遗产名录，主要分布在云南、贵州、四川等的彝族地区。

彝族火把节是所有彝族地区的传统节日，历史悠久，群众基础广泛，覆盖面广，影响深远。火把节充分体现了彝族崇火的民族特色，是彝族传统文化中最具有标志性的象征符号之一，保留着彝族起源发展的古老信息，具有重要的历史和文化价值；火把节同时也是彝族传统音乐、舞蹈、饮食、农耕、天文等文化要素的载体，对强化彝族的民族自我认同、促进社会和谐具有重要意义。但如今，彝汉杂居地区的火把节因群众参与面逐步减小，节日习俗随之逐渐淡化，特别是居住城市及郊区的彝族群众传统的节日习俗观念日趋淡忘，亟须采取措施保护。

As a folk custom, *Torch Festival of Yi People* was selected into the first batch of the intangible cultural heritage of China in 2006. It prevails in Yi People gathering areas in Yunnan, Guizhou and Sichuan.

Torch Festival of Yi People is a traditional festival in all areas of Yi People. It has a long history, broad mass base, wide coverage and far-reaching influence. *Torch Festival* fully embodies the national character of worshipping fire of the Yi people, being one of their most typical symbols. It is with important historical and scientific value for its retaining of the ancient Yi people, including their origin and development. At the same time, *Torch Festival of Yi People* is also the carrier of traditional music, dance, diet, farming, astronomy and other cultural elements of the Yi people, with great significance for them to equipped with the sense of national self-identity and to promote social harmony. However, nowadays, *Torch Festival of Yi People* has gradually ignored due to the gradual reduction of people's participation, especially in the areas inhabited by Yi and Han people together. Therefore, effective protection measures need to be taken.

73. 羌族瓦尔俄足节　*Waer'ezu Festival of Qiang People*

羌族瓦尔俄足节，又称之为"妇女节"，民俗，2006 年入选国家级第一批非物质文化遗产名录，分布区域主要在四川省茂县北部的曲谷乡，传承方式为亲族传承和师徒传承，现有国家级传承人余无子满。

羌族瓦尔俄足节集歌舞、饮食、宗教、习俗、服饰、建筑等于一体，是研究羌族历史文化的"活标本"，对古羌族宗教文化内涵、民间歌曲、原始舞蹈、教育等都有很高的研究价值。每年农历五月初五，茂县羌族妇女不分老幼、身着鲜艳民族服饰，佩戴银首饰参加这古老的传统妇女节。但因外来文化冲击，组织传承的妇女年事已高，细节难以传承，盛大场面难以再现，瓦尔俄足节面临失传危机，须进行抢救性保护。

As a folk custom, *Waer'ezu Festival of Qiang People* was selected into the first batch of the intangible cultural heritage of China in 2006. It prevails in Qugu town in Maoxian County of Sichuan Province, which is mainly inherited within family members as well as between masters and apprentices. At present, there exists 1 national inheritor: Yu-Wuziman.

The *Waer'ezu Festival of Qiang People* has combined music, dance, diet, religion, customs, costume and architecture. Therefore, it is regarded as the "living fossil" of studying history and culture. It has special research value to religion and culture, the custom of Goddess worship, folk songs, primitive dances as well as education. On May 5th of the lunar calendar, both old and young women in bright-colored traditional costume and silver accessories, participate in this traditional woman's festival. However, because of the influence of external cultures and the aging of inheritors, some details and grand spectacle are difficult to reproduce, which means that further rescue and protection is badly needed.

74. 都江堰放水节　*Dujiangyan Water-releasing Festival*

都江堰放水节，民俗，2006 年入选国家级第一批非物质文化遗产名录，主要分布在四川省都江堰市。

清明放水节是世界文化遗产都江堰水利工程所在地都江堰市自从公元 978 年开始举办一项民间习俗，其目的在于纪念率众修建都江堰水利工程、造福成都平原的李冰父子。每到清明时节，都江堰市的人们都会举行隆重热烈的仪式，既祭祀李冰父子，又祈求五谷丰登、国泰民安，表达了勤劳勇敢的劳动人民对美好生活的热爱、向往和追求。但随着科学技术的革新，如何在现代化发展浪潮中做好尊重民间习俗和传承优秀历史文化，已然成为亟待探讨和解决的问题。

As a folk custom, *Dujiangyan Water-releasing Festival* was selected into the first batch of the intangible cultural heritage of China in 2006. It prevails in Dujiangyan City, Sichuan Province.

The *Water-releasing Festival* during Qingming Festival in Dujiangyan city is a traditional folk custom starting from 978BC. The tradition is to commemorate Libing and his son who build *Dujiangyan Irrigation Project*, benefiting Chengdu people for thousands of years. In ancient times, at every Qingming Festival, people there would hold a grand and warm ceremony to worship Li Bing and his son, as well as to pray for a bumper harvest of grain and peace in the next year. It expresses the love, yearning and pursuit of a life of hardworking and brave working people. However, with the innovation of science and technology, how to respect folk customs and inherit excellent historical culture at modern time is a problem demanding urgent discussion and solution.

75. 灯会（自贡灯会） *Zigong Lantern Festival*

灯会（自贡灯会），民俗，2008 年入选国家级第二批非物质文化遗产名录，主要分布在四川省自贡市。

自贡灯会历史悠久，早在唐宋年间这里就有了新年燃灯的习俗。自贡灯彩构思巧妙，制作精细，用料独特。如今，传统制作技艺与现代科学技术相结合，制成的灯彩五光十色，呈现出绚丽多姿的面貌，令人目不暇接，将自贡灯会推向了更高的艺术境界。但随着社会的发展，人民生活水平日益提高，老百姓对自贡灯会的期望越来越高，如何在这个大环境下传承自贡灯会这一中国传统文化亟需思考。

As a folk custom, *Zigong Lantern Festival* was selected into the second batch of the intangible cultural heritage of China in 2008. It prevails in Zigong City, Sichuan Province.

Zigong Lantern Festival has a long history. As early as Tang and Song Dynasties, there was the custom of lighting lanterns during the new year. Zigong lanterns are ingenious in conception, exquisite in making and unique in materials. Nowadays, the combination of traditional making techniques and modern scientific technology has made the lanterns more colorful and dazzling, showing a gorgeous appearance, which has pushed *Zigong Lantern Festival* to a higher artistic level. However, with the development of society and the improvement of people's living standard, People's expectation of *Zigong Lantern Festival* is now becoming higher and higher, and how to inherit this Chinese traditional culture needs to be considered.

76 ~ 79. 羌年 *New Year of Qiang People* （见四川省世界级非物质文化遗产项目中英文简介）

80. 抬阁（芯子、铁枝、飘色）（大坝高装）

High-stage Play of Daba Town

抬阁（芯子、铁枝、飘色）（大坝高装），民俗，2008 年入选国家级第二批非物质文化遗产名录，主要分布于四川南部兴文县境内的大坝苗族乡，现有国家级传承人钟郁文。

大坝高装是源于清代康熙年间的一种特殊的民间造型艺术，是文化艺术与宗教活动相结合的产物。每年农历二月初一、初二举行大坝高装游街表演，游行活动气势宏大、形象生动活泼。队伍长达 200 米，势如游龙，围观之人不计其数，深受当地和周边人民的喜爱，独具民间传统艺术特色。但由于民间技艺的传承条件苛刻，加上现代文化的冲击，严重阻碍了年轻人对民间文化技艺的传承和延续。因此大坝高装的传承之路异常艰辛，亟须采取措施进行保护。

As a folk custom, *High-stage Play of Daba Town* was selected into the second batch of the intangible cultural heritage of China in 2008. It prevails in Daba Miao Village in Xingwen County, Sichuan Province. At present, there exists 1 national inheritor: Zhong Yuwen.

High-stage Play of Daba Town is a kind of special folk arts originated from Kangxi period in Qing Dynasty. It is the product combining culture, art and religious activities. Every year on the first and second day of February in the lunar calendar, the high-stage play would be performed, with a grand and vivid parade. There would be an over 200-meter-long team in the parade, which is like a dragon, with people watching and chasing after. It is very popular with local people and has unique characteristics of traditional folk art. However, due to the harsh conditions for the inheritance of folk arts and the impact of modern culture, it has seriously hindered its inheritance. Therefore, effective measures should be taken immediately to protect *High-stage Play*.

81. 抬阁（芯子、铁枝、飘色）（青林口高抬戏）

High-stage Play of Qinglinkou Town

抬阁（芯子、铁枝、飘色）（青林口高抬戏），民俗，2008年入选国级第二批非物质文化遗产名录，主要分布于川西北地区江油青林口古镇，现有国家级传承人邓均朝、符恒余。

青林口高抬戏历史悠久，表演形式独特。每台戏根据剧情由数名孩童装扮成戏剧人物形象进行表演，人物形象基本采用传统民间年画的构图方式，造型十分夸张。而且高抬戏表演无需舞台戏楼，全靠老一辈艺人一代代口授身教相传传统绑扎手段，工艺讲究，富有原生态形式。鲜活的民间传说故事化作戏剧片段与艺术形象呈现在高台之上，以人力托起，配以相应的鼓乐，上街巡游，以供大众观赏。但随着现代文明的冲击，高抬戏逐渐受到冷落，年轻人不愿意学而导致高抬戏濒临失传，因此青林口高抬戏的传承方式亟须改进。

As a folk custom, *High-stage Play of Qinglinkou Town* was selected into the second batch of the intangible cultural heritage of China in 2008. It prevails in Qinglinkou Town of Jiangyou City in northwest Sichuan province. At present, there exist 2 national inheritors: Deng Junchao and Fu Hengyu.

High-stage Play of Qinglinkou Town has a long history and unique performance form. According to the plot, each play is performed by several children dressed as drama characters. The characters are basically in the composition of traditional folk New Year pictures, and the modeling is exaggerated. Moreover, there is no need for a stage theater to perform a high-stage play. It relies on the older generation of artists to teach the traditional binding means to make a mobile stage, which is exquisite and full of original ecological form. The vivid folklore turns into drama fragments and artistic images, which are shown on the high platform supported by human power. The performance is accompanied by corresponding drum music for the public to watch. However, with the impact of modern civilization, *High-stage Play of Qinglinkou Town* is gradually neglected. Young people are not willing to learn it, which leads to the loss of high-stage play. Therefore, the inheritance mode needs to be improved.

82. 三汇彩亭会 *Caiting Gathering of Sanhui Town*

三汇彩亭会，民俗，2008 年入选国家级第二批非物质文化遗产名录，主要分布于四川省渠县三汇镇。传承方式为民间自发的师徒传承，现有国家级传承人王安大。

三汇彩亭会是每年农历 3 月 16~18 日开展的地方传统民俗文化表

演活动。其艺术表演以亭子造型和表演为主要特点。它是一种融铁工、木工、刺绣、缝纫、建筑、文学、绘画、雕刻等多项艺术内容和知识技能的民间盛会。彩亭结构巧妙，造型奇特，色彩绚丽，工艺精湛，被誉为川东地区民间艺术瑰宝，倾注着当地劳动人民的朴素情感，并以其独特的艺术思维与浓厚的生活气息焕发出中国传统文化的独特光彩。但也因其"高、惊、险、奇、巧"的艺术特点，优秀工匠和民间艺人青黄不接。传承人培养困难，加上彩亭器材、道具、服装、曲目以及加工工具等方面的储存与保存不力，三汇彩亭会的传承面临诸多困难，亟须采取多重措施加以保护。

As a folk custom, *Caiting Gathering of Sanhui Town* was selected into the second batch of the intangible cultural heritage of China in 2008. It prevails in Sanhui Town, Quxian County, Sichuan Province, which is mainly inherited spontaneously between masters and apprentices. At present, there exists 1 national inheritor: Wang Anda.

Caiting Gathering of Sanhui Town is a local traditional folk culture performance held from the 16th to 18th day of March in the lunar calendar. The main features of its artistic performance are pavilion modeling and performance. It is a grand folk gathering integrating iron art, carpentry, embroidery, sewing, architecture, literature, painting, sculpture and other artistic contents and skills. With ingenious structure, peculiar shape, gorgeous color and exquisite craftsmanship, it is known as the gem of folk arts in eastern Sichuan, showing the feelings of local working people and radiating the unique luster of Chinese traditional culture with its artistic thinking and strong life atmosphere. However, it is the specific characteristics of "high, startling, dangerous, strange and ingenious" that results in the lack of excellent craftsmen and folk artists.

Due to the difficulty of cultivating qualified craftsmen and the poor storage and preservation of equipment, props, clothing, repertoire and processing tools, the inheritance of *Caiting Gathering of Sanhui Town* is facing many difficulties. Therefore, it is urgent to take multiple measures to protect it.

83. 薅草锣鼓（川东土家族薅草锣鼓）

Weeding Songs of Tujia People in Eastern Sichuan

薅草锣鼓（川东土家族薅草锣鼓），又名"打闹歌"，俗称"打闹"，传统音乐，2008 年入选国家级第二批非物质文化遗产名录，主要分布于四川宣汉县各乡镇及周边的万源、开江、重庆开县等地区。

川东土家族薅草锣鼓是与劳动生产、声乐、器乐相结合的一种奇特的音乐文化艺术形式，在传承巴人古乐、原生态保留古巴人生活习俗的基础上，展现了川东土家族人在田地间薅草时边打锣鼓边唱歌的场景，属于川东特有的民间文化现象。几千年来，川东土家族薅草锣鼓被视为川东土家人口头历史的重要载体，留下了土家人生产生活的真实写照，蕴含重要的艺术欣赏与研究价值。但随着现代化进程的加速，当地年轻人对传统民俗活动已逐渐失去了兴趣，加之老艺人年事已高，川东土家族薅草锣鼓面临传承无人的困境，亟待抢救和保护。

As a folk custom, *Weeding Songs of Tujia People in Eastern Sichuan* is also called "Danao Songs". It was selected into the second batch of the intangible cultural heritage of China in 2008, which prevails in towns in Xuanhan County, Sichuan Province as well as Wan yuan, Kai jiang and Kai Xian of Chongqing Province.

Weeding Songs of Tujia People in Eastern Sichuan is a unique music culture and art form combined with labor production, vocal music and instrumental music. Based on inheriting the ancient music of Ba people and preserving their life customs, it shows the scene of Tujia people singing while weeding in the fields, being the unique folk cultural phenomenon in Eastern Sichuan. For thousands of years, it has been regarded as an important carrier of the history of Tujia people in East Sichuan, leaving a true portrayal of Tujia people, which contains important artistic and research value. However, with the acceleration of the modernization process, young people's lack of interest and the death of old artists, nobody is willing to inherit this traditional custom. Therefore, *Weeding Songs of Tujia People in Eastern Sichuan* needs to be rescued and protected.

84. 多声部民歌（羌族多声部民歌）

Multi-voice Folk Songs of Qiang People

多声部民歌（羌族多声部民歌），传统音乐，2008 年入选国家级第二批非物质文化遗产名录，主要分布于四川省松潘县小姓乡与镇坪乡的少数羌族山寨，仅在当地的羌族人民中世代相传，现有国家级传承人郎加木。

羌族多声部民歌，作为羌族文化传播的载体之一，具有独特的历史、审美与研究价值。羌族多声部民歌所流布的松潘县小姓乡与红原县毗邻，当地人生活受藏族文化影响，各方面都呈现出藏羌文化交融的特征，其多声部民歌为研究其他藏缅语族多声部民歌提供了借鉴。但外来文化冲击，多声部民歌所依存的基础不断消失，再加之民族审美意识的改变，多声部民歌演唱难度大，培养传承人的难度大，羌族多声部民歌的生存和发展面临危机，亟待进一步抢救性保护。

As a traditional music, *Multi-voice Folk Songs of Qiang People* was selected into the second batch of the intangible cultural heritage of China in 2008. It prevails in a small number of Qiang Villages in Xiaoxing

Town and Zhenping Town of Songpan County, Sichuan Province. It is only handed down from generation to generation among the local Qiang people. At present, there exists 1 national inheritor: Langjiamu.

As one of the carriers of Qiang culture, *Multi-voice Folk Songs of Qiang People* has unique historical, aesthetic and research value. Xiaoxing township of Songpan County, where the multi-voice songs of Qiang people prevails, is adjacent to Hongyuan County. The local people's life is deeply influenced by Tibetan culture, showing combination of Tibetan culture and Qiang Culture in all aspects. And *Multi-voice Folk Songs of Qiang People* provides a reference for the study of multi-voice folk songs of other Tibetan and Burmese languages. However, due to the impact of foreign culture, the foundation of multi-voice folk songs has been disappearing. In addition, with the change of national aesthetic consciousness, the difficulties of singing multi-voice folk songs and cultivating successors, its survival and development are facing a crisis. Therefore protection measures should be taken immediately.

85. 多声部民歌（硗碛多声部民歌）

Multi-voice Folk Songs of Qiaoqi Town

多声部民歌（硗碛多声部民歌），传统音乐，2008 年入选国家级第二批非物质文化遗产名录，主要分布在四川省雅安市宝兴县硗碛乡。

硗碛多声部民歌历史悠久，当地藏族人民将自己的信仰、渴望及喜怒哀乐都融入古朴脱俗的乐声和舞蹈之中，民歌以其独特的风格、浓厚的宗教色彩和恢弘的气势在硗碛歌舞之乡中占据着主要位置，已然成为当地藏民精神生活的重要组成部分，为藏族文化研究工作提供了宝贵的借鉴材料。但随着社会生产方式的变化和传统习俗的消失，硗碛多声部民歌正面临消亡的危险，亟待抢救。

As a traditional music, *Multi-voice Folk Songs of Qiaoqi Town* was selected into the second batch of the intangible cultural heritage of China in 2008. It prevails in Qiaoqi Town, Baoxing County, Ya'an City, Sichuan Province.

Multi-voice Folk Songs of Qiaoqi Town has a long history. The local Tibetan people integrate their beliefs, aspirations, emotions into music and dance. With its unique style, strong religious color and magnificent momentum, it occupies the main position among all the songs and dances in Qiaoqi Town. It has become an important part of the local Tibetan spiritual life and supplied valuable research material for studying the Tibetan culture. However, with the change of social production mode and the disappearance of traditional customs, it is facing the danger of extinction. Therefore, protection measures should be taken immediately.

86. 龙舞（黄龙溪火龙灯舞）

Fire-dragon Dance of Huanglongxi Town

龙舞（黄龙溪火龙灯舞），传统舞蹈，2008 年入选国家级第二批非物质文化遗产名录，主要分布在四川省双流县。

川西水上古镇黄龙溪，历史悠久，拥有丰富的人文资源与秀丽的自然风光。起源于南宋时期的火龙灯舞是黄龙溪每遇年节和典礼盛会必不可少的传统民俗，富含民间韵味，远近闻名，流传广泛。黄龙溪火龙灯舞融龙、灯、舞、火于一体，以浓郁的川西地方特色展示了川西的民俗风情和乡土文化，成为传承优秀民族文化、弘扬中华民族精神的重要手段。但随着社会生产方式的变化和传统习俗的消失，近年来在现代文明的冲击下黄龙溪火龙灯舞面临生存危机，亟须抢救。

As a traditional dance, *Fire-dragon Dance of Huanglongxi Town* was selected into the second batch of the intangible cultural heritage of China in 2008. It prevails in Shuangliu County, Sichuan Province.

Huanglongxi, an ancient water town in Western Sichuan, has a long history, rich human resources and beautiful natural scenery. The fire-dragon dance originating in Southern Song Dynasty is an indispensable traditional folk custom for every year's ceremony in Huanglongxi. It is rich in folk charm, well-known far and near, and widely spread. *Fire-dragon Dance of Huanglongxi Town* integrates dragon, lantern, dance and fire, which displays the folk customs and local culture of Western Sichuan. It has become an important means to inherit excellent national culture and carry forward the spirit of the Chinese nation. However, with the change of social production mode, the disappearance of traditional custom and the impact of modern civilization, *Fire-dragon Dance of Huanglongxi Town* is facing a survival crisis. Therefore, it is in urgent need of rescue.

87 ~ 91. 锅庄舞（甘孜锅庄、马奈锅庄）   *Guozhuang Dance*

锅庄舞，传统舞蹈，2008年入选国家级第二批非物质文化遗产名录，主要分布在四川省石渠县、德格县、新龙县、雅江县、金川县境内。

锅庄意为"圆圈舞"，是藏族十分流行的民间舞蹈，以反映藏民族社会的农牧业生产和经商贸易活动为主，具备极高的艺术、文化和教育价值。锅庄舞多为集体表演，不限人数，男女分队围成圆圈，面朝圈内，翩翩起舞，歌词内容丰富，舞蹈动作较为灵活。根据流行地域的不同，锅庄舞可分为甘孜锅庄、马奈锅庄等。甘孜锅庄形成于甘孜州地区，舞蹈风格古朴舒展，在快节奏阶段旋律热情明快；男舞者动作粗犷雄健，女舞者秀丽活泼，具有鲜明的地方特色。马奈锅庄长期在四川省金川县境内流传，最初属于苯教的祭祀活动，因此在表演中融入大量苯教文化内容，形成一套特殊的表演程式，宗教色彩浓厚。但由于社会的更迭发展与外来文化的冲击，锅庄舞传承面临"断代"的危险，亟待进一步抢救性保护。

As a traditional dance, *Guozhuang Dance* was selected into the second batch of the intangible cultural heritage of China in 2008. It prevails in Shiqu County, Dege County, Xinlong County, Yajiang County and Jinchuan County, Sichuan Province.

Guozhuang Dance, which means "circle dance" in Tibetan language, is a very popular folk dance in Tibetan areas. It mainly reflects the agricultural, animal husbandry production as well as business and trade activities in Tibetan society, with high artistic, cultural and educational values. Most *Guozhuang Dances* are performed in groups, with no limit to the number of people. The male and female teams form a circle and dance face to face in the circle, with flexible lyrics and dance movements. According to the different popular regions, it can be divided into *Ganzi Guozhuang* and *Manai Guozhuang*. Formed in Ganzi Prefecture, *Ganzi Guozhuang* is fast and simple in dance style, with fast-paced steps in warm and lively melody. In performances, the male dancers are rough and vigorous while the female dancers are beautiful and lively, with distinct local characteristics. *Manai Guozhuang*, which has long been spread in Jinchuan County, was originally a sacrifice activity of Bon religion. Therefore, a lot of Bon culture contents were integrated into its performance, giving it strong religious color. However, due to the development of society and the impact of foreign culture, the inheritance of *Guozhuang Dance* is facing challenges. Therefore, further rescue measures should be taken immediately.

92. 藏戏(德格格萨尔藏戏)   *Gesar Tibetan Opera of Dege County*

藏戏（德格格萨尔藏戏），传统戏剧，2008 年入选国家级第二批非物质文化遗产名录，主要分布在四川省德格县（属藏传佛教宁玛教派），传承方式为家族传承或师徒传承。

发源于四川德格县竹庆寺（属藏传佛教宁玛教派）的格萨尔藏戏，至今已有一百三十多年的历史，一般在每年的藏历年、祭祀活动、宗教节庆中表演。格萨尔藏戏的主题主要为歌颂、缅怀史诗英雄格萨尔，蕴含厚重的高古文化的神秘气息。但由于藏戏演员普遍受教育程度偏低，藏戏人才培养困难，加之艺术表现手段的滞后，格萨尔藏戏的传承与发展面临危机，亟须进一步采取措施进行保护。

As a folk drama, *Gesar Tibetan Opera of Dege County* was selected into the second batch of the intangible cultural heritage of China in 2008. It prevails in Dege County, Sichuan Province, which is mainly inherited within family members as well as between masters and apprentices.

Gesar Tibetan Opera originated from Zhuqing Temple in Dege County, Sichuan Province. With a history of over 130 years, it has been usually performed in sacrificial activities and religious festivals as Tibetan New Year. The opera theme is mainly to praise and commemorate the epic hero Gesar, containing mysterious ancient culture. However, due to the low education level of actors, the difficulty of talents cultivation and the backwardness of performing techniques, *Gesar Tibetan Opera* is now facing crisis in its inheritance and development. Therefore, further protection should be taken immediately.

93. 藏戏（巴塘藏戏）   *Tibetan Opera of Batang County*

藏戏（巴塘藏戏），传统戏剧，2008 年入选国家级第二批非物质文化遗产名录，主要分布在四川省巴塘县，传承方式为家族传承或师徒传承。

巴塘藏戏属于康巴藏戏的其中一个支派，至今已有三百多年的历史，已经形成了自己的一套系统完整的艺术形式，表演风格独特，是藏族生活化的表演艺术和宗教仪式结合体。但由于藏戏演员普遍受教育程度偏低，藏戏人才培养困难，艺术表现手段的滞后与不足，以及全社会的文化遗产保护意识缺少，巴塘藏戏面临严重的传承危机，亟须进一步采取措施进行保护。

As a folk drama, *Tibetan Opera of Batang County* was selected into the second batch of the intangible cultural heritage of China in 2008. It prevails in Bangtang County, Sichuan Province, which is mainly inherited within family members as well as between masters and apprentices.

Tibetan Opera of Batang County belongs to one branch of *Kangba Tibetan Opera*. With a history of over 130 years, it has already set its systematic and complete art style, being a combination of Tibetan performing arts and religious rituals. However, due to the low education level of actors, the difficulty of talents cultivation, the backwardness of performing techniques, as well as the lack of protection awareness, *Tibetan Opera of Batang County* is on the verge of extinction. Therefore, further protection should be taken immediately.

94. 藏戏（色达藏戏） *Tibetan Opera of Seda County*

藏戏（色达藏戏），又称"面具舞"，传统戏剧，2008 年入选国家级第二批非物质文化遗产名录，主要分布在四川省色达县，传承方式为家族传承或师徒传承，现有国家级继承人塔洛。

四川省色达县拥有丰富的格萨尔文化底蕴与深厚的藏戏艺术传

统，为色达藏戏的形成与发展奠定了基础。作为北派藏戏的代表，色达藏戏在寺庙乐舞的基础上，在藏戏的独特唱腔中融入折嘎说唱等艺术形式，它念诵道白清晰，注重人戏表演，以地区白话风格的生活化表演形式为特色，表演效仿歌舞话剧又呈现喜剧艺术效果，观赏效果良好，成为当地普及面最广的民间艺术。但由于藏戏演员普遍受教育程度偏低，藏戏人才培养困难，加之艺术表现手段的滞后，格色达藏戏的传承与发展面临危机，亟须进一步采取措施保护。

As a folk drama, *Tibetan the Opera of Seda County* is also called "Mask Dance". It was selected into the second batch of intangible cultural heritage of China in 2008. It prevails in Seda County, Sichuan Province, which is mainly inherited within family members as well as between maters and apprentices. At present, there exists 1 national inheritor: Taluo.

Seda County of Sichuan Province has rich Gesar culture and profound Tibetan opera art tradition, which has laid the foundation for the formation and development of *Tibetan Opera of Seda County*. As a representative of the northern Tibetan opera, it takes the temple music and dance as its basis, and further integrates Zhega rap singing and other artistic forms into its unique singing. It is characterized by its clear recitation of sermons, emphasis on human drama performance and the local vernacular style of daily performance, and the performance imitates opera focus on sing and dancing, and presents the comic artistic effect. Thus, *Tibetan Opera of Seda County* has a good viewing effect and becomes the most popular folk art in the local area. However, due to the low education level of actors, the difficulty of talents cultivation and the backwardness of performing techniques, *Tibetan Opera of Seda County* is now facing crisis in its inheritance and development. Therefore, further protection should be taken immediately.

95 ~ 96. 皮影戏（四川皮影戏）　*Sichuan Shadow Play*

皮影戏（四川皮影戏），又叫"灯影戏"，传统戏剧，2008 年入选国家级第二批非物质文化遗产名录，主要分布在以阆中市为中心的南充、广安等地区的 36 个县市地区，现有国家级继承人王彪。

四川皮影戏，地方特色浓厚，影人造型夸张、动态滑稽、脸谱服饰多仿川剧，注重人物性格的刻画。所演剧目以反映四川地区的风俗习惯、社会风貌和人文传统为主，具有重要的民俗学、艺术学研究价值。但由于高素质皮影表演人才紧缺致使后继无人、观众对皮影认识缺乏导致观众锐减、政策落实不到位，造成四川皮影戏传承发展困难，渐渐淡出人们的视野，甚至面临生死存亡的危机，亟须采取措施对其进行传承和保护。

As a traditional drama, *Sichuan Shadow Play* is also known as "Lantern play". It was selected into the second batch of the intangible cultural heritage of China in 2008. It prevails in Nanchong and Guangan City. At present, there exists 1 national inheritor: Wang Biao.

With strong local characteristics, *Sichuan Shadow Play* owns exaggerated, dynamic and funny characters. Its facial makeup and costumes mostly imitate Sichuan Opera which attaches great importance to the characterization. Its repertoires mainly reflect the customs, social features and cultural traditions of Sichuan, equipping the play with important research value of folklore and art. However, due to the shortage of high-quality shadow puppet performers, the sharp decrease of audience and the ill implementation of policies, *Sichuan Shadow Play* is now facing a crisis of extinction in its inheritance and development.

Therefore, effective measures should be taken immediately to inherit and protect *Sichuan Shadow Play*.

97. 竹刻（江安竹簧）　*Bamboo Reed of Jiang'an County*

竹刻（江安竹簧），传统美术，2008 年入选国家级第二批非物质文化遗产名录，主要分布在四川省江安县，传承方式主要为家族传承与师徒传承，现有国家级传承人何华一。

代表四川省竹文化的江安竹簧，为江安竹工艺的总称，其产生、发展与当地人的日常生活密切相关，独具粗犷、质朴、精美的艺术特色。在造型和雕刻中保留中国书画笔墨神韵的同时显示出高超的民族工艺技巧，既显示了中国民间美术典型的文化特征，又呈现出鲜明的时代性和社会性。

但由于现存竹簧作坊仅有六家，工艺艺人均年事已高，江安竹簧举步维艰，日渐陷于濒危境地，亟待抢救性保护。

As a traditional art, *Bamboo Reed of Jiang'an County* was selected into the second batch of the intangible cultural heritage of China in 2008. It prevails in Jiang'an County of Sichuan Province, which is mainly inherited within family members as well as between masters and apprentices. At present, there exists 1 national inheritor: He Huayi.

As the general name of Jiang'an bamboo craft, *Bamboo Reed of Jiang'an County* represents the remarkable bamboo culture of Sichuan Province. Its emergence and development is closely related to local daily life, being rough, simple and exquisite. In modeling and carving, it retains the charm of Chinese calligraphy and painting, showing superb national craft skills, typical cultural characteristics of Chinese folk art, as well as distinctive characteristics of the times and society. However, since there are only six existing bamboo reed workshops and the aging of existing craftsmen, *Bamboo Reed of Jiang'an County* is facing the crisis of extinction. Therefore, rescue and protection are badly needed.

98. 泥塑（徐氏泥彩塑）　*Colored Clay Sculpture of Xu Clan*

泥塑（徐氏泥彩塑），传统美术，2008 年入选国家级第二批非物质文化遗产名录，主要分布在四川省大英县一带，传承方式主要为家族传承与师徒传承，现有国家级传承人徐兴国。

徐氏泥彩塑始于清末民初，以泥塑圆雕、浮雕、单尊、群像为主，以宗教或历史故事为题材，并以"传统的人物造型、服饰彩画、贴金、绘画工笔重彩"等特征闻名，是一种具有地方特色的民间泥塑艺术。其泥塑造像，造型惟妙惟肖，描绘精致，色彩鲜亮，堪称"五十年不变色，百年不变形"，在旅游景点及宗教寺庙极受欢迎。但徐氏泥彩塑传统工艺繁复，技艺学习不易，再加之现代工艺、高科技产品的冲击，传统塑神形式缺乏实用性，压缩纯手工技艺的生存空间，徐氏泥彩塑传承与发展受限，面临失传，亟须保护。

As traditional art, *Colored Clay Sculpture of Xu Clan* was selected into the second batch of the intangible cultural heritage of China in 2008. It prevails in Daying county and its surrounding areas, which is mainly inherited within family members as well as between masters and apprentices. At present, there exists 1 national inheritor: XuXingguo.

Colored Clay Sculpture of Xu Clan began in the late Qing Dynasty and the early Republic of China. It is mainly composed of round sculpture, relief sculpture, single statue and group image, whose main contents are religious or historical stories. And it is famous for its "traditional character modeling, clothing color, covering gold leaf, meticulous heavy color painting". Its clay sculptures have vivid shapes,

209

delicate descriptions and bright colors, which is known for "no color change in 50 years, no deformation in 100 years". The clay sculptures are popular in tourist attractions and religious temples. However, due to the complex process, the difficulty of learning this skill, the impact of modern technology and high-tech products and the decreasing application of clay sculpture in religious temples squeeze the living space of *Colored Clay Sculpture*. Its inheritance and development are limited. Therefore, rescue and protection are badly needed.

99. 竹编（渠县刘氏竹编）

Bamboo Weaving of Liu Clan in Quxian County

竹编（渠县刘氏竹编），传统美术，2008 年入选国家级第二批非物质文化遗产名录，主要分布在四川省渠县一带，现有国家级传承人刘嘉峰。

渠县刘氏竹编，"以竹作画"，作品设计新颖，技艺精湛，极富笔情墨趣，各种图案逼真、细腻、传神，具有浓郁的民族风格和地方特色。渠县刘氏竹编以编工精细见长，将竹文化与多种其他文化相结合进行竹艺的再创作，是一项集造型、设计、工艺等于一体的综合艺术，兼具观赏和实用功能，深受国内外朋友的喜爱。但由于渠县刘氏竹编属于纯手工制作，编织耗时耗神，生产成本高，经济效益低，大量艺人鉴于生存压力被迫转行，同时学习技艺的年轻人也越来越少，竹编业人才十分匮乏，其传承与发展前景令人担忧，亟需善筹长策，予以保护。

As traditional art, *Bamboo Weaving of Liu Clan in Quxian County* was selected into the second batch of the intangible cultural heritage of China in 2008. It prevails in Quxian County and its surrounding areas. At present, there exists 1 national inheritor: Liu Jiafeng.

Bamboo Weaving of Liu Clan in Quxian County is characterized by novel design, exquisite craftsmanship, rich affection, whose pattern is vivid and delicate. It has a strong national style and local characteristics. *Bamboo Weaving of Liu Clan in Quxian County* is famous for its fine weaving. It combines bamboo culture with various cultures, making it a comprehensive art of modeling, design, craft and other aspects. It has both ornamental and practical functions, and is deeply loved by friends at home and abroad. However, due to the fact that *Bamboo Weaving of Liu Clan in Quxian County* is purely hand-made as well as high production costs and low economic benefits, a large number of artists are forced to change careers in view of the survival pressure. At the same time, fewer and fewer young people are willing to learn this skill, which leads to the shortage of talents. Its inheritance and development prospects are uncertain. Therefore, effective measures should be taken to protect *Bamboo Weaving of Liu Clan in Quxian County.*

100. 竹编（青神竹编） *Bamboo Weaving of Qingshen County*

竹编（青神竹编），传统美术，2008 年入选国家级第二批非物质文化遗产名录，主要分布在四川省眉山市青神县一带，现有国家级传承人陈云华。

青神竹编发展历史悠久，手工技艺娴熟，在当地具有完整的产业生产链条，在青神县当地的经济发展中占据重要地位。青神竹编以平面竹编、立体竹编、瓷胎竹编为主要类别，制成制品以"新、奇、特、绝"的神韵著称，被联合国教科文组织称为"竹编史上的奇迹，艺术中的艺术"。但目前青神竹编已陷入濒危境地，主要是因为一是环境恶化，竹节变短，韧性减弱，原材料出现问题；二是人们的消费观念发生很大改变，不少竹编制品为工业制品所取代；三是老艺人年事已高，年轻人不愿传承，导致这一民间手工艺后继乏人。在此情势下，有必要迅速制订一套可行的方案，对青神竹编进行抢救和保护。

As traditional art, *Bamboo Weaving Qingshen County* was selected into the second batch of the intangible cultural heritage of China in 2008. It prevails in Qingshen County and its surrounding areas. At present, there exists 1 national inheritor: Chen Yunhua.

Bamboo Weaving of Qingshen County has a long history and skilled craftsmanship, occupying an important position in the local economic development of Qingshen county where exists a complete industrial production chain. It is mainly classified into plane weaving, stereoscopic weaving and porcelain weaving. For the "new, strange, special and unique" characteristic of its products, this bamboo weaving is named a "miracle in history and gem in art" by UNESCO. However, *Bamboo Weaving of Qinghen County* is now in danger for mainly three reasons: firstly, the environmental deterioration results in shortages of raw materials by shortening bamboo knots as well as weakening its toughness; secondly, due to the great change of people's consumption concept nowadays, they prefer industrial products to handmade bamboo works; thirdly, the current craftsmen are aging and the young people are unwilling to inherit this skill, leading to the lack of successors of this folk handicraft. Therefore, it is necessary to work out a feasible scheme to rescue and protect *Bamboo Weaving of Qingshen County*.

101. 竹编（瓷胎竹编） *Bamboo Weaving over Porcelain*

竹编（瓷胎竹编），传统美术，2008 年入选国家级第二批非物质文化遗产名录，主要分布在四川省邛崃市一带。

瓷胎竹编，产品技艺独特，以精细见长，是四川地区独特的传统手工艺品，具有"精选料、特细丝、紧贴胎、密藏头、五彩图"等技艺特色。瓷胎竹编起源于清代中叶，当时主要做贡品。瓷胎竹编通常是以彩色或素色的精细竹丝，均匀地编贴于洁白的瓷上，紧扣瓷器，以胎成型，有很高的观赏价值和装饰价值，但由于瓷胎竹编附加值不高，技艺要求十分严格，年轻人多不愿学习，其传承越来越困难，如不及时加以抢救和保护，将逐渐从人们的生活中消失。

As traditional art, *Bamboo Weaving over Porceilain* was selected into the second batch of the intangible cultural heritage of China in 2008. It prevails in Qionglai County and its surrounding areas.

Bamboo Weaving over Porcelain is a unique traditional handicraft in Sichuan Province with peculiar and fine craftsmanship. It has the technical characteristics of "elaborate material selection, extra-fine silk, close to porcelain, hidden weaving end, rich color". It originated in the middle Qing dynasty, which was used as a tribute to the imperial court. Usually, with a fine-color or plain-color bamboo stripe, it is woven evenly and tightly over the white porcelain. *Bamboo Weaving over Porcelain* has a high ornamental value and decorative value. However, due to the low added value and strict technical requirements and the reluctance of young people to learn it, its inheritance is becoming more and more difficult. If it is not rescued and protected in time, it will gradually disappear from people's life.

102. 扎染技艺（自贡扎染技艺）

Tie-dye Techniques of Zigong City

扎染技艺（自贡扎染技艺），传统技艺，2008 年入选国家级第二批非物质文化遗产名录，主要分布在四川省自贡市，现有国家级传承人张晓平。

自贡扎染以古代传统工艺为基础，历经数代民间艺人地不断探索和总结，整理出绞、缝、扎、捆、撮、叠、缚、夹等数十种扎染手法，形成一套独特的制作技艺。自贡扎染色彩斑斓，扎痕耐久，艺术效果奇异；图案设计富于情趣，手法出神入化，极具地方特色。但随着社会发展，纺织印花的机械化生产的普及大大冲击手工印染行业，自贡扎染技艺的生存和发展空间也受到挤压，匠人大量减少，生产陷于停滞，陷入濒危状态，亟待抢救性保护。

As a traditional skill, *Tie-dye Techniques of Zigong City* was selected into the second batch of the intangible cultural heritage of China in 2008. It prevails mainly in Zigong City, Sichuan province. At present, there exists 1 national inheritor: Zhang Xiaoping.

Tie-dye Techniques of Zigong City is based on ancient traditional crafts and has been explored and developed by generations of folk artists. Dozens of tie-dye techniques have been sorted out, forming a unique set of production techniques. It is colorful and durable, and the artistic effect is novel. The design is full of interest, the technique is superb and is full of local characteristics. However, with the development of society, the popularization of mechanized production of textile and dyeing has greatly impacted the hand-made dyeing industry. The survival and development space of *Tie-dye Techniques of Zigong City* has also been squeezed. A large number of craftsmen have been reduced and the production practice has been stagnated, which make it in an endangered state. Therefore, rescue protection is badly needed.

103. 银饰制作技艺（彝族银饰制作技艺）

Silverware Forging Techniques of Yi People

银饰制作技艺（彝族银饰制作技艺），传统技艺，2008 年入选国家级第二批非物质文化遗产名录，主要分布在四川省凉山州的广大彝族地区，现有国家级传承人勒古沙日。

彝族银饰制作技艺具有鲜明的民族文化传统和独特的审美情趣，所打制的银器、饰品种类繁多，形式多样，造型美观大方，充分体现了彝族人民的审美情趣和独具特色的民族风格。但因社会生活的变迁和时代发展的影响，人们观念随之变化，少数民族的服饰、习俗逐渐现代化，使得彝族银饰制作技艺生存面临挑战，亟待进一步抢救和保护。

As a traditional skill, *Silverware Forging Techniques of Yi People* was selected into the second batch of the intangible cultural heritage of China in 2008. It prevails mainly in the vast area of Liangshan Yi Autonomous Prefecture of Sichuan Province. At present, there exists 1 national inheritor: Legushari.

Silverware Forging Techniques of Yi People has distinct national cultural tradition and unique aesthetic taste. The silverware and ornaments are various in form and shape, fully reflecting the aesthetic taste and unique national style of Yi people. However, due to the influence of the development of the times and social life, the change of people's ideas as well as the gradual modernization of ethnic minority costumes and customs, *Silverware Forging Techniques of Yi People* is facing challenges and needs further protection.

104. 制扇技艺（龚扇）　*Fan-making Techniques of Gong Clan*

制扇技艺（龚扇），传统技艺，2008 年入选国家级第二批非物质文化遗产名录，主要分布在四川省自贡市。

龚扇，又名"宫扇"，因其精细的选料和复杂的工艺堪称艺术珍品。龚扇以透明莹洁、薄如蝉翼、细如发丝的竹丝在扇面上重现名家书画的原作神韵，成品做工巧妙，扇面似绫绸细腻，具有极高的艺术价值。但随着现代科技的发展，人们普遍使用空调或电扇来抵御酷暑，对扇子的需求不高。再加之老一辈制扇名家的相继辞世，制扇工艺濒临失传，相关的抢救与保护工作已迫在眉睫。

As a traditional skill, *Fan-making Techniques of Gong Clan* was selected into the second batch of the intangible cultural heritage of China in 2008. It prevails in Zigong City, Sichuan Province.

Fan of Gong Clan is also called "Palace Fans", because it was used as a tribute to the royal court in Qing dynasty. It can be regarded as an art treasure because of its fine selection of materials and complex technology. Fan of Gong Clan recreates the original charm of famous calligraphers and paintings on the fan surface with translucent and fine bamboo stripes. The finished product is skillful in workmanship, whose surface is delicate like silk, giving it a high artistic quality. However, with the development of modern technology, people generally use air conditioning or electric fans to resist the heat, and the demand for fans is continuously decreasing. In addition, with the death of the old famous fan makers, the fan making technology is on the verge of being lost. Therefore, the relevant rescue and protection work is badly needed.

105. 中药炮制技术（中药炮制技艺）

Traditional Chinese Medicine Processing Techniques

中药炮制技艺，传统医药，2008 年入选国家级第二批非物质文化遗产名录，主要分布在四川省，现有国家级传承人胡昌江。

四川素有"天府之国"和"中医之乡、中药之库"的美称，中草药资源丰富，品种多样。中药炮制是根据中医药理论，按照治病用药需要、药物自身性质以及调剂、贮藏等不同要求，采用的一项制药技术，为中国中医药学的一大特色。对于中医理论和运用，中药炮制作用十分重要，一方面医生可根据不同情况有的放矢地选用恰当的材料炮制药品，以增强方剂的准确性、可靠性和实用疗效；另一方面，中药炮制技艺可以降低或消除药物的毒副作用，保证临床用药的安全。但由于改革开放后国家在大力推进中药发展过程中，废除有毒药物和回避技术难点高的品种，导致许多独有的中药成方制备技术被逐渐淘汰。同时民间掌握这类制剂处方、制备方法、制备设备的老一代技术人员大多已去世，健在的也年事已高，中药炮制技艺呈现"后继无人"的窘境，亟待抢救和保护。

As a traditional medicine, *Traditional Chinese Medicine Processing Techniques* was selected into the second batch of the intangible cultural heritage of China in 2008. It prevails in Sichuan Province. At present, there exists 1 national inheritor: Hu Changjiang.

Sichuan is known as "the land of abundance" and "the hometown of traditional Chinese medicine and the storehouse of traditional Chinese medicine", which has abundant traditional Chinese medicine resources. *Traditional Chinese Medicine Processing* is a pharmaceutical technology based on the theory of traditional Chinese medicine, in accordance with the needs of treatment and medication, the nature of the drug itself, as well as the different requirements of dispensing and storage. It is a major feature of Chinese medicine. It is of great importance for the theory, application as well as processing of traditional Chinese medicine. On the one hand, doctors can select appropriate processed medicine according to different situations to enhance the accuracy, reliability and practical efficacy of prescriptions; on the other hand, *Traditional Chinese Medicine Processing Techniques* can reduce or eliminate the toxic and side effects of medicine and ensure the safety of a clinical medication. However, in the process of promoting the development of traditional Chinese medicine after the reform and opening up, the government abolished toxic drugs and avoided varieties with high technical difficulties, which led to the gradual elimination of many unique processing techniques of traditional Chinese medicine. At the same time, due to the aging or death of the old technical personnel who mastered the prescription, processing method and processing equipment, *Traditional Chinese Medicine Processing Techniques* is in a dilemma of "no successor". Therefore, rescue protection is badly needed.

106~107. 禹的传说 *Legend of King Yu*

禹的传说，民间文学，2011 年入选国家级第三批非物质文化遗产名录，主要分布在四川北川、汶川、茂县、理县等地，方式传承主要是口耳相传。

据史学记录，"禹兴于西羌"，"平水土定九州"，一生功绩在于治水；大禹传说"西兴东渐"，已流传数千年。我国羌族更将大禹奉为神灵与民族保护神，对其顶礼膜拜，四川羌族地区被视为大禹故里。禹的传说所体现的自强不息、艰苦奋斗的精神，为华夏民族带来了深远的影响，是我国古代人民力量和智慧的象征，也是中华民族应当永续传承的文化精神。但"5·12"大地震后，羌族自然环境遭到严重破坏，加之能够完整口传大禹传说的老一辈艺人过世，禹的传说处于几近失传的困境，保护工作迫在眉睫。

As folk literature, *Legend of King Yu* was selected into the third batch of the intangible cultural heritage of China in 2011 It prevails in Beichuan County, Wenchuan County, Maoxian County and Lixian County of Sichuan Province, which is mainly inherited through word of mouth.

According to historical records, "King Yu flourished in Xiqiang", and the biggest contribution in his whole life was to control the floods and "to stabilize the soil and water and to stabilize Jiuzhou"; *Legend of King Yu* that "prospered in the West and spread to the East" has been handed down for thousands of years. The Qiang people regard Yu as the God of National Protection and worship him, and the inhabited areas of Qiang people in sichuan are regarded as the hometown of Yu. *Legend of King Yu* shows the spirit of self-improvement and hard struggle, which has brought far-reaching influence on the Chinese nation. It is a symbol of the strength and wisdom of the ancient Chinese people and the cultural spirit that the Chinese nation should inherit forever. However, in the "5.12" earthquake in Wenchuan County, the natural environment of Qiang inhabited areas was seriously damaged. Besides, the old artists who could completely narrate the *Legend of King Yu* passed away. It is almost on the verge of disappearing. Therefore, protection work is urgently needed.

108. 羌戈大战　*Battles between Qiang and Geji People*

羌戈大战，民间文学，2011 年入选国家级第三批非物质文化遗产名录，主要分布在四川省阿坝藏族羌族自治州茂县、汶川县等羌族聚集区。

羌戈大战以古羌语演唱，其史诗形式为羌族释比等少数人掌握，以神话故事的形式在民间流传，有鼓舞斗志、教化人心的作用，被誉为"羌族口诉历史教科书"、形象化的古代羌族历史、中国少数民族民间文学宝库的瑰宝，具有极高的史学、文学和文化价值，涵盖羌民族历史、宗教、哲学、习俗、社会等。但因羌戈大战的史诗掌握者羌族释比对传承人的语言、记忆能力要求很高，加之现代的年轻人缺乏学习传统文化的兴趣，羌戈大战传承难度大，亟待进一步抢救和保护。

As folk literature, *Battles between Qiang and Geji People* was selected into the third batch of the intangible cultural heritage of China 2011. It prevails in Wenchuan County and Maoxian County of Aba Tibetan and Qiang Autonomous Prefecture, Sichuan Province.

Battles between Qiang and Geji People has been sung in ancient Qiang language. Its epic form is mastered by a few people as Shibi and its mythology form is spread among the Qiang people, which equipped the Battles between Qiang and Geji People with the function of education. Being one dictated history textbook of the Qiang people and its visualization, the *Battles between Qiang and Geji People* is the treasure of Chinese minority folk literature. It has great values of history, literature and culture, reflecting all aspects of folk life, from religion, philosophy, custom to society. However, the Shibi culture sets high requirements on the language and memory abilities of inheritors of the *Battles between Qiang and Geji People*. In addition, nowadays, most young people lack interest in learning traditional cultures. These factors have made *Battles between Qiang and Geji People* in danger. Therefore, further rescue protection is urgently needed.

109. 跳曹盖 *Mask Dance*

跳曹盖，传统舞蹈，2011年入选国家级第三批非物质文化遗产名录，主要分布在四川省平武县、九寨沟县和甘肃文县的白马地区，现有国家级传承人格格。

跳曹盖是一种白马藏族的古老的驱邪祭祀祈福活动。"曹盖"是白马藏语音译，意为"面具"，跳曹盖即是戴着面具跳舞。白马藏族信奉原始宗教，"跳曹盖"中以夸张的舞姿祭祀山神，祈祷来年风调雨顺、无病无灾。但"文革"时期，"跳曹盖"被冠以"封建迷信"，导致了传承断层；另外因时代与交通发展，白马地区受到外来文化影响，其长期封闭的局面被逐渐打破。加之白马藏族没有文字，"跳曹盖"的文化传承难度大，亟待抢救和保护。

As a traditional dance, *Mask Dance* was selected into the third batch of the intangible cultural heritage of China in 2011. It prevails in Liangshan Yi Autonomous Prefecture, Sichuan Province. At present, there exists 1 national inheritor: Gege.

Mask Dance is an ancient exorcism, sacrifice and blessing activity of Baima Tibetans. "Caogai" is the pronunciation of Baima Tibetan, meaning "Mask". Therefore, originally it means dancing with a mask. Baima Tibetan believe in primitive natural religion, so they worship the mountain god with exaggerated dance posture in "mask dance", praying for good weather and harvest in the coming year. However, during the Cultural Revolution, *Mask Dance* was labeled as "feudal superstition", which led to the suspension of its inheritance. Besides, with the development of the times and transportation, Baima area was eroded by foreign culture, and its long-term closed situation was gradually broken. Furthermore, Baima Tibetan has no written language, which endangered the inheritance of *Mask Dance*. Therefore, rescue protection is badly needed.

110. 棕编（新繁棕编） *Palm Fiber Weaving of Xinfan Town*

棕编（新繁棕编），传统美术，2011 年入选国家级第三批非物质文化遗产名录，主要流行于四川省成都市新都区新繁地区。

新繁棕编起源于清代嘉庆末年，心灵手巧的新繁妇女用棕丝编织物品以补贴家用，是新繁劳动人民智慧的结晶。其保持中国民间传统手工艺品的原生态特点，凝聚着中华民族自强不息的传统美德和朴素自然的审美情趣，具备较高的艺术审美价值和一定的经济价值。但近年来，新繁棕编的老艺人相继去世，年轻人不愿研习这门技艺，新繁棕编濒临后继乏人的困境，亟须采取措施对其加以保护。

As traditional art, *Palm Fiber Weaving of Xinfan Town* was selected into the third batch of the intangible cultural heritage of China in 2011. It prevails in Xinfan Town, Xindu District, Chengdu City of Sichuan Province.

Palm Fiber Weaving of Xinfan Town originated in the late Jiaqing period of the Qing Dynasty. The ingenious women in Xinfan Town weaved different kinds of products to subsidize the household. It is the crystallization of the wisdom of working people, which is inherited from generation to generation. It also maintains the original ecological characteristics of Chinese traditional folk handicrafts, and condenses the traditional virtues as well as a simple and natural aesthetic taste of the Chinese nation, having high artistic and aesthetic value and certain economic value. However, in recent years, due to the death of old craftsmen and the lack of interest in learning this skill, *Palm Fiber Weaving of Xinfan Town* is on the verge of lacking successors. Therefore, effective measures should be taken to protect it immediately.

111. 藏族编织、挑花刺绣工艺

Tibetan Weaving & Embroidery Techniques

藏族编织、挑花刺绣工艺，传统美术，2011 年入选国家级第三批非物质文化遗产名录，主要分布在四川省阿坝藏族羌族自治州，现有国家级传承人杨华珍。

藏族善于刺绣、纺织，精巧的工艺为其服饰增添了无穷的魅力。

藏族编织、挑花刺绣工艺依附于服饰，实用性与装饰性的统一，是藏族审美价值的集中体现，也是其历史、文化、习俗和宗教信仰的记录。作为藏族物质文化和精神文化的有形载体和无形表征，其编织品具有极高的艺术审美价值。但由于外来文化和机绣产品的冲击，绣品使用空间日渐缩小，藏绣手工艺人越来越少，藏族编织、挑花刺绣工艺市场生存困难，亟待进一步抢救性保护。

As a traditional art, *Tibetan Weaving & Embroidery Techniques* was selected into the third batch of the intangible cultural heritage of China in 2011. It prevails in Aba Tibetan and Qiang Autonomous Prefecture, Sichuan Province. At present, there exists 1 national inheritor: Yang Huazhen.

Tibetan is good at weaving and embroidery. Affiliated to clothing, the unity of practicality and decoration is not only the typical embodiment of Tibetan aesthetic value, but also the record of its history, culture, customs, religion and beliefs. As the tangible carrier and intangible representation of Tibetan material culture and spiritual culture, *Tibetan Weaving & Embroidery Techniques* has high artistic and aesthetic value. However, due to the impact of foreign culture and machine-made embroidery products, the shrinking of use space for embroidery products and the decrease of craftsmen, *Tibetan Weaving & Embroidery Techniques* is difficult to survive Therefore, further rescue protection is badly needed.

112. 彝族年 *New Year of Yi People*

彝族年，民俗，2011 年入选国家级第三批非物质文化遗产名录，主要分布在四川省凉山彝族自治州各个地区。

彝族年，彝语称"库史"，意思是新年，是四川省凉山彝族自治州大小凉山彝族传统的祭祀兼庆贺性节日。彝族年每年在秋收的农历十一月二十四日左右进行，期间集祭祀祖先、游艺竞技、餐饮娱乐、服饰制度等诸多民俗事项为一体，是彝族远古文明和祖先崇拜的活态见证，也反映了彝族历史文化、经济生活、人伦规范、风俗礼制、服装民俗、审美情趣、禁忌事宜等诸多文化内容。但因外来文化冲击和文化生长环境的变化，传承人年事已高，年轻人对传统文化的兴趣缺乏，彝族年的生存和发展面临危机，亟待进一步抢救和保护。

As a folk custom, *New Year of Yi People* was selected into the third batch of the intangible cultural heritage of China in 2011. It prevails in Liangshan Yi Autonomous Prefecture, Sichuan Province.

New Year of Yi People is called "Kushi" in Yi dialect which means New Year. It is a traditional sacrificial and celebratory festival of Yi people in Liangshan Yi Autonomous Prefecture of Sichuan Province. It is held every year around November 24 according to Yi calendar. It integrates many folk customs such as ancestor worship, entertainment, food and clothing system. It is a living witness of Yi People's ancient civilization and ancestor worship. It also reflects the Yi People's history and culture, economic life, ethical norms, custom and etiquette, clothing and folk customs, aesthetic taste, taboos, etc. However, due to the impact of foreign culture and the change of cultural growth environment, the aging of the inheritors and lack of interest in inheriting traditional culture, the survival and development of *New Year of Yi People* are in crisis. Therefore, it needs further protection.

113. 婚俗（彝族传统婚俗） *Marriage Custom of Yi People*

婚俗（彝族传统婚俗），民俗，2011 年入选国家级第三批非物质文化遗产名录，主要分布在四川省凉山彝族自治州各个地区。

彝族婚俗是彝族民俗文化精华，是研究彝族人类学、民族学、宗教学的基因库。彝族婚俗的内容极其丰富、独特别致，将婚姻缔结从一家一户的个体行为上升为整个家族、姻亲、邻居等关联的集体行为，是彝族族群认同和文化传承的重要礼俗活动，具有极强的研究、艺术和教育价值。但因外来文化的冲击和生产生活方式的变迁，现代社会中比较传统、典型、完整的彝族婚礼形式越来越少，彝族婚俗的沿袭和传承状况堪忧，亟待进一步抢救性保护。

As a folk custom, *Marriage Custom of Yi People* was selected into the third batch of the intangible cultural heritage of China in 2011. It prevails in Liangshan Yi Autonomous Prefecture, Sichuan Province.

Marriage Custom of Yi People is the essence of Yi culture, as well as research basis of the anthropology, ethnology, religion of Yi people. Its content is extremely rich and unique, transferring the marriage from the individual behavior to the collective behavior of the whole family, the clan or even neighbors. Being the important etiquette and custom activity of ethnic identity and cultural heritage for the Yi people, it has enormous values in research, art and education. However, due to the impact of foreign culture, the decreasing of typical and complete traditional marriage of Yi people, *Marriage Custom of Yi People* is in danger. Therefore, further rescue protection is urgently needed.

114. 藏族民歌（藏族赶马调） *Tibetan Horse-driving Tunes*

藏族民歌（藏族赶马调），传统音乐，2011 年入选国家级第三批非物质文化遗产名录，主要分布在四川省冕宁县，传承方式为口耳相传，现有国家级传承人伍德芬。

藏族赶马调在藏语里称"木弱加"，包括旋律和歌词两部分。旋律高亢、悠长，音域宽广，跌宕起伏，头尾常有吆喝马的呼唤性腔调的特点；歌词内容主要反映赶马、牧马，有关赶马人的生活、思想感情、愿望追求。藏族赶马调诞生于古代"南丝绸之路"川滇高原的零关古道，具有很高的历史价值、社会价值和艺术价值。但随着历史的变迁和社会的发展，越来越少的年轻人对藏族赶马调感兴趣，亟须采取有效措施对其加以保护。

As traditional music, *Tibetan Horse-driving Tunes* was selected into the third batch of the intangible cultural heritage in 2011. It mainly prevails in Mianning County of Sichuan Province, which is mainly inherited through word of mouth. At present, there exists 1 national inheritor: Wu Defen.

Tibetan Horse-driving Tunes is called "Muruojia" in Tibetan language, which includes melody and lyrics. The melody is high and long, the range is wide. There often have the characteristics of calling for horses both at the beginning and the ending. The content of the lyrics mainly reflects the life, thoughts and feelings of the people who drive horses. *Tibetan Horse-driving Tunes* originated in the ancient "South Silk Road" in Sichuan and Yunnan Plateau which has high historical, social and artistic value. However, due to the development and change of history and society, fewer and fewer young people are interested in *Tibetan Horse-driving Tunes*. Therefore, effective measures should be taken to protect it.

116. 佛教音乐（觉囊梵音） *Sanskrit Chant of Jonang*

觉囊梵音，传统音乐，2011 年入选国家级第三批非物质文化遗产名录，主要分布在四川阿坝州壤塘县，现有国家级传承人嘉阳乐住。

觉囊梵音是中国藏传佛教现存最古老的乐种之一，已有 1000 多年的历史，至今仍在四川阿坝州壤塘县的觉囊藏哇寺活态传承。觉囊梵音不仅是被用来表演与欣赏的，更是一种修行。它用古老空灵的音乐传达智慧与慈悲的境界，将修行的艺术呈现在世人面前，保存了中国传统藏传佛教音乐的基本风貌，为研究中国传统藏传佛教文化的内涵与变迁提供了典型的生动实例，被音乐界评为"中国音乐历史的活化石"。但由于觉囊梵乐无论是内修还是外在的演奏技巧，都对演奏者有很高的要求，所有的领唱者都需要接受大德们严格而完整的传承训练，加之觉囊法脉在雪域传承千载，一直奉行避世禅修、精研实证的佛门宗风，多不为外世所知。这种随着觉囊一派而存在的原汁原味的古代音乐，濒临灭绝，亟须采取措施对其加以保护。

As traditional music, *Sanskrit Chant of Jonang* was selected into the third batch of the intangible cultural heritage of China in 2011. It prevails in Rangtang County of Aba Prefecture, Sichuan Province, At present, there exists 1 national inheritor: Jiayanglezhu.

Sanskrit Chant of Jonang is one of the oldest existing music types of Tibetan Buddhism in China, which has been inherited in Tibet for 1000 years, and is still alive in Jonang zangwa temple in Rangtang County, Aba Prefecture, Sichuan Province. It is not only used for performance and appreciation, but also for Buddhism practice. It uses the ancient ethereal music to convey the realm of wisdom and compassion, presents the art of Buddhism practice in front of the world, preserves the basic features of Chinese traditional Tibetan Buddhist music and provides a typical and vivid example for the study of the connotation and changes of Chinese traditional Tibetan Buddhist culture, which is rated as "the living fossil of Chinese music history" by the music circle. However, it has high requirements for performers in both internal Buddhism practice and external performance skills. All the leading singers need to accept the strict and complete inheritance of eminent monks. In addition, after thousands of years of inheritance in snow-covered Plateau, it pursues the belief of avoiding the mortal world and emphasizing empirical studies, which means that it is mysterious and unknown to the outside world. This kind of original ancient music, which existed with the school of Jonang, is on the verge of extinction. Therefore, effective measures should be taken to protect it.

117. 盆景技艺（川派盆景技艺） *Sichuan Bonsai Techniques*

盆景技艺（川派盆景技艺），传统美术，2011 年入选国家级第三批非物质文化遗产名录，主要分布在四川省成都市及其周边地区，现有国家级传承人周厚西。

川派盆景技艺历史悠久、造型多样，极具美感，因其所独有的造型格律和鲜明的艺术特征，被誉为"立体画、无声诗""高等艺术、美化自然"。川派盆景善于借小盆景展现大自然精神，用有限的景观表达无限的精神，体现的是一种哲理性思考和诗意的结晶。但由于现代生活的快节奏致使很少有人对山石、树石组合盆景制作产生兴趣，因此缺乏能进一步提高川派盆景技艺的优秀匠人，需要采取措施对其加以保护和传承。

As a traditional art, *Sichuan Bonsai Techniques* was selected into the third batch of the intangible cultural heritage of China in 2011. It prevails in Chengdu City and its surrounding areas. At present, there exists 1 national inheritor: Zhou Houxi.

Sichuan Bonsai Techniques has a long history, diverse shapes and great aesthetic feeling. It is known as "three-dimensional painting, silent poetry", "superior art, beautifying nature" because of its unique modeling and distinctive artistic characteristics. *Sichuan Bonsai*

Techniques is good at using the small bonsai to show the spirit of nature and express the infinite spiritual mood with the limited landscape, which reflects a kind of philosophical thinking and poetic crystallization. However, due to the rapid pace of modern life, few people are interested in the production of bonsai. There is a lack of outstanding craftsmen who can further promote the *Sichuan Bonsai Techniques*. Therefore, effective measures should be taken to protect and inherit *Sichuan Bonsai Techniques*.

118. 蜡染技艺（苗族蜡染技艺） *Batik Techniques of Miao People*

蜡染技艺（苗族蜡染技艺），传统技艺，2011 年入选国家级第三批非物质文化遗产名录，主要分布在四川省珙县。

苗族蜡染技艺历史悠久，早在秦汉时期苗族人民就已掌握了蜡染技术。珙县苗族蜡染以图案精美，结构严谨，线条流畅为主要特点。珙县地区苗族人民常将蜡染成品做成衣饰、围腰、卧单等，朴实大方，富有民族特色，极具人类学、美学、工艺学的重要价值。但由于现代文明的渗透与冲击，传统蜡染艺术不断被先进生产力和产品所替代。加之蜡染制作耗工、耗时、耗物，缺乏批量外销，经济效益不明显，造成大量艺人迫于生计而改行，技艺传承人越来越少，亟待抢救性保护与传承。

As a traditional skill, *Batik Techniques of Miao People* was selected into the third batch of the intangible cultural heritage of China in 2011. It prevails in Gongxian County, Sichuan Province.

Batik Techniques of Miao People has a long history. As early as Qin and Han Dynasties, Miao people have mastered the batik technology. The batik of Miao People of Gongxian is characterized by exquisite patterns, rigorous composition and smooth lines. Miao people in Gongxian County often make batik products into clothes, waists, sleeping sheets, etc., which are simple and natural, rich in national characteristics. It is of great value in anthropology, aesthetics and technology. However, because of the penetration and impact of modern civilization, traditional batik art has been replaced by advanced productivity and products. In addition, batik production consumes labor, time and materials, and lacks export channels on a large scale, so its economic benefits are not obvious. As a result, a large number of artists are forced to change their careers under the pressure of livelihood, which leads to fewer and fewer art inheritors. Therefore, rescue protection and inheritance are urgently needed.

119 ~ 120. 碉楼营造技艺（羌族碉楼营造技艺）

Watchtower Building Techniques of Qiang People

碉楼营造技艺（羌族碉楼营造技艺），传统技艺，2011 年入选国家级第三批非物质文化遗产名录，传承方式主要为亲族传承和师徒传承，主要分布在阿坝藏族自治州汶川县、茂县、理县、绵阳北川等地。

羌族碉楼，以石砌建筑、黏土建筑、石粘混合建筑为特色，兼具居住和防御功能，集民族意识、宗教信仰、自然环境、历史变迁、科技进步、经济发展于一体，体现了羌族的历史、经济、建筑、军事、宗教、审美、文化，具有极强的研究价值。但因"5·12"地震严重破坏自然环境，羌寨被埋，碉楼被毁，再加之年轻人对传统技艺的兴趣缺失，碉楼营造技艺传承难度大，生存面临危机，亟待进一步抢救和保护。

As a traditional skill, the *Watchtower Building Techniques of Qiang People* was selected into the third batch of the intangible cultural heritage of China in 2011. It is mainly inherited within family members as well as between masters and apprentices. It mainly prevails in

Wenchuan County, Maoxian County and Lixian County of Aba Tibetan Autonomous Prefecture, as well as Beichuan County of Mianyang City, Sichuan Province.

Watchtower of Qiang People is characterized by stone buildings, clay buildings and stone-concrete buildings, with the combined functions of living and defence. It integrates national consciousness, religious beliefs, natural environment, historical changes, scientific and technological progress, and economic development. *Watchtower Building Techniques of Qiang people* has extremely high research value because it reflects the history, economy, architecture, military, religion and aesthetic and culture of the Qiang people. However, due to the 5·12 earthquake, the natural environment was seriously damaged, the village buried, the tower destroyed, and also because the young people's interest in traditional skills was lacking, it's difficult to pass on the skills. The *Watchtower Building Techniques* is in crisis. Therefore, further rescue protection was urgently needed.

121. 毕阿史拉则传说 *Legend of Biashilaze*

毕阿史拉则传说，民间文学，2014年入选国家级第四批非物质文化遗产名录，主要分布在四川省金阳县、美姑、昭觉等地的彝族聚居区，主要传承方式为口耳相传。

毕阿史拉则，又称阿史拉则，是彝族宗教中赫赫有名的毕摩宗师。阿史拉则的系列故事在凉山彝族流传广泛，具有深厚的群众基础。在其近800年的流传过程中，经过不断地创造、加工、丰富，成为四川凉山地区口承传统中最具代表性的传说，在深入了解研究彝族的历史、文化、宗教、哲学、文学、医学等方面具有重要的价值。但随着现代社会的发展，年轻一代的彝族人缺乏对传统文化的兴趣，其传承面临危机，亟待采取措施对其加以传承与保护。

As folk literature, *Legend of Biashilaze* was selected into the fourth batch of the intangible cultural heritage of China in 2014. It prevails in Yi inhabited areas in Jinyang County, Meigu County and Zhaojue County in Sichuan Province. It is mainly inherited through word of mouth.

Biashilaze is a famous Bimo patriarch of Yi religion. Biashilaze's series of stories are widely spread among the Yi people in Liangshan Prefecture and have a deep mass foundation. During the 800 year's spreading history, through continuous creation, processing and enrichment, it has become the most representative oral legend in Liangshan area. It has important historical value in understanding and studying the history, culture, religion, philosophy, literature and medicine of Yi people. However, with the development of modern society and young people's lack of interests in traditional culture, its inheritance is facing a crisis. Therefore, effective measures should be taken to inherit and protect *Legend of Biashilaze* immediately.

122. 玛牧 *Mamu—Revelation of Yi People*

玛牧，又称玛牧特依，民间文学，2014 年入选国家级第四批非物质文化遗产名录，主要分布在四川省凉山彝族聚集地区，传承方式主要为背诵、口耳相传和手抄，现有国家传承人沙马史体。

玛牧是彝族人民口头流传的传统教育经典，影响和维系着彝族地区社会几千年的秩序。它是彝族人民生活智慧与经验的总汇，是集体智慧的结晶，是凉山彝族社会内部人与自然、人与人之间关系的行为准则和道德规范，对研究彝族传统道德规范具有重要价值。但因玛牧为古彝语诗句，对传承人的语言和记忆能力要求很高，加之年轻人缺少对传统文化的兴趣，其传承面临危机，亟待采取措施对其加以传承与保护。

As folk literature, *Mamu—Revelation of Yi People* was selected into the fourth batch of the intangible cultural heritage of China in 2014. It prevails in Yi inhabited areas of Liangshan Yi Autonomous Prefecture, Sichuan Province, which is mainly inherited through recitation, word of mouth and handwriting. At present, there exists 1 national inheritor: Shamashiti.

Mamu is a traditional education classic handed down orally by the Yi people, whith has influenced and maintained the social order of Yi area for thousands of years. It is the collection of Yi People's life wisdom and experience, the crystallization of collective wisdom, and the code of conduct and ethics of the relationship between human and nature, and between people. It is of great value for the study of Yi traditional ethics. However, due to the fact that *Mamu* is expressed in ancient Yi language which has a high demand on the inheritors' language and memory ability, and the lack of interest of young people in traditional culture, its inheritance is facing a crisis. Therefore, effective measures should be taken to inherit and protect *Mamu—Revelation of Yi People*.

123. 西岭山歌　*Xiling Folk Songs*

西岭山歌，传统音乐，2014 年入选国家级第四批非物质文化遗产名录，主要分布在四川省大邑县，主要通过口耳相传的方式进行传承。

西岭山歌历史悠久、原始古朴、旋律流畅，其艺术创作来源于西岭山民的生产、生活、劳动过程，色彩、调式包含了藏、羌、汉族的民歌元素，属于山民"道法自然"的原创作品。西岭山歌富含真情实感，反映了山民勤劳、朴实、不畏艰辛追求真善美行美德。但随着现代社会的发展和外来文化的冲击，年轻一代缺少对传统文化的兴趣，其传承面临危机，亟待采取措施对其加以传承与保护。

As traditional music, *Xiling Folk Songs* was selected into the fourth batch of the intangible cultural heritage of China in 2014. It prevails in Dayi County, Sichuan Province, and it is mainly inherited through word of mouth.

Xiling Folk Songs has a long history, characterized by primitive simplicity and smooth melody. Its artistic creation comes from the production, life and labor process of Xiling mountainous people, integrating the folk song elements of Tibetan, Qiang and Han People, and reflecting the hard-working, simple and brave people's virtue of pursuing truth, goodness and beauty. However, with the development of modern society and the impact of foreign culture as well as young people's lack of interests, it is now facing the crisis of extinction. Therefore, effective measures should be taken to rescue and protect it immediately.

124. 毕摩音乐 *Chanting of Bimo*

毕摩音乐，传统音乐，2014 年入选国家级第四批非物质文化遗产名录，主要分布在四川省凉山等彝族聚集区，传承方式主要为师徒传承，现有国家级传承人曲比拉火。

毕摩文化源远流长。毕摩是古代彝族社会的祭司和部落首领，具有崇高的威望与地位。而毕摩音乐则是毕摩在仪式活动以诵和唱的方式来叙述故事、讲述历史、探究万物起源、塑造人物形象，借此抒发思想情感，表达志向和愿望的远古音乐艺术。毕摩音乐旋律绚丽多彩，调式富于变化，内容涵盖了彝族政治、经济、哲学、文学、艺术、医学、军事、风俗礼制等，凝聚了彝族民众的智慧，被誉为音乐史上的"活化石"，具有极强的历史、文化和艺术价值。但因彝族历史文化受到现代文明的挑战和冲击，同时人为损坏和自然的破坏仍然存在，加上传承后继无人的现实情况，亟须对毕摩音乐进行抢救性保护。

As traditional music, *Chanting of Bimo* was selected into the fourth batch of the intangible cultural heritage of China in 2014. It prevails in Yi People inhabited areas in Liangshan Yi Autonomous Prefecture, Sichuan Province. It is mainly inherited between masters and apprentices. At present, there exists1 national inheritor: Qubilahuo.

Bimo culture has a long history. In the ancient Yi society, Bimo was the priest and tribal leader, having high prestige and status. Bimo music is a kind of ancient music art in which Bimo narrates the story, tells the history, explores the origin of all things and shapes the character image in the way of reciting and singing in the ritual activities, so as to express the thoughts, feelings and aspirations. It has colorful melody and varied tunes, covering Yi People's politics, culture, economy, philosophy, literature, art, medicine, military affairs, customs and rituals, and embodying the wisdom of the Yi people. Therefore, it is known as the "living fossil" in the history of music, with strong historical, cultural and artistic value. However, due to the challenges and impact of modern civilization on Yi People's history and culture, human damage and natural damage as well as the reality that there is no successor, it is urgent to rescue and protect *Chanting of Bimo*.

125. 古蔺花灯　*Lantern Dance of Gulin County*

古蔺花灯，传统舞蹈，2014 年入选国家级第四批非物质文化遗产名录，主要流传于四川省泸州市古蔺县，主要通过师带徒、家族流传等方式进行传承。

古蔺花灯是一种民间传统歌舞艺术，集唱、念、跳、打为一体，一般为双人对舞形式，舞步造型丰富，舞蹈技巧极高，被誉为南方的"二人转"，表演风格深受古蔺县民众喜爱。古蔺花灯因其丰富的文化内涵、特殊的地理位置和民族风情，展现出独特的功能性与重要的社会价值。但因现代文明社会的发展，越来越少的年轻人对这种传统舞蹈感兴趣，加上老一辈艺人的离世，亟须采取措施对古蔺花灯进行保护。

As a traditional dance, *Lantern Dance of Gulin County* was selected into the fourth batch of the intangible cultural heritage of China in 2014. It prevails in Gulin County, Luzhou City, Sichuan Province, which is mainly inherited within family members as well as between masters and apprentices.

Lantern Dance of Gulin County is a kind of traditional folk song and dance art, combining singing, reciting, dancing and playing together. It is generally a duet dance, which has rich dance steps and high dance skills. It is known as the "Errenzhuan" in South China, and its funny and lively performance style makes it popular among local people in Gulin County. Because of its rich cultural connotation, special geographical location and ethnic customs, *Lantern Dance of Gulin County* shows unique functionality and important social value. However, due to the development of modern civilization, young people's lack of interest and the death of the old artists, effective measures should be taken to protect *Lantern Dance of Gulin County* immediately.

126. 登嘎甘伯（熊猫舞）　*Panda-worshiping Dance*

登嘎甘伯（熊猫舞），传统舞蹈，2014 年入选国家级第四批非物质文化遗产名录，主要分布在四川省阿坝藏族羌族自治州九寨沟县，主要以家族方式进行传承。

熊猫舞是白马藏族人的传统祭祀舞蹈，每年正月十五、十六日，九寨沟县草地乡上草地村的白马藏族会头戴动物头骨，拟兽起舞，以原始形态的跳舞进以驱邪。熊猫舞是白马藏人"万物有灵"动物崇拜的活态遗存，展现的是远古先民最初的立体造型艺术和审美意识，是独具特色的白马藏族民风民俗的体现。但由于这种用以驱邪的祭祀舞蹈对表演者体力要求高、舞步复杂变化多，老一辈艺人大多年事已高或已离世，而年轻一代又不愿意学习，项目传承后继无人，亟须采取抢救性保护措施。

As a traditional dance, *Panda-worshiping Dance* was selected into the fourth batch of the intangible cultural heritage of China in 2014. It prevails in Jiuzhaigou County, Aba Tibetan and Qiang Autonomous Prefecture, Sichuan Province, and it is mainly inherited within family members.

Panda-worshiping Dance is a traditional sacrificial dance of Baima Tibetans. On the 15th and 16th of the first lunar month each year, Baima Tibetans would dance with a panda mask which to passed down from the ancient time just in the traditional way exorcise evil spirits. The dance is a living remains of animal worship of Baima Tibetan, which shows ancient ancestors' three-dimensional contouring and aesthetics and typical Baima Tibetan custom. However, due to its energy-demanding, complex dance steps, the aging or death of old artists and the lack of interest of young people, there is no inheritor. Therefore, effective measures should be taken to protect *Panda-worshiping Dance* immediately.

127. 毕摩绘画 *Painting of Bimo*

毕摩绘画，传统美术，2014 年入选国家级第四批非物质文化遗产名录，主要分布在川、滇、黔、桂四省的彝族地区，尤其以四川省大小凉山美姑、昭觉、布拖等彝区为代表，现有国家级传承人吉克伍沙。

毕摩绘画承袭岩画风格，以彝族历史文化为绘画背景，以图腾、神话故事和祭祀舞蹈等为表现题材，反映了彝族的历史文化和宗教信仰等内容，堪称彝族远古绘画艺术的"活化石"。毕摩绘画以其"书画合一"的独特风格和仿自然万物之像的原始美感，展现了毕摩仪式的宗族信仰，具有鲜明的民族特色，集历史、文化、艺术与社会价值于一身。但由于高远山区气候环境的影响，以及对文化资源的保护、利用、创新不足等问题，毕摩绘画的传承面临危机，亟须采取进一步抢救性保护措施。

As traditional art, *Painting of Bimo* was selected into the fourth batch of the intangible cultural heritage of China in 2014. It prevails in the provinces of Sichuan, Yunnan, Guizhou and Guangxi. Among them, the most distinctive *Painting of Bimo* is in Meigu county, Zhaojue County and Buocuo County in Sichuan Province. At present, there exists 1 national inheritor: Jikewusha.

Painting of Bimo inherits the style of rock painting, takes the Yi People's history and culture as the painting background, totem, myth story and sacrificial dance as a theme. It uses unique Chinese traditional painting method and materials to reflect the Yi People's history, cultuve and religion and beliefs, which is called the "living fossil" of Yi People's ancient painting art. *Painting of Bimo*, with its unique style of "integration of calligraphy and painting" and the original aesthetic of imitating the image of all things in nature, shows the patriarchal belief of Bimo ceremony and has distinct national characteristics. It integrates historical, cultural, artistic and social values. However, due to the impact of climate and environment in mountainous areas, lack of protection, utilization and innovation of cultural resources, it is now facing the crisis of extinction. Therefore, further rescue protection is urgently needed.

128. 彝族服饰　*Clothing of Yi People*

彝族服饰，民俗，2014年入选国家级第四批非物质文化遗产名录，主要分布在四川、云南的大小凉山及毗邻的金沙江地区，现有国家级传承人贾巴子则。

彝族服饰是凉山彝族物质文化的杰出代表，与彝族生产生活息息相关，是彝族族群的标志和宗教文化的体现，具备极高的历史文化价值。彝族服饰色彩丰富，款式变化多姿，并且以大量银制品和刺绣装饰，全部都由彝人手工完成，体现了彝族的审美特征，具有较高的文化底蕴与价值。但由于彝族服饰制作一般由纯羊毛手工制造，对技艺要求较高，加上传承人年事已高以及现代化纺织品的冲击，传统纺织品市场生存困难，彝族服饰制作技艺面临"断代"的危险，亟待对其进行抢救性保护。

As a traditional folk custom, *Clothing of Yi People* was selected into the fourth batch of the intangible cultural heritage of China in 2014. It prevails in Lianghan Yi autonomous areas in Yunnan and Sichuan as well as Jinshajiang area. At present, there exists 1 national inheritor Jiabazize.

Clothing of Yi People is an outstanding representative of the material culture of Yi people, which is closely related to the production of Yi people. It is the symbol of Yi ethnic group and the highlight of religious culture, which has high historical and cultural value. *Clothing of Yi People* is rich in color, varied in style, and decorated with a large number of silver products and embroidery. All the clothing is hand-made, which reflects the aesthetic characteristics of the Yi people and has a high cultural heritage value. However, due to the fact that *Clothing of Yi People* is generally made by pure wool by hand and its complicated procedures, it has high requirements for skills. Because of the aging of inheritors and the impact of modern textiles, *Clothing of Yi People* is facing the danger of extinction. Therefore, further rescue protection is urgently needed.

129. 多声部民歌（阿尔麦多声部民歌）

Multi-voice Songs of Almai

多声部民歌（阿尔麦多声部民歌），传统音乐，2014 年入选国家级第四批非物质文化遗产名录，主要分布在四川省阿坝州黑水、松潘、茂县交汇处的广大地区，以口耳相传的方式进行传承。

阿尔麦多声部民歌是阿尔麦人这一特殊族群的情感纽带和文化基因。阿尔麦人是生活在川西"藏羌走廊"大山深处的一支特殊族群，其语言、生活、生产方式和文化习俗都与其他藏羌族群有着明显的区别。他们身处三个彼此毗邻的不同地区，但在演唱多声部民歌时都使用古羌语。阿尔麦多声部民歌以古老朴素的音乐语言代代传承，是其地理环境和多元文化交融所孕育的特殊艺术形式，成为维系族群的情感纽带，更是族群认同的内在基因和文化符号。但随着社会文化交流的加深和交通的发展，四川省阿坝州逐渐摆脱原有的封闭状态，外来文化的冲击导致阿尔麦多声部民歌赖以生存的农耕时代逐渐走向没落。再加之现在健在的会唱民歌的老艺人越来越少，年轻一代不愿学习，多声部民歌传承处于高度濒危状态，亟待抢救性保护。

As traditional music, *Multi-voice Songs of Almai* was selected into the fourth batch of the intangible cultural heritage of China in 2014. It prevails in Heishui County, Songpan County and Maoxian County, Sichuan Province. It is mainly inherited through word of mouth.

Multi-voice Songs of Almai is the emotional ties and cultural genes of this special ethnic group. Almai people are a special ethnic group living in the mountains of the "Tibetan and Qiang corridor" in Western Sichuan. Their language, mode of life and cultural customs are different from other Tibetan and Qiang ethnic groups. They live in three different areas adjacent to each other, but they all use the ancient Qiang language when singing *Multi-voice Songs of Almai* which is handed down from generation to generation in the ancient and simple musical language. It is the special artistic form bred by their geographical environment and multi-cultural integration. It is also the emotional ties that maintain the ethnic groups, and internal genes and cultural symbols of ethnic identity. However, with the deepening of social and cultural exchanges and the development of convenient transportation, Aba Prefecture of Sichuan Province has gradually got rid of the original closed state. The impact of foreign culture has led to the decline of the farming era which *Multi-voice Songs of Almai* relies on. In addition, with the decrease of old singers and the lack of interests in young people, the inheritance of *Multi-voice Songs of Almai* is in a highly endangered state. Therefore, rescue protection is urgently needed.

130. 洞经音乐（邛都洞经音乐） *Dongjing Chant of Qiongdu*

洞经音乐（邛都洞经音乐），传统音乐，2014 年入选国家级第四批非物质文化遗产名录，主要分布在四川省西昌市，传承方式主要为口传心授，现有国家级传承人韩定生。

洞经音乐渊源于道教音乐，并受到佛教音乐、宫廷音乐和民间音乐的影响，是中国特有的文人雅集型音乐。洞经音乐以文昌文化为载体，通过音乐来宣扬儒家经典，教化人民敬天畏地，忠于国、孝于亲、和于人。邛都洞经古乐以其悠久的历史和多元的文化特征，被音乐界认为它在人类学、语言学、民俗学、中外文化交流史等学术研究方面同样有很高的价值。可是，一旦离开具体的"口传"，洞经就将变为"天书"，无法解读。尤其近代以来，社会剧变，洞经主要依托的文化环境消失，洞经音乐急速衰退，面临着消亡的危机，抢救性保护迫在眉睫。

As traditional music, *Dongjing Chant of Qiongdu* was selected into the fourth batch of the intangible cultural heritage of China in 2014. It prevails in Xichang City, Sichuan Province, and it is mainly inherited through word of mouth. At present, there exists 1 national inheritor Han Dingsheng.

Originated from Taoist music and influenced by Buddhist music, court music and folk music, *Dongjing Chant of Qiongdu* is unique refined music of literati in China. It takes Wenchang culture as its carrier, and promotes confucian classics through music. It aims at educating the people to respect heaven and earth, be loyal to the country, be filial to their relatives, and be friendly to others. However, once without oral interpretation, it is too difficult to understand. Especially since modern times, the society has changed dramatically, the cultural environment that *Dongjing Chant of Qiongdu* mainly relies on disappears. *Dongjing Chant of Qiongdu* declines rapidly and faces the crisis of extinction. Therefore, rescue protection is urgently needed.

131. 堆谐（甘孜踢踏） *Tap Dance of Ganzi Prefecture*

堆谐（甘孜踢踏），传统舞蹈，2014 年入选国家级第四批非物质文化遗产名录，主要分布在四川省甘孜县，主要传承方式为师徒传承，现有国家级传承人陈邦文。

甘孜是康藏高原上踢踏舞之乡，甘孜踢踏保留了民间舞蹈传统而自成一派，其舞步充满了跳跃性，活泼而欢快，音乐也多运用传统的藏族民间音乐，形式不拘一格，舞蹈形式非常自由，是甘孜人民文化生活中不可或缺的重要内容之一，充分展示了甘孜人民热情洋溢的情怀和积极向上的气质。但随着现代社会生活和习俗的改变，越来越少的年轻人喜欢甘孜踢踏并愿意将其发扬光大，亟须采取措施对其进行传承和保护。

As traditional dance, *Tap Dance of Ganzi Prefecture* was selected into the fourth batch of the intangible cultural heritage of China in 2014. It prevails in Ganzi Tibetan Autonomous Prefecture in Sichuan Province, which is mainly inherited between masters and apprentices. At present, there exists 1 national inheritor: Chen Bangwen.

Ganzi Prefecture is the hometown of *Tap Dance of Ganzi Prefecture* on Tibetan plateau. *Tap dance of Ganzi Prefecture* retains the folk-dance tradition and forms of its school with traditional Tibetan folk music, which is very freestyle and becomes one of the indispensable parts in the cultural life of people in Ganzi, reflecting their enthusiastic feelings and upward temperament. However, with the changes modern social life and customs, few people are interested in it and willing to carry it forward. Therefore, effective measures should be taken to protect it immediately.

132. 木偶戏（中型杖头木偶戏）　*Middle-sized Puppet Show*

木偶戏（中型杖头木偶戏），传统戏剧，2014 年入选国家级第四批非物质文化遗产名录，主要分布在四川省资中县，现有国家级传承人胡海。

中型杖头木偶戏通过独特而传统的表演技艺，将木偶呆滞愚钝的神态变得灵巧传神，为其注入生命力和艺术感染力。作为资中县的文化名片，中型杖头木偶在传播资中文化、传承艺术技艺、丰富群众文化生活方面极具有重要价值，是资中县民间传统艺术的瑰宝。但随着现代社会的发展，木偶戏的生存空间不断缩小，再加之老一辈艺人年事已高、年轻人不愿从事此项技艺，中型杖头木偶戏已经到了濒临灭绝的地步，亟须采取措施对其进行传承和保护。

As a traditional drama, *Middle-sized Puppet Show* was selected into the fourth batch of the intangible cultural heritage of China in 2014. It prevails in Zizhong County, Sichuan Province. At present, there exists 1 national inheritor: Hu Hai.

The unique and traditional performing skills of *Middle-sized Puppet Show* make the puppet's dull expression become dexterous and vivid and also inject vitality and artistic appeal into it. As the cultural card of Zizhong County, the medium-sized puppet show is of great value in spreading Zizhong culture, inheriting art skills and enriching people's cultural life. It is a treasure of folk traditional art in Zizhong County. However, with the development of modern society, the living space of *Middle-sized Puppet Show* is shrinking. In addition, due to the aging of old artists and the lack of interest of young people, *Middle-sized Puppet Show* is on the verge in extinction. Therefore, effective measures should be taken to protect it.

133. 阳戏（射箭提阳戏）　*Nuo Play of Shejian Town*

阳戏（射箭提阳戏），传统戏剧，2014 年入选国家级第四批非物质文化遗产名录，主要分布在四川省广元市。

射箭提阳戏历史悠久，由人和木偶同台演出，其演出形式十分独特。射箭提阳戏是宗教与艺术相结合的原始古朴的戏剧形式，是目前中国保存最完整、传承最正宗、内容最丰富的傩戏品种，堪称中国傩戏的"活化石"，具有独特的学术价值和实用价值，一直得到国内外专家的高度关注。但随着现代社会的发展，射箭提阳戏的生存空间不断缩小，加之老一辈艺人年事已高、年轻人不愿从事此项技艺，射箭提阳戏的传承发展面临诸多挑战，急需采取必要措施对其加以传承和保护。

As a traditional drama, *Nuo Play of Shejian Town* was selected into the fourth batch of the intangible cultural heritage of China in 2014. It prevails in Guangyuan City, Sichuan Province.

Nuo Play of Shejian Town has a long history, which is performed by people and puppets on the same stage. Its performance form is very unique. *Nuo Play of Shejian Town* is a primitive and simple drama form combining religion and art. It is the most complete, authentic and rich Nuo Play in China which is regarded as the "living fossil" of Chinese Nuo Play. It has unique academic value and practical value, and has been highly concerned by experts at home and abroad. However, with the development of modern society, the living space of Nuoplay is shirnking. In addition, due to the aging of artists and the lack of interests in young people, its inheritance and development face many challenges. Therefore, effective measures should be taken to protect it.

134. 竹编（道明竹编）　*Bamboo Weaving of Daoming Town*

竹编（道明竹编），传统美术，2014 年入选国家级第四批非物质文化遗产名录，主要分布在四川省崇州市道明镇，现有国家级传承人赵思进。

道明竹编距今已有 300 多年的编织历史，其花色品种繁多，造型别致，精巧细腻，经久耐用，具有较强的实用性和观赏性，具有生活和工艺品的双重价值。但由于道明竹编属于纯手工操作，编织耗时耗神，生产成本高，经济效益低，大量艺人鉴于生存压力被迫转行，同时学习技艺的年轻人也越来越少，竹编业人才十分匮乏，其传承与发展前景令人担忧，亟须善筹长策，积极应对。

As a traditional skill, *Bamboo Weaving of Daoming Town* was selected into the fourth batch of the intangible cultural heritage of China in 2014. It prevails in Daoming Town, Chongzhou City, Sichuan Province. At present, there exists 1 national inheritor: Zhao Sijin.

Bamboo Weaving of Daoming Town has a history of more than 300 years, and it has the dual value of life and handicraft for its wide variety of colors, unique shape, exquisite craftsmanship, durability, and strong practicability and ornamental features. However, due to the fact that *Bamboo Weaving of Daoming Town* is purely hand-made and it is time and energy-consuming, high cost and low economic benefits, a large number of artists are forced to change careers in face of the survival pressure. At the same time, few young people are willing to learn bamboo weaving skills. Its inheritance and development prospects are worrisome. Therefore, effective measures should be taken to protect it.

135. 地毯织造技艺（阆中丝毯织造技艺）

Silk Carpet Weaving Techniques of Langzhong City

地毯织造技艺（阆中丝毯织造技艺），传统技艺，2014 年入选国家级第四批非物质文化遗产名录，主要分布在四川省阆中市。

四川阆中完整地保留了传统丝毯编织全流程技艺，一些在国内外早已消失的绝技在这里得以良好传承，如让平面的图案呈现浮雕感的"片剪饰花"绝技以及"每作百幅而无一尽同"的"织活图"绝技。阆中丝毯织造技艺因其工艺复杂，手工精细，质地优良，被国外专家誉为"东方软浮雕"，片剪技工被誉为"片剪皇后"。丝毯图案古朴典雅，构图严谨，造型活泼新颖，具有较高的艺术、历史研究价值。但由于阆中丝毯织造技艺对原料讲究，又因全用手工，耗时极长，精细度极高，产量一直较低，无法做到市场性大规模量售，购买者有限，加之熟练手艺人稀少，项目生存困难，技艺亟待进一步抢救性保护。

As a traditional skill, *Silk Carpet Weaving Techniques of Langzhong City* was selected into the fourth batch of the intangible cultural heritage of China in 2014. It prevails in Langzhong City and its surrounding areas, Sichuan Province.

Langzhong of Sichuan province has completely retained the whole process of traditional silk carpet weaving. Some unique skills that have long disappeared at home and abroad have been well inherited here, such as the unique skill of "cutting and decorating flowers" which makes the plane patterns present the relief feeling, and the unique skill of "weaving mobile-picture" which makes silk carpet completely different from each other. It is known as "Oriental soft relief" by foreign experts because of its complex technology, fine craftsmanship and excellent texture. Silk carpet weaving craftsman of Langzhong city is also known as the "Queen of silk carpet weaving". The pattern of the silk carpet is simple and elegant, the composition rigorous, and the shape lively and novel. It has high artistic and historical research value. However, due to its special and picky requirements to raw materials, hand-made and time-consuming nature, high degree of fineness and low output, the buyers are scarce. In addition, because of the decreasing of skilled craftsmen, its survival is facing a crisis. Therefore, further rescue protection is urgently needed.

136. 酱油酿造技艺（先市酱油酿造技艺）

Soy Sauce Fermenting Techniques of Xianshi Town

酱油酿造技艺（先市酱油酿造技艺），传统技艺，2014 年入选国家级第四批非物质文化遗产名录，主要分布在四川省合江县，现有国家级传承人陈思维。

先市酱油酿造技艺历史悠久，始于汉，兴于唐，盛于清。先市酱油风味独特，具有"酱香浓郁，色泽棕红，体态澄清，味道鲜美，挂碗不沾碗，久储不变质"的优良品质，被誉为"中国酱油传统酿造的活化石"，是珍贵的文化遗产。但由于在全球化、工业化、现代化的大环境下，面临新工艺、新技术垄断市场，"效益至上"观念影响下而产生的酱油勾兑制作方式的威胁，以及传承人员的断代，先市酱油酿造技艺受到强烈的冲击，处于高度濒危状态，亟待抢救和保护。

As a traditional skill, *Soy Sauce Fermenting Techniques of Xianshi Town* was selected into the fourth batch of the intangible cultural heritage of China in 2014. It prevails in Hejiang County, Sichuan Province. At present, there exists 1 national inheritor: Chen Siwei.

Soy Sauce Fermenting Techniques of Xianshi Town has a long history, which began in the Han Dynasty, developed in the Tang Dynasty and flourished in Qing Dynasty. Soy sauce of Hejiang Town has a unique flavor and excellent quality. It is characterized by strong flavor, rich red color, pure and delicious taste and long-term storage without deterioration. It is regarded as the "living fossil of traditional Chinese soy sauce fermenting techniques" and precious cultural heritage. However, under the environment of globalization, industrialization and modernization, it faces the threat of monopolizing the market with new skills and new technologies. "The soy sauce blending craftmanship produced urder the influence of "Profit-oriented" concept poses a threat to *Soy sauce Fermenting Techniques of Xianshi Town*. The lack of inheritors brings strong impacts to *Soy Sauce Fermenting Techniques of Xianshi Town*. It is in a highly endangered state. Therefore, rescue protection is badly needed.

137. 传统棉纺织技艺（傈僳族火草织布技艺） *Hemp Weaving Techniques of Lisu People*

传统棉纺织技艺（傈僳族火草织布技艺），传统技艺，2014 年入选国家级第四批非物质文化遗产名录，主要分布在四川省凉山州德昌县地区，现有国家级传承人李从会。

传统火草织布技艺历史久远，是傈僳族人在长期的生产生活实践中利用自然的伟大成果，是傈僳族文明的重要组成部分。相传远古时代，傈僳族青年为蔽体御寒以荨麻、火草织成麻布长衫替代简陋的兽皮衣服。傈僳族火草织布技艺，全靠手工完成，程序繁多，工艺考究，难度大，周期长，具有重要的工艺和经济价值。但随着工业化进程的加快，各种新型服装面料涌入市场，现代纺织品代替了手工织品，给传统手工纺织技艺造成了很大的冲击，导致手工纺织的市场需求减少，手工织布专业户骤减，而年轻人又不愿意继承传统的手工纺织技艺，傈僳族火草织布技艺正濒临灭绝，亟须引起关注。

As a traditional skill, *Hemp Weaving Techniques of Lisu People* was selected into the fourth batch of the intangible cultural heritage of China in 2014. It prevails in Dechang County, Sichuan Province. At present, there exists 1 national inheritor: Li Conghui.

Hemp Weaving Technique of Lisu People is a great achievement of Lisu People using nature in their long-term production and living practice, being an important part of Lisu civilization, and has a long history. It is said that in ancient times, Lisu youngsters used nettle and hemp fiber to weave linen clothes instead of simple animal skin clothes. It is completely hand-made and has a variety of procedures, exquisite technology and a long producing cycle. Therefore, it has important technological and economic value. However, with the acceleration of industrialization, all kinds of new clothing fabrics have poured into the market and modern textiles have replaced hand weaving, which has caused a great impact on the traditional manual textile technology and a decrease in the market demand for manual weaving. In addition, with a sharp decrease in the number of manual weaving professionals and young people's lack of interest, *Hemp Weaving Technique of Lisu People* is on the verge of extinction. Therefore, special attention should be paid to it.

138. 民间信俗（康定转山会） *Folk Belief and Custom*

民间信俗（康定转山会），民俗，2014 年入选国家级第四批非物质文化遗产名录，主要分布在四川省康定县。

康定转山会源自为佛祖沐浴的祭祀庆典活动。每年农历四月初八的浴佛节，传说是佛祖释迦牟尼的诞辰，四川康定地区藏族人民会举办转山会。其与藏族历史、环境、经济、文化、习俗、宗教等密切相关，并且经过历史的变迁与演变，如今更多地融汇了踏青游览的内容，同时增添了物资交流、文艺演出等，有重要的文化研究价值与经济价值。但因外来文化冲击，传承人年事已高，年轻人对传统文化的兴趣缺失，康定转山会的生存和发展面临危机，亟待进一步抢救性保护。

As a folk custom, *Folk Belief and Custom　（Zhuan-shan Festival of Kangding City）* was selected into the fourth batch of the intangible cultural heritage of China in 2014. It prevails in Kangding County and its surrounding areas, Sichuan Province.

Zhuan-shan Festival of Kangding City originated from the sacrificial ceremony of Buddha Bathing. The Buddha Bathing Festival falls on the eighth day of the fourth lunar month every year which is Sakyamuni's birthday according to legend. Tibetan people in Kangding area of Sichuan Province hold *Zhuan-shan Festival* to celebrate Buddha's birthday. It is closely related to Tibetan history, environment, economy, culture, customs, religion etc. After historical change and evolution, *Zhuan-shan Festival of Kangding City* has integrated spring outing, goods exchange, artistic performance and other new contents. It has important cultural research value and economic value. However, due to the impact of foreign culture, the aging of inheritors and the lack of interest of young people in traditional culture, the survival and development of *Zhuan-shan Festival of Kangding City* is in crisis. Therefore, further rescue protection is urgently needed.

139. 祭祖习俗（凉山彝族尼木措毕祭祀）

Ancestor Worship of Yi People

祭祖习俗（凉山彝族尼木措毕祭祀），民俗，2014 年入选国家级第四批非物质文化遗产名录，主要分布在四川省凉山州美姑县。

彝俗行火葬，自古亦然，而凉山彝族尼木措毕祭祀是彝族火葬与送灵文化的具体体现。在"人死归祖"观念影响下，尼木措毕仪式展现了凉山彝族遵循古礼、恪守祖制的社会规范，深蕴着极其悠远而深长的"人死归祖"的文化情结与落叶归根的民族心性，是彝族传统社会实践和民俗生活的集中表现，包含着彝族人民的生活环境、宗教信仰、心理状态、思想感情等，成为当地民俗生活传统的重要内容，对于历史学、民俗学、宗教学等的研究具有极高的价值。但由于外来文化的冲击，加之现有传承人毕摩年事已高，年轻一代对传统文化缺少兴趣，凉山彝族尼木措毕祭祀的生存和发展面临危机，亟待进一步抢救性保护。

As a folk custom, *Ancestor Worship of Yi People* was selected into the fourth batch of the intangible cultural heritage of China in 2014. It prevails in Meigu County, Liangshan Yi Autonomous Prefecture, Sichuan

Province.

Since ancient times, Yi people adopted cremation. *Ancestor Worship of Yi People* is the concrete embodiment of the cremation and spirit sending culture of Yi people. Under the influence of the concept of "people returning to their ancestors after death", *Ancestor Worship of Yi People* shows the social norms of the Yi people in Liangshan Prefecture to follow the ancient rites and strictly abide by the patriarchal system. It contains a very profound cultural complex of returning to the ancestors after death and the national spirit of returning to their roots. It is the concentrated expression of the traditional social practice and folk life of the Yi people, which is closely related to the living environment, religion, belief, psychological state and ideological feelings of the Yi people. It has become an important part of folk life tradition in mountainous society. It is of great value to history, folklore and religion. However, due to the impact of foreign culture, the aging of current inheritor and young people's lack of interest, its survival and development are facing a crisis. Therefore, further rescue protection is urgently needed.

140. 端公戏（旺苍端公戏） *Duan-gong Opera of Wangcang*

端公戏（旺苍端公戏），传统戏剧，2021 年入选国家级第五批非物质文化遗产名录。主要分布地区为四川省北部米仓山南麓旺苍县境内及陕南山区。

旺苍端公戏属于傩戏的一种，以巫师歌舞戏剧为载体，内容涵盖汉族原始宗教、民情民俗、文学艺术等，集文学、音乐、舞蹈、戏剧、绘画、书法、雕刻、剪纸于一体，表现形式丰富多样，艺术感染力强烈。旺苍端公戏是承载川北人情、生活习性的重要载体，对研究川北发展史、文化史具有极其重要的意义。但由于历史原因影响，旺苍端公戏被少数人视为"封建迷信活动",这在一定程度上压制了它的发展，如今能表演该戏剧的人越来越少，旺苍端公戏高度濒危，亟待抢救和保护。

As a traditional drama, *Duan-gong Opera of Wangcang* was selected into the fifth batch of intangible cultural heritage of China in 2021, which mainly prevails in the southern foot of Micang Mountain, Wangchang County, northern Sichuan Province as well as in the southern mountain areas of Shaanxi Province.

As one kind of Nuo Play, *Duan-gong Opera of Wangcang* owns typical features of the wizard drama, covering primitive religion, folk customs, literature and art of Han nationality. With various forms of literature, music, dance, play, painting, calligraphy, carving as well as paper cutting, it is equipped with rich artistic appeal, having valuable meaning for studies and researches about the development history and cultural history of North Sichuan Province. However, due to the historical reasons, it was once regarded as feudal superstition, which has greatly hindered its inheritance and development. Nowadays, there are fewer and fewer people who can perform this drama. The *Duan-gong Opera of Wangcang* is facing high endangerment and urgently needs rescue and protection.

141. 藏棋 *Tibetan Chess*

藏棋，又称传统体育、游艺与杂技，2021年入选国家级第五批非物质文化遗产名录。主要分布地区为四川省阿坝藏族羌族自治州的藏族聚集区。

藏棋在藏语中称"密芒"，意思为"多眼棋"。藏棋起源于西藏苯教时期，传说已有3000多年的历史，其道理常运用于军事和民间体育活动。在藏族聚集区，无论是达官贵人还是牧民僧人，随时随地都可以进行棋赛，藏棋成为一种男女老少咸宜的竞技游戏。然而，随着时代发展，原本藏族聚集区相对封闭的生产生活方式快速地变迁，业余时间的休闲娱乐生活得到极大的丰富，日渐压榨藏棋的生存空间，对其进行传承与保护迫在眉睫。

As traditional sports, entertainment and acrobatics, *Tibetan Chess* was selected into the fifth batch of intangible cultural heritage of China in 2021. It mainly prevails in the Tibetan gathering area of Aba Tibetan and Qiang Autonomous Prefecture in Sichuan Province.

Tibetan Chess is called "Mimang" in Tibetan language, which means "Multi-eyed chess". It originated in the period of Bon Religion in Tibet, owing a history of more than 3,000 years, whose principles are often applied to military and civilian sports activities. Now it is popular among all people in Tibetan areas, and the match could be played anytime and anywhere. However, with the modernization of society, due to the great enrichment of leisure time and entertainment means, the traditional life style in Tibetan area is changing rapidly, gradually shrinking its living space. Therefore, the inheritance and protection is badly needed.

142. 青城武术　*Qingcheng Martial Arts*

青城武术，传统体育、游艺与杂技，2021 年入选国家级第五批非物质文化遗产名录。主要分布地区为四川省成都市都江堰市青城山。

有近两千年历史的青城武术，属于中国古代武术四大门派之一。其动作轻灵飘逸，小手连环，擅吐纳养生，重自卫防身，尤以玄门太极和剑术见长。但由于武术学习难度大，对学习者身体素质与精神毅力要求较高，这在一定程度上压制了它的传承与发展，青城武术的生存空间越来越小，亟待抢救和保护。

As traditional sports, entertainment and acrobatics, *Qingcheng Martial Arts* was selected into the fifth batch of intangible cultural heritage of China in 2021. It mainly prevails in Qingcheng Mountain of Dujiangyan City, Sichuan Province.

With a history of nearly two thousand years, *Qingcheng Martial Arts* belongs to one of the four schools of ancient Chinese martial arts. Being skilled in deep breathing so as to help keep good health and emphasize in self-defense, it is light and elegant in movements, wish most famous ones as Xuanmen Taichi and swordsmanship. However, its inheritance and development has greatly suppressed due to the difficulties in learning as well as the high requirements in physical quality and mental perseverance. The living space has been gradually shrinking. Therefore, effective protection is urgently needed.

143. 滑竿（华蓥山滑竿抬幺妹） *Slide of Huaying Mountain*

滑竿（华蓥山滑竿抬幺妹），传统体育、游艺与杂技，2021 年入选国家级第五批非物质文化遗产名录。主要分布地区为四川省广安市一带。

华蓥山滑竿抬幺妹始于唐宋时期，而"幺妹"是农耕时期对农家小妹的俗称，过去因华蓥山坡陡林密，道路崎岖，滑竿是人们常见的出行代步工具，每年农历三月初九（观音菩萨生日）期间华蓥上还会举行滑竿抬幺妹、祈求五谷丰朝山仪式。如今，华蓥山滑竿抬幺妹已成为华蓥山地区特有的民俗文体活动，并打造出以"幺妹文化"为特色的独特文化品牌，深受大众喜爱与好评。但随着时间的推移，老一辈的轿夫和幺妹们渐渐老去，传承人数量不断减少，该项目面临着高度濒危，亟待抢救和保护。

As traditional sports, entertainment and acrobatics, *Slide of Huaying*

Mountain was selected into the fifth batch of intangible cultural heritage of China in 2021. It mainly prevails in Guang'an City, Sichuan Province.

Slide of Huaying Mountain began in the Tang and Song dynasties, and "youngest sister" is a common name for young females of one family in the farming period. In the past, due to the steep slopes and rugged roads, slides became common travel tools at Huaying mountain. At the ninth day of the third lunar month every year, the birthday of Guanyin Bodhisattva, this ceremony would be held to pray for harvest of the coming year. Nowadays, *Slide of Huaying Mountain* has become the unique folk sports activities and cultural brand in Huaying Mountain, being loved and praised by the public. However, there have emerged development obstacles and market challenges for *Slide of Huaying Mountain*, as well as the aging of the old generation and decreasing of inheritors, gradually shrinking its living space. Therefore, the inheritance and protection is badly needed.

144. 藤编（怀远藤编）　*Rattan Weaving of Huaiyuan County*

藤编（怀远藤编），传统美术，2021 年入选国家级第五批非物质文化遗产名录，主要分布在四川省成都市崇州市一带。

怀远藤编起源于三国时期，至今已有千余年的历史。制品色泽素雅、光洁凉爽、轻巧灵便，是四川地区独特的传统手工艺品。怀远藤编密实、坚固、轻盈，加之古雅自然的创意，具有很强的实用性和艺术性。但由于怀远藤编附加值不高，技艺要求十分严格，年轻人多不愿学习，其传承越来越困难，如不及时加以抢救保护，将逐渐从人们的生活中消失。

As traditional art, *Rattan Weaving of Huaiyuan County* was selected into the fifth batch of intangible cultural heritage of China in 2021. It mainly prevails in Chongzhou City, Sichuan Province.

Rattan Weaving of Huaiyuan County originated in the Three Kingdoms Period, having a history of more than one thousand years. It is a unique traditional handicraft in Sichuan Province with peculiar and fine craftsmanship. Its products are simple and elegant in color, cool and convenient in using. With the dense, solid and light features, as well as the quaint and natural activities, *Rattan Weaving of Huaiyuan County* has strong practicability and artistry. However, due to its low added value and strict technical requirements and the reluctance of young people to learn the skill, its inheritance is becoming more and more difficult. If it is not rescued and protected in time, it will gradually disappear from people's life.

145. 彝族刺绣（凉山彝族刺绣）

Embroidery of Yi People in Liangshan Prefecture

彝族刺绣（凉山彝族刺绣），传统美术，2021 年入选国家级第五批非物质文化遗产名录，主要分布地区为四川等地彝民族聚居区。

凉山彝族刺绣，种类繁多、丰富多姿、制作精美、异彩纷呈，是彝族传统文化的一种体现，是彝族服饰中不可缺少的部分。彝族刺绣一般都是以黑色和天蓝色做底色，充分展示了人与自然和谐的服饰生态文化，反映出彝族民众对自然的崇敬尊重和对美好生活的向往。然而，如今的彝族刺绣面临发展的瓶颈与市场的挑战，不仅传承人数量不断减少，另外还有旅游业快速发展的影响，日渐压榨其生存空间，对其进行传承与保护迫在眉睫。

As a traditional art, *Embroidery of Yi People in Liangshan Prefecture* was selected into the fifth batch of intangible cultural heritage of China in 2021. It mainly prevails in some gathering areas of Yi People in Sichuan Province.

Embroidery of Yi people in Liangshan is various in style and color, and exquisite in making. It is a manifestation of the traditional Yi culture, being indispensable part of their clothing. Mostly, it takes black and sky blue as the background colors, showing the ecological culture of harmony between man and nature of Yi people, as well as their longings for better lives. However, nowadays there have emerged development obstacles and market challenges for *Embroidery of Yi People in Liangshan Prefecture*, as well as the decreasing of inheritors and influence of tourism, gradually shrinking its living space. Therefore, the inheritance and protection is badly needed.

146. 川菜烹饪技艺 *Cooking Techniques of Sichuan Cuisine*

川菜烹饪技艺，传统技艺，2021年入选国家级第五批非物质文化遗产名录，主要分布在四川省各地区。

川菜是中国汉族传统的四大菜系之一、中国八大菜系之一、中华料理集大成者。川菜烹饪技艺综合炒、滑、熘、爆、煸、炸、煮、煨等传统烹饪技艺，尤为小煎、小炒、干煸和干烧擅长且独具特色。川菜烹饪在"炒"的方面有其独到之处。它的很多菜式都采用"小炒"的方法，特点是时间短、火候急、汁水少、口味鲜嫩，合乎营养卫生要求。菜肴烹饪看似简单，实际上包含着高度的科学性、技术性和艺术性，显示出劳动人民的无穷智慧和创造能力。但随着时代发展，年轻人追求口味的创新与多变的影响下，川菜烹饪技艺需要在烹饪原材料与菜品研制方面不断进行求新，其传承面临传统与创新的博弈，需要在传承中进行保护。

As traditional skills, *Cooking Techniques of Sichuan Cuisine* was selected into the fifth batch of intangible cultural heritage of China in

2021. It mainly prevails in Sichuan Province.

Being one of the four traditional Han Chinese cuisines and the eight traditional Chinese cuisines, Sichuan cuisine has integrated various kinds of traditional cooking techniques, like frying, boiling, simmering etc., with quick-fry, stir-fry and dry roast as its unique characteristics. Most dishes in Sichuan cuisine prefer to use the technique of "stir-fry", which is characterized by short time, urgent heat, little juice, fresh and tender taste, in line with the requirements of nutrition and health. Sichuan cuisine seems simple, but in fact it contains a high degree of scientific, technical and artistic, showing the infinite wisdom and creative ability of the working people. However, with the advancement of time and society, young people would like to pursue innovation and change of taste constantly, which has set high requirements on the materials and dishes. Thus, the inheritance of *Cooking Techniques of Sichuan Cuisine* is facing the battle between tradition and innovation, and it needs to be preserved in the inheritance.

147. 彝族传统建筑营造技艺 （凉山彝族传统民居营造技艺）

Traditional Building Techniques of Yi People in Liangshan Prefecture

彝族传统建筑营造技艺（凉山彝族传统民居营造技艺），传统技艺，2021 年入选国家级第五批非物质文化遗产名录，主要分布在四川省凉山彝族自治州。

彝族传统建筑以石土墙与木构架共同出现的榫卯连接为基本建筑特点，在挡风防御、透光排烟的同时，具备族祖灵崇拜的精神意义。彝族传统建筑主要依山而建，遵循地理环境的变化，充分利用地形的高低差异来调整建筑，布局较为灵活，并与水域形成紧密的联系，形成天人相亲的生态伦理观念，体现了彝族人民敬畏自然、信仰自然、万物平等、人与自然和谐相处等观念。但随着社会的发展，原来相对封闭的农耕文明不断受到现代文明的冲击，四川凉山现存仅有两个村落（四季吉村与古拖村）中还保留着彝族传统建筑，再加之彝族聚集区能熟练掌握传统建筑营造技艺的匠人已经不多，古老的彝族传统建筑营造技艺濒临失传，亟待抢救保护。

As traditional skills, *Traditional Building Techniques of Yi People in Liangshan Prefecture* was selected into the fifth batch of intangible cultural heritage of China in 2021. It mainly prevails in Liangshan Yi Autonomous Prefecture, Sichuan Province.

Traditional Building Techniques of Yi People is basically featured by mortise and tenon joints appearing in both stone walls and wood frames in Yi architecture. Beside shielding, defending, transmitting, and exhausting, it also has the spiritual meaning of worshiping the ancestors of the ethnic group. The traditional buildings of the Yi people are mainly built on the mountains, following the changes of the geographical environment, making full use of the height difference of the topography, being flexible in layout and close with the water, which shows the ethical concepts of Yi people, such as the respect and belief in nature, equality in all, and harmony between man and nature. However, with the development of society, the original farming civilization has been constantly impacted by modern civilization. Even in Liangshan prefecture, only two villages (Sijiji village and Gutuo village) still retain traditional Yi buildings. In addition, the number of skilled workers is shrinking rapidly, which endangers the existence and development of building techniques. Therefore, it is urgent to rescue and protect

Traditional Building Techniques of Yi People in Liangshan Prefecture.

148. 龙舞（安仁板凳龙）　*Bench-dragon Dance of Anren County*

龙舞（安仁板凳龙），传统舞蹈，2021 年入选国家级第五批非物质文化遗产名录，主要分布在四川省达州市一带。

安仁板凳龙是以板凳为道具的一种地方传统舞蹈，是"湖广填四川"时湖南籍移民引入的，至今已有 300 多年的历史。安仁板凳龙工艺原始，形状古朴，演出方式灵活，可单龙独舞，也可多龙共舞。演出场地不受局限，可在乡村院坝进行，也可在街头、广场、舞台演出。舞龙的人随着激昂的锣鼓声，舞动板凳，翻滚腾越矫健洒脱，充满阳刚之美，很受广大人民群众喜爱。但随着社会生产方式的变化和传统习俗的消失，近年来在现代文明冲击下安仁板凳龙面临生存危机，亟须抢救。

As a traditional dance, *Bench-dragon Dance of Anren County* was selected into the fifth batch of intangible cultural heritage of China in 2021. It mainly prevails in Dazhou City, Sichuan Province.

With the bench as its property *Bench-dragon Dance of Anren County* was introduced by immigrants from Hunan Province during Qing dynasty, having a history of more than 300 years. It is primitive in craftsmanship, simple in shape, and flexible in performances, which could be played either singly or in group, with little limitation about the performance venue. It could be in a rural courtyard, or on the street, square and stage. During performance, the performers would dance the bench together with the passionate sound of gongs and drums, full of masculine beauty, which makes the dance very popular among the people. However, with the change of time and society, the disappearance of traditional custom and the impact of modern civilization made *Bench-dragon Dance of Anren*

County facing a survival crisis in recent years. Therefore, it is in urgent need of rescue.

149. 藏族唐卡（郎卡杰唐卡） *Langkaj Thangka*

藏族唐卡（郎卡杰唐卡），传统美术，2021 年入选第五批国家级非物质文化遗产名录。分布区域主要在四川省甘孜藏族自治州。其传承方式为师徒传承。

郎卡杰唐卡指的是以唐卡画师郎卡杰绘画风格为特色的唐卡艺术。400 多年前誉为"神变画师"的郎卡杰所开创的画风，集众家之长，技艺精细绝妙，成为整个川西藏区最具标准性的风格，并被后来的画师们传承。其嫡传弟子进一步继承和吸收了郎卡杰的绘画风格，至今已经传至第十二代，使郎卡杰唐卡画派的绘画艺术得到了稳固传承和发扬光大，是甘孜州最为古老，传承最为久远的唐卡画派。但与所有唐卡艺术一样，郎卡杰唐卡因其传统天然颜料的制作方法和使用技法纷繁复杂，以及其考究的技艺和口耳相传的传承方式，传承与维系难度较高。再加之近年来，以价格低廉的现代合成颜料替代传统颜料对其产生巨大冲击，现如今郎卡杰唐卡面临着失传的危险，亟需保护和抢救。

As a traditional art, *Langkaj Thangka* was selected into the fifth batch of intangible cultural heritage of China in 2021. It mainly prevails in Ganzi Tibetan Autonomous Prefecture, Sichuan Province, whose inheritance method is from masters to apprentices.

Langkaj Thangka refers to the thangka characterized by the style of Thangka painter Langkaj who was well-known for his magical painting skills 400 years ago. Then it had also derived good points and qualities from others, becoming the most standard style in the Tibetan area of western Sichuan Province, and its exquisite craftsmanship was passed down by later painters. Langkaj's apprentices has further inherited and absorbed his painting style. Up to now, it has been passed down to the 12th generation, which has steadily inherited and carried forward the painting art. *Langkaj Thangka* is regardes as the oldest Thangka school in Ganzi prefecture. However, like all the other thangka, due to the complexity of the production and use of traditional natural pigments as well as the exquisite skills and oral inheritance, it is difficult to inherit and maintain *Langkaj Thangka*. In addition, in recent years, the replacement of traditional pigments with cheap modern synthetic pigments has had a huge impact on it. Now *Langkaj Thangka* is facing the danger of being lost, and it is in urgent need of protection and rescue.

150. 酿造技艺（保宁醋传统酿造工艺）

Brewing Techniques of Baoning Vinegar

保宁醋传统酿造工艺，传统技艺，2021 年入选国家级第五批非物质文化遗产名录，主要分布地区在四川省南充市一带。

保宁醋传统酿造工艺起源于公元 936 年，距今已有千余年历史，其工艺的核心是中药制曲、麦麸酿醋。保宁醋通过 42 道工序酿制而成，具有色泽红棕、酸味柔和、醇香回甜、久存不腐的特点，深受消费者喜爱。但由于保宁醋传统酿造技艺传承人的保护、管理和培养都存在一定难度，亟须采取具体措施进行保护。

As traditional skills, *Brewing Techniques of Baoning Vinegar* was selected into the fifth batch of intangible cultural heritage of China in 2021. It mainly prevails in Nanchong City, Sichuan Province.

Brewing Techniques of Baoning Vinegar originated in 936 and has a history of more than one thousand years, with the core technology of making yeast with traditional Chinese medicine and brewing vinegar with wheat bran. It is brewed through 42 processes, which equipped it with the characteristics of red-brown color, soft-sour taste, mellow sweet and durability, popular among consumers. However, due to the difficulties in the protection, management and cultivation of inheritors of *Brewing Techniques of Baoning Vinegar*, it is urgent to take specific measures to protect it.

151. 工艺制鞋技艺（唐昌布鞋制作技艺）

Cloth Shoes Making Techniques in Tangchang Town

唐昌布鞋制作技艺，传统技艺，2021 年入选国家级第五批非物质文化遗产名录，主要分布在四川省成都市郫都区。

作为千层底布鞋的一个分支流派和中国南派布鞋的代表，唐昌布鞋距今已有 700 多年历史。唐昌布鞋为纯手工制作，尤其是其中的毛边槽眼布鞋鞋底、鞋帮的基础工序为川西独有，见证了川西地区民俗审美近千年发展变化。唐昌布鞋制作需经过打布壳、裁剪、制帮、烘烤定型等 32 道大工艺和 100 道小工艺，每一道工序都要求极其严格，容不得半点马虎。虽然目前虽仍有人沿袭传统技艺制作唐昌布鞋，但受原材料供给困难的影响，布鞋生产陷于窘境，加上制鞋匠人大都年事已高，年轻人不愿学习，唐昌布鞋制作技艺传承乏人，亟待保护和抢救。

As traditional skills, *Cloth Shoes Making Techniques in Tangchang Town* was selected into the fifth batch of intangible cultural heritage of China in 2021. It mainly prevails in Pidu District, Sichuan Province.

As a branch of multi-layered cloth shoes and a representative of southern China cloth shoes, Tangchang cloth shoes have a history of more than 700 years. It is purely hand-made with some basic making processes being unique to western Sichuan, which has witnessed the development and change of folk aesthetics there. There are in-total 32 stages and 100 procedures from material selection to product making, and every step is extremely strict allowing no sloppiness. At present, although some people still follow the traditional cloth shoes making techniques in Tangchang town, the production is still in a dilemma for the difficult supply of raw materials. In addition, most of the shoemakers are old and young people are not willing to learn it. Therefore, rescue and protection to *Cloth Shoes Making Techniques* is urgently needed.

152. 绿茶制作技艺（蒙山茶传统制作技艺）

Making Techniques of Mengshan Tea

绿茶制作技艺（蒙山茶传统制作技艺），传统技艺，2021 年入选国家级第五批非物质文化遗产名录，主要分布在四川省雅安市。

蒙山茶是中国众多名茶中唯一多品类茶，包含蒙顶甘露、蒙顶黄芽、蒙顶石花、万春银叶、玉叶长春等五种代表性茶品，其中以"红锅杀青，三炒三揉"为技艺核心的"蒙顶甘露"极负盛名。蒙山茶传统制作技艺，主要为采摘、摊凉、杀青、揉捻、三炒三揉、烘焙提香六大步骤。步骤看似简单，可温度高低、手法轻重，全凭制茶人的积累的经验掌握，传统手工炒制技艺严谨、细腻，出品的茶叶呈现色、香、味、形兼具的特质。但随着时代的发展，经济社会水平不断提高，使得人们在茶叶品质、口感上的要求也越来越高，茶叶市场竞争激烈，加之老一辈的制茶大师离世，年轻匠人缺少，技艺传承陷入青黄不接的困境，亟待保护和抢救。

As traditional skills, *Making Techniques of Mengshan Tea* was selected into the fifth batch of intangible cultural heritage of China in 2021. It mainly prevails in Ya'an City, Sichuan Province.

Mengshan Tea is the only multi-category tea among many famous teas in China, having 5 representative branches with different flavors, and it is famous for its unique making techniques. There are mainly 6 steps in *Making Techniques of Mengshan Tea*, and the steps seem simple, but all depending on the experience of the tea makers. The rigorous and delicate traditional making techniques provide the tea with features of color, smell, taste and shape. However, with the continuous development of economic and social economy, people set higher and higher requirements on tea quality and taste, intensifying competition in the tea market. In addition, the inheritance of skills is in a difficult situation due to the passing-away of old masters and lack of young craftsmen. Therefore, rescue and protection to *Making Techniques of Mengshan Tea* is urgently needed.

153. 中医诊疗法（李忠愚杵针疗法）

Pestle Needle Therapy of Li-zhongyu

李忠愚杵针疗法，传统医药，2021年入选国家级第五批非物质文化遗产名录，主要分布在四川省各地区。

杵针疗法起源于明末清初，距今已有300余年的历史，而且目前全球仅有"李仲愚杵针疗法"一支，别无旁系，是中国乃至世界独有的中医诊疗法。李仲愚杵针疗法有"四大工具、五种手法、三大穴位"，是指利用杵针（七曜混元杵、五星三台杵、金刚杵、奎星笔）这一特殊工具，运用点叩、升降、开阖、运转、分理等不同的手法，在针灸常用的腧穴和杵针疗法的特殊穴位（八阵穴、八廓穴、河车路等）上进行治疗的一种方法。虽然有"针"字，但杵针与针灸不同，杵针治疗疾病时，不刺入皮肤肌肉，没有疼痛之苦，也不用担心交叉感染，兼具针灸与推拿的优点。由于李仲愚杵针疗法传统上为家族传承与师徒传承，传承难度较大，虽然现在成都中医药大学已组建李仲愚杵针疗法传承人团队，拓展"师带徒"为主的传承方式，将传承群体扩展成工作室传承人及广大临床工作者，但普及面与力度仍十分有限，需要继续不断被再创造，才能更好地促进技艺的传承与发展。

As traditional skills, *Pestle Needle Therapy of Li-zhongyu* was selected into the fifth batch of intangible cultural heritage of China in 2021. It mainly prevails in Shichuan Province.

Originated in the late Ming and early Qing dynasties, the pestle needle therapy has a history of more than 300 years, and currently *Pestle Needle Therapy of Li-zhongyu* has no branches. It is a unique traditional Chinese medical treatment in China and even the world, using 4 pestle needles, 5 technicians and 3 acupoints in therapy. It has the advantages of acupuncture and massage, but totally different from acupuncture for not piercing the skin and muscles, so there is little pain and no worries about cross-infection. However, in the past, the *Pestle Needle Therapy of Li-zhongyu* was traditionally passed on among the families and from the master to the apprentice, so it is difficult to be carried on. Nowadays, Chengdu University of Traditional Chinese Medicine has established a team of inheritors of *Pestle Needle Therapy of Li-zhongyu*, which has expanded the inheritance group into workshop inheritors and clinical workers to some extent. However, its popularization is still very limited, and more innovative ways are in urgent demand so as to promote its inheritance and development.

第九章
四川省省级非物质文化遗产名录列表
（611项）

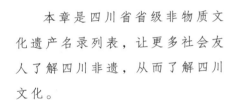

　　本章是四川省省级非物质文
化遗产名录列表，让更多社会友
人了解四川非遗，从而了解四川
文化。

序号	编号	项目名称	类型	申报地区及单位
		一、四川省第一批非物质文化遗产名录（189项）		
1	I-1	※格萨（斯）尔	民间文学	甘孜州文化局
2	I-2	苗族古歌	民间文学	珙县文化体育局
3	I-3	阿嫫妮惹	民间文学	凉山州语委
4	I-4	支格阿龙	民间文学	凉山州民间文艺家协会
5	I-5	月儿落西下	民间文学	巴中市文化体育新闻出版局
6	I-6	十里坪	民间文学	巴中市文化体育新闻出版局
7	I-7	毕摩经诵	民间文学	马边彝族自治县教育文化体育局
8	I-8	彝族克智	民间文学	美姑县人民政府、喜德县人民政府
9	I-9	蚕丝祖神传说	民间文学	盐亭县文化旅游局
10	I-10	安安送米传说	民间文学	德阳市旌阳区孝泉镇人民政府
11	I-11	巴渠童谣	民间文学	达州市通川区文化体育局
12	I-12	"苏济川"虫虫歌	民间文学	长宁县文化体育局
13	II-1	薅秧歌	民间音乐	开江县文化馆
14	II-2	薅草锣鼓（※川北薅草锣鼓、川东薅草锣鼓、川东土家族薅草锣鼓）	民间音乐	青川县人民政府、万源市文化局、宣汉县文化局
15	II-3	※巴山背二歌	民间音乐	巴中市文化体育新闻出版局、万源市文化局
16	II-4	滚板山歌	民间音乐	泸州市纳溪区文化体育广播电视局
17	II-5	高腔山歌	民间音乐	合江县文化体育广播电视局
18	II-6	彝族阿都高腔	民间音乐	布拖县人民政府
19	II-7	朵乐荷	民间音乐	布普格县人民政府、拖县人民政府

序号	编号	项目名称	类型	申报地区及单位
20	Ⅱ-8	顶毪衫歌	民间音乐	丹巴县文化馆
21	Ⅱ-9	玛达咪山歌	民间音乐	九龙县文化馆
22	Ⅱ-10	康定溜溜调	民间音乐	康定县文化馆
23	Ⅱ-11	阿惹妞	民间音乐	马边彝族自治县教育文化体育局
24	Ⅱ-12	川西藏族山歌	民间音乐	甘孜州文化馆、康定市文化旅游局、丹巴县文化旅游局、炉霍县文化旅游局、九龙县文化旅游局、甘孜县文化旅游局、雅江县文化旅游局、新龙县文化旅游局、道孚县文化旅游局、白玉县文化旅游局、理塘县文化旅游局、德格县文化旅游局、乡城县文化旅游局、石渠县文化旅游局、稻城县文化旅游局、色达县文化旅游局、巴塘县文化旅游局、德荣县文化旅游局、马尔康市文化体育局、九寨沟县文化体育局、红原县文化体育局、阿坝县文化体育局、理县县文化体育局、若尔盖县文化馆、小金县文化体育局、黑水县文化体育局、金川县文化体育局、松潘县文化体育局、壤塘县文化旅游局、茂县县文化体育局、木里县文化局
25	Ⅱ-13	义诺彝族民歌	民间音乐	雷波县文化体育局
26	Ⅱ-14	※川江号子	民间音乐	四川省音乐舞蹈研究所
27	Ⅱ-15	金沙江下游船工号子	民间音乐	屏山县文化体育旅游局

序号	编号	项目名称	类型	申报地区及单位
28	Ⅱ-16	永宁河船工号子	民间音乐	纳溪区文化体育广播电视局
29	Ⅱ-17	沱江船工号子	民间音乐	内江市东兴区文化体育局
30	Ⅱ-18	嘉陵江中游船工号子	民间音乐	南充市高坪区文化体育局
31	Ⅱ-19	竹麻号子	民间音乐	邛崃市群众艺术馆
32	Ⅱ-20	巴山石工号子	民间音乐	达县文化体育局、开江县文化馆
33	Ⅱ-21	抬工号子	民间音乐	仁寿县文化馆
34	Ⅱ-22	婚嫁歌	民间音乐	南充市高坪区文化体育局、蓬安县文化馆、华蓥市文化馆
35	Ⅱ-23	南坪小调	民间音乐	九寨沟县文化体育局
36	Ⅱ-24	多声部民歌（阿尔麦多声部民歌、硗碛多声部民歌、羌族多声部民歌）	民间音乐	黑水县文化体育局、宝兴县文化馆、松潘县文化体育局、茂县文化体育局
37	Ⅱ-25	※羌笛演奏及制作技艺	民间音乐	茂县文化体育局
38	Ⅱ-26	大竹竹唢呐及制作工艺	民间音乐	大竹县文化馆
39	Ⅱ-27	唢呐艺术（咪苏唢呐、福宝贯打唢呐、苗族大唢呐、丹棱唢呐）	民间音乐	叙永县文化体育广播电视局、合江县文化体育广播电视局、筠连县文化体育局、丹棱县文化馆
40	Ⅱ-28	口弦	民间音乐	北川县文化馆、布拖县人民政府
41	Ⅱ-29	四川耍锣鼓（渠县耍锣鼓、李家耍锣鼓、象山花锣鼓、复兴耍锣鼓）	民间音乐	渠县土溪镇人民政府、渠县临巴镇人民政府、广元市朝天区文化体育局、大英县文化体育局、洪雅县文化馆
42	Ⅱ-30	川中大乐（仓山大乐、蓬莱大乐）	民间音乐	中江县文化体育旅游局、大英县文化体育局

序号	编号	项目名称	类型	申报地区及单位
43	Ⅱ-31	文昌洞经古乐	民间音乐	梓潼县文物管理所
44	Ⅱ-32	青城洞经古乐	民间音乐	都江堰市文化馆
45	Ⅱ-33	峨眉山佛教音乐	民间音乐	峨眉山市文化体育局
46	Ⅱ-34	成都道教音乐	民间音乐	成都市道教协会
47	Ⅲ-1	龙舞（※泸州雨坛彩龙、安仁板凳龙、船山桃子龙、盐亭桃子龙、遂宁耍旱龙、马潭火龙、双流火龙、宜宾小彩龙）	民间舞蹈	泸县文化体育广播电视局、达县文化体育局、遂宁市船山区文化体育局、遂宁市船山区南京路街道办事处、盐亭县文化旅游局、遂宁市民间文化研究会、泸州市龙马潭区胡市镇文化体育中心、双流县文化馆、宜宾县文化体育局
48	Ⅲ-2	高台狮子	民间舞蹈	金堂县文化馆
49	Ⅲ-3	巴象鼓舞	民间舞蹈	阆中市文化局
50	Ⅲ-4	翻山铰子	民间舞蹈	平昌县文化体育新闻出版局、达县文化体育局、营山县文化体育局
51	Ⅲ-5	泸县百和莲花枪	民间舞蹈	泸县百和镇人民政府
52	Ⅲ-6	花灯（古蔺花灯、白龙花灯）	民间舞蹈	古蔺县文化体育广播电视局、剑阁县文化局
53	Ⅲ-7	罗城麒麟灯	民间舞蹈	犍为县文化体育旅游局
54	Ⅲ-8	云童舞	民间舞蹈	广安市广安区文化体育局
55	Ⅲ-9	白马跳曹盖	民间舞蹈	平武县文化旅游局
56	Ⅲ-10	甲措	民间舞蹈	盐源县人民政府
57	Ⅲ-11	锅庄[达尔嘎、马奈锅庄、马尔锅庄、真达锅庄、木雅锅庄、得荣学羌、丹巴阿克日翁（兔儿锅庄）、乡城恰热（疯装锅庄）、新龙锅庄、德格卓且]	民间舞蹈	马尔康市文化体育局、金川县文化体育局、小金县文化体育局、石渠县文化旅游局、雅江县文化馆、得荣县文化旅游局、丹巴县文化馆、乡城县文化旅游局、新龙县文化馆、德格县文化馆

序号	编号	项目名称	类型	申报地区及单位
58	Ⅲ-12	扎坝嘛呢舞	民间舞蹈	道孚县文化旅游局
59	Ⅲ-13	热巴舞	民间舞蹈	巴塘县文化旅游局
60	Ⅲ-14	甘孜踢踏	民间舞蹈	甘孜县文化馆
61	Ⅲ-15	弦子舞（※巴塘弦子舞）	民间舞蹈	巴塘县人民政府
62	Ⅲ-16	羌族羊皮鼓舞	民间舞蹈	汶川县文化体育局
63	Ⅲ-17	哈玛（战神舞）	民间舞蹈	马尔康市文化体育局
64	Ⅲ-18	金冠舞	民间舞蹈	若尔盖县文化馆
65	Ⅲ-19	博巴森根	民间舞蹈	理县文化体育局
66	Ⅲ-20	※卡斯达温舞	民间舞蹈	黑水县文化体育局
67	Ⅲ-21	※偱舞	民间舞蹈	九寨沟县文化体育局
68	Ⅳ-1	※川剧	传统戏剧	四川省川剧艺术研究院
69	Ⅳ-2	"泸州河"川剧艺术	传统戏剧	泸州市川剧团
70	Ⅳ-3	四川皮影戏（阆中皮影戏、何家班皮影戏、高观皮影戏、巴中皮影戏、成都皮影戏）	传统戏剧	阆中市文化局、南部县文化馆、剑阁县文化局、巴中市巴州区文化馆、成都市艺术剧院
71	Ⅳ-4	灯戏（※川北灯戏、岳池灯戏、峨眉堂灯戏、夹江麻柳堂灯戏、许家湾十二花灯戏）	传统戏剧	南充市川剧团、岳池县文体局、峨眉山市文化体育局、夹江县文化体育广播电视旅游局、北川县文化馆
72	Ⅳ-5	木偶戏（※川北大木偶戏、手掌木偶戏、成都木偶戏）	传统戏剧	南充市四川省大木偶剧院、邻水县文化体育局、成都市艺术剧院
73	Ⅳ-6	射箭提阳戏	传统戏剧	广元市元坝区射箭乡人民政府
74	Ⅳ-7	旺苍端公戏	传统戏剧	旺苍县人民政府
75	Ⅳ-8	藏戏（德格藏戏、巴塘藏戏、色达藏戏）	传统戏剧	德格县文化旅游局、巴塘县文化旅游局、色达县文化馆

273

序号	编号	项目名称	类型	申报地区及单位
76	V-1	四川扬琴	曲艺	四川省曲艺团、成都市艺术剧院、泸州市歌舞团、四川省音乐舞蹈研究所
77	V-2	四川清音	曲艺	四川省曲艺团、泸州市歌舞团、成都市艺术剧院
78	V-3	四川竹琴	曲艺	四川省曲艺团、成都市艺术剧院
79	V-4	金钱板	曲艺	成都市艺术剧院、南充市高坪区文化体育局
80	V-5	百汪说唱	曲艺	红原县文化体育局
81	V-6	飞刀花鼓	曲艺	成都市青羊区文化馆
82	VI-1	拗棒	杂技与竞技	开江县文化馆
83	VI-2	搬打狮子	杂技与竞技	泸州市纳溪区文化体育广播电视局
84	VI-3	大坝高装	杂技与竞技	兴文县文化体育局
85	VI-4	华蓥山滑竿抬幺妹	杂技与竞技	华蓥市文化体育局
86	VI-5	高亭	杂技与竞技	岳池县文化体育局
87	VI-6	峨眉武术	杂技与竞技	夹江县文化体育广播电视旅游局、峨眉山市文化体育局
88	VI-7	五通桥龙舟竞技	杂技与竞技	乐山市五通桥区体育总会
89	VI-8	青林口高抬戏	杂技与竞技	江油市文化馆
90	VII-1	唤马剪纸	民间美术	苍溪县唤马镇人民政府
91	VII-2	麻柳刺绣	民间美术	广元市朝天区文化体育局
92	VII-3	石刻工艺（白花石刻、雾山石刻、安岳石刻）	民间美术	广元市市中区文化体育旅游局、江油市李白纪念馆、安岳县文化体育局

序号	编号	项目名称	类型	申报地区及单位
93	Ⅶ-4	江安竹簧工艺	民间美术	江安县旅游文化局
94	Ⅶ-5	宜宾面塑	民间美术	宜宾市翠屏区文化局
95	Ⅶ-6	德格藏文书法	民间美术	德格县文化馆
96	Ⅶ-7	夹江年画	民间美术	夹江县文化体育广播电视旅游局
97	Ⅶ-8	※绵竹木版年画	民间美术	德阳市绵竹年画博物馆
98	Ⅶ-9	※藏族格萨尔彩绘石刻	民间美术	色达县文化旅游局
99	Ⅶ-10	※藏族唐卡（噶玛嘎孜画派）	民间美术	甘孜州藏画研究所
100	Ⅶ-11	※蜀绣	民间美术	成都市蜀绣厂
101	Ⅷ-1	※蜀锦织造技艺	手工技艺	成都市蜀锦文化发展有限责任公司
102	Ⅷ-2	自贡扎染工艺	手工技艺	自贡市扎染工艺厂
103	Ⅷ-3	凉山彝族毛纺织及擀制技艺	手工技艺	昭觉县人民政府
104	Ⅷ-4	隆昌夏布编织工艺	手工技艺	隆昌县文化体育局
105	Ⅷ-5	康巴藏族服装配饰制作工艺	手工技艺	甘孜州文化局
106	Ⅷ-6	藏族牛羊毛手工编织工艺	手工技艺	色达县文化馆
107	Ⅷ-7	羌绣传统刺绣工艺	手工技艺	汶川县文化体育局、茂县文化体育局
108	Ⅷ-8	龚扇	手工技艺	自贡市龚扇竹编工艺厂
109	Ⅷ-9	德阳潮扇传统工艺	手工技艺	德阳市旌阳区文化局
110	Ⅷ-10	油纸伞传统制作技艺	手工技艺	泸州市江阳区旅游局
111	Ⅷ-11	渠县刘氏竹编工艺	手工技艺	渠县刘氏竹编工艺有限公司
112	Ⅷ-12	青神竹编工艺	手工技艺	青神县文化馆
113	Ⅷ-13	沐川草龙编扎技艺	手工技艺	沐川县文化体育局
114	Ⅷ-14	道明日用竹编技艺	手工技艺	崇州市文化馆

序号	编号	项目名称	类型	申报地区及单位
115	Ⅷ-15	瓷胎竹编工艺	手工技艺	邛崃市群众艺术馆
116	Ⅷ-16	※德格印经院藏族雕版印刷技艺	手工技艺	德格县文化旅游局
117	Ⅷ-17	※竹纸制作技艺	手工技艺	夹江县文化局
118	Ⅷ-18	徐氏泥彩塑工艺	手工技艺	大英县文化体育局
119	Ⅷ-19	珙县珙石雕	手工技艺	珙县文化体育局
120	Ⅷ-20	自贡彩灯传统制作工艺	手工技艺	自贡市彩灯艺术协会
121	Ⅷ-21	高桩彩绘绑扎技艺	手工技艺	峨眉山市文化体育局、夹江县文化体育广播电视旅游局
122	Ⅷ-22	中型杖头木偶制作工艺	手工技艺	资中县木偶剧团
123	Ⅷ-23	藏族民间车模技艺	手工技艺	得荣县文化旅游局
124	Ⅷ-24	藏族建筑砌石技艺	手工技艺	丹巴县文化馆
125	Ⅷ-25	重华烟火架制作工艺	手工技艺	江油市文物保护管理所
126	Ⅷ-26	※自贡井盐深钻汲制技艺	手工技艺	自贡市四川久大盐业集团公司
127	Ⅷ-27	※大英井盐深钻汲制技艺	手工技艺	大英县文化局
128	Ⅷ-28	※成都漆艺	手工技艺	成都市漆器工艺厂
129	Ⅷ-29	凉山彝族漆器制作工艺	手工技艺	喜德县人民政府
130	Ⅷ-30	凉山彝族银饰手工技艺	手工技艺	布拖县人民政府
131	Ⅷ-31	白玉河坡藏族金属手工技艺	手工技艺	白玉县文化馆
132	Ⅷ-32	银花丝技艺	手工技艺	成都市青羊区文化馆
133	Ⅷ-33	荣经砂器	手工技艺	荣经县文化体育管理局
134	Ⅷ-34	阿西土陶烧制工艺	手工技艺	稻城县旅游文化局
135	Ⅷ-35	桂花土陶传统制作工艺	手工技艺	彭州市群众艺术馆

序号	编号	项目名称	类型	申报地区及单位
136	Ⅷ-36	邛陶烧造技艺	手工技艺	邛崃市群众艺术馆
137	Ⅷ-37	南路边茶传统手工制作技艺	手工技艺	雅安市茶业协会
138	Ⅷ-38	蒙山茶传统制作技艺	手工技艺	名山县非物质文化遗产保护中心
139	Ⅷ-39	※泸州老窖酒酿制技艺	手工技艺	泸州老窖股份有限公司
140	Ⅷ-40	五粮液酒传统酿造技艺	手工技艺	四川省宜宾五粮液集团有限公司
141	Ⅷ-41	水井坊酒传统酿造技艺	手工技艺	成都市四川全兴股份有限公司
142	Ⅷ-42	剑南春酒传统酿造技艺	手工技艺	德阳市四川剑南春集团有限责任公司
143	Ⅷ-43	古蔺郎酒传统酿造技艺	手工技艺	泸州市四川郎酒集团有限责任公司
144	Ⅷ-44	沱牌曲酒传统酿造技艺	手工技艺	遂宁市四川沱牌曲酒股份有限公司
145	Ⅷ-45	民间藏酒酿造技艺	手工技艺	丹巴县文化馆
146	Ⅷ-46	渠县呷酒酿造技艺	手工技艺	渠县宕府王食品有限公司
147	Ⅷ-47	中江手工挂面工艺	手工技艺	中江县文化体育旅游局
148	Ⅷ-48	富顺豆花制作工艺	手工技艺	自贡市富顺豆花文化协会
149	Ⅷ-49	东柳醪糟酿造技艺	手工技艺	大竹县文化馆、达州市四川东柳醪糟有限责任公司
150	Ⅷ-50	护国陈醋传统酿制技艺	手工技艺	泸州市纳溪区文化体育广播电视局
151	Ⅷ-51	泸州市先市酱油传统酿制技艺	手工技艺	合江县文化体育广播电视局
152	Ⅷ-52	南溪豆腐干制作工艺	手工技艺	南溪区文化体育旅游局
153	Ⅷ-53	郫县豆瓣传统制作技艺	手工技艺	成都市郫县文化馆
154	Ⅷ-54	临江寺豆瓣传统工艺	手工技艺	资阳市雁江区文化体育局
155	Ⅷ-55	潼川豆豉制作技艺	手工技艺	三台县文化体育局

序号	编号	项目名称	类型	申报地区及单位
156	Ⅷ-56	糖画技艺	手工技艺	成都市锦江区文化馆
157	Ⅷ-57	酥油花制作技艺	手工技艺	道孚县文化旅游局
158	Ⅷ-58	达县灯影牛肉传统加工技艺	手工技艺	达州市文化馆、达州四川妙达饴美厨食品有限公司
159	Ⅸ-1	藏医药（※甘孜州南派藏医药）	传统医药	甘孜州藏医院
160	Ⅸ-2	李仲愚针疗法	传统医药	成都中医药大学附属医院
161	Ⅸ-3	成都中药炮制技术	传统医药	成都中医药大学
162	Ⅸ-4	成都中医传统制剂方法	传统医药	成都中医药大学
163	Ⅹ-1	彝族年	民俗	凉山州文化局、马边县教育文化体育局
164	Ⅹ-2	藏历年	民俗	甘孜州文化局、阿坝州文化局、木里县文化局
165	Ⅹ-3	羌年	民俗	茂县文化体育局、汶川县文化体育局、理县文化体育局、北川县文化旅游局
166	Ⅹ-4	※火把节（彝族火把节）	民俗	凉山州文化局
167	Ⅹ-5	新龙藏历十三节	民俗	新龙县文化馆
168	Ⅹ-6	苏布士（羌年庆典）	民俗	阿坝州中国古羌释比文化传承研究会
169	Ⅹ-7	※都江堰放水节	民俗	成都市都江堰风景名胜管理局
170	Ⅹ-8	三汇彩亭会	民俗	渠县三汇镇人民政府
171	Ⅹ-9	文昌出巡	民俗	梓潼县文物管理所
172	Ⅹ-10	广汉保保节	民俗	广汉市文化体育局
173	Ⅹ-11	川南苗族踩山节	民俗	叙永县文化体育广播电视局
174	Ⅹ-12	硗碛上九节	民俗	宝兴县文化馆
175	Ⅹ-13	八月彩楼会	民俗	芦山县民族民间文化

序号	编号	项目名称	类型	申报地区及单位
				传承中心
176	X-14	※羌族瓦尔俄足节	民俗	茂县文化达州局
177	X-15	康定"四月八"跑马转山会	民俗	康定县文化馆
178	X-16	赛马节（会）	民俗	理塘县文化馆
179	X-17	泸沽湖摩梭人母系氏族习俗	民俗	盐源县人民政府
180	X-18	雅砻江河谷扎巴藏族母系氏族习俗	民俗	雅江县文化馆
181	X-19	成人仪式	民俗	丹巴县文化馆
182	X-20	阿依美格	民俗	马边县教育文化体育局
183	X-21	通家山女儿碑庙会	民俗	射洪县青岗镇人民政府
184	X-22	环山鸡节	民俗	石棉县文化体育旅游局
185	X-23	广元女儿节	民俗	广元市文化局
186	X-24	山岩帕措习俗	民俗	白玉县文化馆
187	X-25	凉山彝族"尼木措毕"祭祀	民俗	美姑县人民政府
188	X-26	峨眉山大庙庙会	民俗	峨眉山市文化体育局
189	X-27	新山傈僳族约德节	民俗	攀枝花市文化局

二、四川省第二批非物质文化遗产

（一）四川省第二批非物质文化遗产名录（共137项）

序号	编号	项目名称	类型	申报地区及单位
1	I-1	望娘滩传说	民间文学	成都市都江堰市文化馆
2	I-2	卓文君与司马相如的故事	民间文学	成都市邛崃市群众艺术馆
3	I-3	甘嫫阿妞的传说	民间文学	乐山市峨边彝族自治县文化馆
4	I-4	王幺贡爷系列故事	民间文学	达州市宣汉县文化馆

序号	编号	项目名称	类型	申报地区及单位
5	I-5	羌戈大战（羌族古典叙事长诗）	民间文学	阿坝州汶川县文化体育局、绵阳市北川羌族自治县文化旅游局
6	I-6	大禹的传说	民间文学	阿坝州汶川县文化体育局、绵阳市北川羌族自治县文化旅游局
7	I-7	阿古登巴的故事	民间文学	甘孜州色达县文化旅游局
8	I-8	勒俄特依	民间文学	凉山州喜德县文化文化馆
9	I-9	玛牧特依	民间文学	凉山州喜德县文化馆
10	II-1	江河号子 [府河号子 （黄龙溪号子） 涪江号子、 涪江船工号子 铜河船工号子、 岷江号子]	传统音乐	成都市双流区黄龙溪风景名胜区管委会、绵阳市三台县潼川镇人民政府、遂宁市文化馆、乐山市沙湾区文化馆、乐山市犍为县文化馆
11	II-2	耍锣（福集耍锣）	传统音乐	泸州市泸县福集镇社会事务服务中心
12	II-3	木格岛苗族祭祀鼓乐	传统音乐	泸州市叙永县分水镇人政府
13	II-4	遂宁叫卖调	传统音乐	遂宁市文化馆
14	II-5	遂宁坐歌堂	传统音乐	遂宁市文化馆
15	II-6	石工号子	传统音乐	遂宁市安居区分水镇人民政府
16	II-7	觉囊梵音（藏哇梵音）	传统音乐	阿坝州壤塘县中壤塘乡藏哇寺
17	II-8	骨笛	传统音乐	甘孜州色达县文化旅游局
18	II-9	彝族挽歌	传统音乐	凉山州宁南县文化馆
19	II-10	藏族赶马调	传统音乐	凉山州冕宁县文化馆
20	II-11	彝族克西举尔	传统音乐	凉山州召觉县文物管理所、凉山州雷波县文化馆

序号	编号	项目名称	类型	申报地区及单位
21	Ⅱ-12	彝族马布音乐	传统音乐	凉山州越西县广播电视文化体育局、凉山州昭觉县文物管理所
22	Ⅱ-13	彝族月琴音乐	传统音乐	凉山州普格县文化艺术馆
23	Ⅱ-14	毕摩音乐	传统音乐	凉山州美姑县文化旅游体育局
24	Ⅱ-15	大号唢呐	传统音乐	凉山州会理县文化馆
25	Ⅱ-16	川北山歌（巴山茅山歌、阆州情歌、嘉绒藏区农耕劳动歌、德格劳动歌曲）	传统音乐	巴中市文化馆、南充市阆中市文化馆、阿坝州嘉绒文化研究会、甘孜德格县文化馆
26	Ⅱ-17	蜀派古琴	传统音乐	四川音乐学院、成都市文化馆
27	Ⅱ-18	四川洞经音乐（迤沙拉谈经古乐）	传统音乐	攀枝花市仁和区文化体育局
28	Ⅲ-1	熊猫舞	传统舞蹈	阿坝州九寨沟县文化馆
29	Ⅲ-2	天全牛儿灯	传统舞蹈	雅安市天全县文体局
30	Ⅲ-3	越溪牛灯舞	传统舞蹈	内江市威远县越溪镇人民政府
31	Ⅲ-4	耍蚕龙	传统舞蹈	绵阳市盐亭县文化旅游局
32	Ⅲ-5	平武虎牙藏族斗牦牛	传统舞蹈	绵阳市平武县文化馆
33	Ⅲ-6	玄滩狮舞	传统舞蹈	泸州市泸县玄滩镇社会事务服务中心
34	Ⅲ-7	阿署达彝族打跳舞	传统舞蹈	攀枝花市东区文化馆
35	Ⅲ-8	蓝田花船	传统舞蹈	泸州市江阳区蓝田街道办事处
36	Ⅲ-9	羌族沙朗	传统舞蹈	绵阳市北川羌族自治县文化旅游局
37	Ⅲ-10	建中高跷狮灯	传统舞蹈	绵阳市三台县建中乡人民政府
38	Ⅲ-11	花灯（得胜花灯、大新花灯）	传统舞蹈	泸州市泸县得胜镇社会事务服务中心、绵阳市梓潼县文化馆

序号	编号	项目名称	类型	申报地区及单位
39	Ⅲ-12	蚌鹤舞	传统舞蹈	达州市万源市文化馆
40	Ⅲ-13	傈僳族嘎且且撒勒舞	传统舞蹈	凉山会州东县文化馆、凉山州德昌县文化馆
41	Ⅲ-14	彝族苏尼舞	传统舞蹈	凉山州布拖县文化馆
42	Ⅲ-15	蹢脚舞	传统舞蹈	凉山州会理县文化馆
43	Ⅲ-16	藏族杜基嘎尔	传统舞蹈	凉山州木里藏族自治县文化馆
44	Ⅳ-1	马鸣阳戏	传统戏剧	绵阳市梓潼县文化馆
45	Ⅳ-2	被单戏	传统戏剧	成都市青羊区文化馆
46	Ⅳ-3	白龙纸偶	传统戏剧	广元市剑阁县文化馆
47	Ⅳ-4	南部傩戏	传统戏剧	南充市南部县文化馆
48	Ⅳ-5	南木达藏戏	传统戏剧	阿坝州壤塘县文化馆
49	Ⅴ-1	四川车灯	曲艺	成都市金牛区文化馆
50	Ⅴ-2	钱棍	曲艺	达州市万源市文化馆
51	Ⅵ-1	青城武术	传统游艺、杂技与竞技	成都市都江堰市文化馆
52	Ⅵ-2	峨眉盘破门武术	传统游艺、杂技与竞技	内江市资中县武术协会
53	Ⅵ-3	三雄夺魁	传统游艺、杂技与竞技	乐山市金口河区文化馆
54	Ⅵ-4	土家余门拳	传统游艺、杂技与竞技	达州市宣汉县文化馆
55	Ⅵ-5	绿林派武术	传统游艺、杂技与竞技	雅安市雨城区文化馆
56	Ⅵ-6	羌族推杆	传统游艺、杂技与竞技	绵阳市北川羌族自治县文化旅游局、阿坝州汶川县文化馆

序号	编号	项目名称	类型	申报地区及单位
57	Ⅵ-7	彝族磨尔秋	传统游艺、杂技与竞技	凉山州甘洛县文化馆
58	Ⅶ-1	草编（柏合草编、草靶龙、峨眉席草龙）	传统美术	成都市龙泉驿区文化馆、自贡市贡井区文化馆、乐山市峨眉山市文化馆
59	Ⅶ-2	汉源彩塑	传统美术	雅安市汉源县文化体育局
60	Ⅶ-3	馍馍印	传统美术	阿坝州马尔康市文化馆
61	Ⅶ-4	郎卡杰唐卡传统绘画艺术	传统美术	甘孜州炉霍县文化馆
62	Ⅶ-5	毕摩绘画	传统美术	凉山州美姑县文化旅游体育局
63	Ⅶ-6	彝文书法	传统美术	凉山州盐源县文化馆
64	Ⅶ-7	四川手工剪纸（平武剪纸、涪城剪纸、仪陇剪纸、武胜剪纸、自贡手工剪纸）	传统美术	绵阳市平武县文化馆、绵阳市涪城区文化馆、南充市仪陇县文化馆、广安市武胜县文化馆、自贡市自流井区文化馆
65	Ⅶ-8	青神捻条画艺术	传统美术	眉山市青神县文化馆
66	Ⅶ-9	石雕（通江石雕、泸县石雕、蓬溪石雕、苴却砚雕刻、黎渊石雕、拉日马玛尼石雕）	传统美术	巴中通江县文化馆、泸州市泸县文物管理所、遂宁市蓬溪县文体旅游局、攀枝花市鑫艺工艺美术制品厂、广元市青川县文化馆、甘孜州新龙县文化馆
67	Ⅶ-10	藤编（怀远藤编）	传统美术	成都市崇州市文化馆
68	Ⅶ-11	棕编（新繁棕编）	传统美术	成都市新都区文化馆
69	Ⅶ-12	竹编（遂宁竹编、安岳竹编）	传统美术	遂宁市安居区石洞镇人民政府、资阳市安岳县文化体育局
70	Ⅶ-13	小凉山彝族刺绣	传统美术	乐山市峨边彝族自治县文化馆
71	Ⅶ-14	苗族刺绣	传统美术	宜宾市筠连县文化体育和旅游局

序号	编号	项目名称	类型	申报地区及单位
72	Ⅷ-1	蒸馏酒传统酿造技艺（彭县肥酒酿造技艺、江口醇酒传统酿造技艺）	传统手工技艺	成都市彭州市群众艺术馆、四川江口醇酒业（集团）有限公司
73	Ⅷ-2	酿造酒传统酿造技艺（彝族杆杆酒酿造技艺）	传统手工技艺	凉山州甘洛县文化馆
74	Ⅷ-3	配制酒传统酿造技艺（彝族民间泡水酒）	传统手工技艺	乐山市峨边彝族自治县文化馆
75	Ⅷ-4	怀远三绝制作技艺	传统手工技艺	成都市崇州市文化馆
76	Ⅷ-5	麻饼制作技艺（汤长发麻饼制作技艺）	传统手工技艺	成都市崇州市文化馆
77	Ⅷ-6	川派盆景制作技艺	传统手工技艺	成都市四川省盆景艺术家协会
78	Ⅷ-7	金鸡风筝扎制技艺	传统手工技艺	成都市崇州市文化馆
79	Ⅷ-8	构树皮造纸工艺	传统手工技艺	泸州市叙永县分水镇宣传文化服务中心
80	Ⅷ-9	羌族水磨漆艺	传统手工技艺	绵阳市北川羌族自治县文化旅游局
81	Ⅷ-10	蜜饯制作技艺（内江蜜饯制作技艺）	传统手工技艺	内江市市中区文化体育局
82	Ⅷ-11	宋笔制作技艺	传统手工技艺	乐山市毛笔厂
83	Ⅷ-12	米花糖制作技艺（苏稽香油米花糖制作技艺）	传统手工技艺	乐山市市中区文化馆
84	Ⅷ-13	峨眉白蜡生产加工技艺	传统手工技艺	乐山市峨眉山市白蜡研究所
85	Ⅷ-14	豆腐菜肴制作技艺（龚氏西霸豆腐制作技艺、五通桥西坝豆腐制作技艺）	传统手工技艺	乐山市龚氏西霸饮食有限公司、西坝镇方德饭店、乐山五通桥天一香酒楼（五通桥）

序号	编号	项目名称	类型	申报地区及单位
86	Ⅷ-15	腐乳酿造技艺（德昌源"桥"牌豆腐乳制作工艺、"长春号"南味豆腐传统手工制作技艺）	传统手工技艺	乐山市五通桥区德昌源酱园厂、眉山市彭山区文化馆
87	Ⅷ-15	豆笋制作技艺（开江豆笋）	传统手工技艺	达州市开江县文化馆
88	Ⅷ-17	保宁醋传统酿造工艺	传统手工技艺	南充阆中市四川保宁醋有限公司
89	Ⅷ-18	四川苗族蜡染	传统手工技艺	宜宾市珙县文化馆
90	Ⅷ-19	芝麻糕制作技艺（裕泰乾马氏芝麻糕制作技艺）	传统手工技艺	眉山市东坡区文化馆
91	Ⅷ-20	传统民居营造技艺（踏板房建筑、羌家石雕房与吊脚楼、新龙民居建造技艺、木雅石砌）	传统手工技艺	阿坝州九寨沟县文化馆、绵阳市北川羌族自治县文化旅游局、甘孜州新龙县文化馆、甘孜州雅江县文化馆
92	Ⅷ-21	申臂桥建造技艺	传统手工技艺	甘孜州新龙县文化馆
93	Ⅷ-22	德格麦宿塑像制作技艺	传统手工技艺	甘孜州德格县文化馆
94	Ⅷ-23	德格麦宿传统土陶技艺	传统手工技艺	甘孜州德格县文化馆
95	Ⅷ-24	木雕（德格麦宿木雕技艺）	传统手工技艺	甘孜州德格县文化馆
96	Ⅷ-25	德沙旋木技艺	传统手工技艺	甘孜州稻城县旅游文化局
97	Ⅷ-26	新龙药泥藏式面具制作技艺	传统手工技艺	甘孜州新龙县文化馆
98	Ⅷ-27	牧区皮革加工技艺	传统手工技艺	甘孜州色达县文化旅游局
99	Ⅷ-28	民族乐器制作技艺（傈僳族葫芦笙制作技艺、南坪土琵琶制作技艺）	传统手工技艺	凉山州德昌县文化馆、阿坝州九寨沟县文化馆

序号	编号	项目名称	类型	申报地区及单位
100	Ⅷ-29	绿釉陶瓷品制作技艺	传统手工技艺	凉山州会理县文化馆
101	Ⅷ-30	红铜火锅制作技艺	传统手工技艺	凉山州会理县文化馆
102	Ⅷ-31	传统茶具制作技艺（藏式竹制茶具制作、藏式木制茶具制作、藏式烧制茶具制作技艺）	传统手工技艺	凉山州木里藏族自治县文化馆
103	Ⅷ-32	嘉绒藏族编织	传统手工技艺	挑花刺绣工艺 阿坝州嘉绒藏族编织挑花刺绣协会
104	Ⅷ-33	羌族碉楼营造技艺	传统手工技艺	阿坝州汶川县文化馆、阿坝州理县文化馆、阿坝州茂县文化馆、阿坝州松潘县文化馆、阿坝州黑水县文化馆、绵阳市北川县文化馆、绵阳市平武县文化馆
105	Ⅷ-34	富顺手工微刻技艺	传统手工技艺	自贡市富顺县文化馆
106	Ⅷ-35	遂宁福锦手工编织技艺	传统手工技艺	遂宁市闻喜阁旅游工艺品有限公司
107	Ⅷ-36	婴儿米粉制作技艺（泸州肥儿粉传统制作技艺）	传统手工技艺	泸州市四川省正味正点食品厂
108	Ⅸ-1	德仁堂中医中药文化	传统医药	成都市青羊区文化馆
109	Ⅸ-2	合江地道中草药热灸技艺	传统医药	泸州市合江县合江镇宣传文化服务中心
110	Ⅸ-3	何天祥传统疗伤手法技艺	传统医药	四川艺术职业学院
111	Ⅸ-4	中医正骨疗法（郑氏骨科）	传统医药	四川省骨科医院
112	Ⅹ-1	巴塘歌卦	民俗	甘孜州巴塘县文化馆
113	Ⅹ-2	客家婚俗	民俗	成都市龙泉驿区文化馆

序号	编号	项目名称	类型	申报地区及单位
114	X-3	端午龙舟会	民俗	成都市新津县文化体育局
115	X-4	观灯习俗（成都灯会）	民俗	成都市灯会办公室
116	X-5	焦滩乡大端阳节	民俗	泸州市合江县焦滩乡人民政府
117	X-6	分水岭乡火龙节	民俗	泸州市江阳区分水岭乡人民政府
118	X-7	大禹祭祀习俗	民俗	绵阳市北川羌族自治县文化旅游局
119	X-8	睢水春社踩桥会	民俗	绵阳市安县文化馆
120	X-9	蚕姑庙会	民俗	绵阳市盐亭县文化馆
121	X-10	达州元九登高节	民俗	达州市通川区文化馆
122	X-11	石桥烧火龙节	民俗	达州市达县文化馆
123	X-12	正月十六登高节	民俗	巴中市巴州区文化馆
124	X-13	五月台会（城隍庙会）	民俗	眉山市洪雅县文化馆
125	X-14	嘉绒藏族春耕仪式	民俗	阿坝州马尔康市文化馆
126	X-15	彝族婚俗（彝族婚礼歌、彝族婚俗）	民俗	凉山州越西县广播电视文化体育局、凉山州美姑县文化体育局
127	X-16	傈僳族服饰	民俗	凉山州德昌县文化馆
128	X-17	彝族服饰（彝族服饰、义诺彝族服饰、彝族奥索布迪服饰艺术）	民俗	凉山州昭觉县文物管理所、凉山州美姑县文化旅游局、凉山州会东县文化馆
129	X-18	傈僳族阔时节	民俗	凉山州德昌县文化馆
130	X-19	傈僳族婚俗	民俗	凉山州德昌县文化馆
131	X-20	摩梭人成丁礼	民俗	凉山州盐源县文化馆
132	X-21	彝族"阿依蒙格"儿童节	民俗	凉山州雷波县语委
133	X-22	藏族尔苏射箭节	民俗	凉山州甘洛县文化馆
134	X-23	彝族换童裙成人仪式	民俗	乐山市峨边彝族自治县文化馆

287

序号	编号	项目名称	类型	申报地区及单位
135	X-24	摩梭人转湖节	民俗	凉山州盐源县文化馆、凉山州木里县文化馆
136	X-25	华蓥山宝鼎庙会	民俗	广安市华蓥市文化馆
137	X-26	说春	民俗	巴中市南江县文化馆

（二）第一批扩展项目（共7项）

序号	编号	项目名称	类型	申报地区及单位
1	Ⅱ-28	口弦（羌族口弦）	第一批扩展——传统音乐	阿坝州汶川县文化馆、阿坝州理县文化体育局
2	Ⅲ-1	龙舞（四川客家龙舞、安仁谭氏子孙龙、永宁火龙、盐亭水龙、双凤龙灯）	第一批扩展——传统舞蹈	成都市龙泉驿区文化馆、达州市达县文化旅游局、广元市苍溪县永宁镇文化站、绵阳市盐亭县文化馆、内江市隆昌县双凤镇政府
3	Ⅲ-11	锅庄（宝兴硗碛锅庄、灯笼卓钦、木里藏族"嘎卓"舞）	第一批扩展——传统舞蹈	雅安市宝兴县文化馆、甘孜州白玉县文化馆、凉山洲木里藏族自治县文化馆
4	Ⅳ-1	川剧（嘉阳河川剧艺术）	第一批扩展——传统戏剧	乐山市市川剧团
5	Ⅳ-4	灯戏[川北灯戏（阆中老观灯戏）]	第一批扩展——传统戏剧	南充市阆中市文化馆
6	Ⅴ-1	四川扬琴（黄家扬琴）	第一批扩展——曲艺	泸州市古蔺县文化馆
7	Ⅶ-11	蜀绣（观音绣）	第一批扩展——传统美术	遂宁市妙善文化艺术坊

三、四川省第三批非物质文化遗产

（一）四川省第三批非物质文化遗产名录（共89项）

序号	编号	项目名称	类型	申报地区及单位
1	Ⅰ-1	诺苏佐木莫	民间文学	乐山市峨边彝族自治县文化馆

序号	编号	项目名称	类型	申报地区及单位
2	Ⅰ-2	《释比古唱经》	民间文学	阿坝州茂县文化体育局
3	Ⅰ-3	木姐珠和斗安珠	民间文学	阿坝州汶川县文化馆
4	Ⅰ-4	毕阿史拉则传说	民间文学	凉山州金阳县文化馆
5	Ⅰ-5	傈僳族民间传说	民间文学	凉山州德昌县文化馆
6	Ⅰ-6	东乡白莲教传说	民间文学	达州市宣汉县文化馆
7	Ⅰ-7	阿都歌谣	民间文学	凉山州布拖县文化馆
8	Ⅰ-8	什喜尼支嘿	民间文学	凉山州布拖县文化馆
9	Ⅱ-1	荥经民间竹号	传统音乐	雅安市荥经县文化馆
10	Ⅱ-2	西充祥龙嫁歌	传统音乐	南充市西充县祥龙乡社会事务服务中心
11	Ⅱ-3	苗族斗釜歌	传统音乐	攀枝花市盐边县文化馆
12	Ⅱ-4	彝族"久觉合"	传统音乐	凉山州甘洛县文化馆
13	Ⅱ-5	木模拉格	传统音乐	凉山州越西县文化馆
14	Ⅱ-6	热打("里惹尔")	传统音乐	凉山州甘洛县文化馆
15	Ⅱ-7	阿古合	传统音乐	凉山州甘洛县文化馆、凉山州越西县文化馆
16	Ⅱ-8	金江鼓乐	传统音乐	凉山州会东县文化馆
17	Ⅱ-9	南溪哈号	传统音乐	宜宾市南溪县文化馆
18	Ⅱ-10	广元煤歌	传统音乐	广元市煤炭工业管理局
19	Ⅱ-11	石坪山歌	传统音乐	内江市威远县观音滩镇人民政府
20	Ⅱ-12	西岭山歌	传统音乐	成都市大邑县文化馆
21	Ⅲ-1	灯舞(羌族麻龙马灯、蛾蛾灯)	传统舞蹈	绵阳市北川羌族自治县文化馆、成都市温江区公平街办文化中心
22	Ⅲ-2	圈德迪	传统舞蹈	阿坝州黑水县文体新闻出版局
23	Ⅲ-3	迪厦	传统舞蹈	阿坝州松潘县文化体育局
24	Ⅲ-4	新山傈僳族舞蹈"斑鸠吃水"	传统舞蹈	攀枝花市米易县文化馆

序号	编号	项目名称	类型	申报地区及单位
25	Ⅲ-5	彝族羊皮鼓舞	传统舞蹈	攀枝花市仁和区文化馆
26	Ⅲ-6	纳西族"金佐措"	传统舞蹈	凉山州木里藏族自治县文化馆
27	Ⅲ-7	苍溪独角兽舞	传统舞蹈	广元市苍江县陵江镇综合文化站
28	Ⅲ-8	古蔺苗族舞蹈	传统舞蹈	泸州市古蔺县民宗办
29	Ⅲ-9	水族闹春	传统舞蹈	达州市开江县文化馆
30	Ⅲ-10	高跷（夹关高跷）	传统舞蹈	成都市邛崃市群众艺术馆
31	Ⅲ-11	春牛舞	传统舞蹈	阿坝州松潘县文化体育局
32	Ⅴ-1	折嘎说唱	曲艺	阿坝州阿坝县文化馆
33	Ⅴ-2	四川评书（南部评书）	曲艺	南充市南部县文化馆
34	Ⅴ-3	相书（宣汉背篼戏、四川相书）	曲艺	达州市宣汉县文化馆、成都市武侯区文化馆
35	Ⅴ-4	四川莲箫（峨眉莲箫、四川莲箫）	曲艺	乐山市峨眉山市文化馆、成都市青羊区文化馆
36	Ⅵ-1	太极拳（李雅轩太极拳）	传统游艺、杂技与竞技	成都市李雅轩太极拳武术馆
37	Ⅶ-1	壤塘藏经石刻技艺	传统美术	阿坝州壤塘县文化馆
38	Ⅶ-2	彝族传统刺绣技艺	传统美术	凉山州甘洛县彝族妇女刺绣协会
39	Ⅶ-3	傈僳族刺绣技艺（傈僳族刺绣技艺、新山傈僳族刺绣技艺）	传统美术	凉山州德昌县文化馆、攀枝花市米易县文化馆
40	Ⅶ-4	民间画匠技艺（合江匠笔画）	传统美术	泸州市合江县甘雨镇政府
41	Ⅶ-5	成都面人	传统美术	成都市成华区文化馆
42	Ⅶ-6	竹雕（聚源竹雕）	传统美术	成都市都江堰市文化馆
43	Ⅷ-1	家禽菜肴传统烹制技艺（周记棒棒鸡制作技艺、桥头堡凉拌鸡传统制作技艺、徐鸭子传统制作技艺、观音场月母鸡汤制作技艺）	传统手工技艺	雅安市荥经县文化馆、雅安市天全县文化馆、达州市宣汉县文化馆、泸州市云龙观音场月母鸡汤餐馆

序号	编号	项目名称	类型	申报地区及单位
44	VIII-2	川北凉粉传统制作技艺	传统手工技艺	四川川北凉粉饮食文化有限公司
45	VIII-3	梓潼片粉制作技艺	传统手工技艺	绵阳市梓潼县文化馆
46	VIII-4	梓潼酥饼制作技艺	传统手工技艺	绵阳市梓潼县文化馆
47	VIII-5	金属制品加工工艺（藏族金属制品加工工艺）	传统手工技艺	阿坝州阿坝县文化馆
48	VIII-6	羌族传统编织技艺	传统手工技艺	阿坝州四川羌寨绣庄有限责任公司
49	VIII-7	羌族银饰锻制技艺	传统手工技艺	阿坝州茂县文化体育局
50	VIII-8	麻布制作技艺	传统手工技艺	阿坝州汶川县文化馆
51	VIII-9	傈僳族织布技艺（新山傈僳族织布技艺、傈僳族火草织布技艺）	传统手工技艺	攀枝花市米易县文化馆、凉山州德昌县文化馆
52	VIII-10	彝族金属锻造技艺（喜德彝族叶形双耳腰刀制作技艺）	传统手工技艺	凉山州喜德县文化馆
53	VIII-11	藏族手工皮制品制作技艺	传统手工技艺	凉山州木里藏族自治县文化馆
54	VIII-12	擦窝制作技艺	传统手工技艺	凉山州木里藏族自治县文化馆
55	VIII-13	饵块手工制作技艺	传统手工技艺	凉山州会理县文化馆
56	VIII-14	宜宾燃面传统制作技艺	传统手工技艺	宜宾市益康饮食服务有限责任公司
57	VIII-15	什邡晾晒烟传统生产技艺	传统手工技艺	四川省川渝中烟工业公司
58	VIII-16	泸州邓氏桂圆干果传统制作技艺	传统手工技艺	泸州市邓氏土特产品有限公司

291

序号	编号	项目名称	类型	申报地区及单位
59	Ⅷ-17	牛肉烹制技艺（阆中盐叶子牛肉制作、自贡火边子牛肉制作）	传统手工技艺	四川阆中市华珍风味食品有限公司、自贡市文化馆
60	Ⅷ-18	酱菜制作技艺（"周萝卜"酱菜制作技艺、"丰源"资中冬尖生产工艺）	传统手工技艺	内江市威宝食品有限公司、四川省资中县丰源食品有限责任公司
61	Ⅷ-19	赖汤圆传统制作技艺	传统手工技艺	成都市饮食公司
62	Ⅷ-20	夫妻肺片传统制作技艺	传统手工技艺	成都市饮食公司
63	Ⅷ-21	钟水饺传统制作技艺	传统手工技艺	成都市饮食公司
64	Ⅷ-22	仁和曲药制作技艺	传统手工技艺	泸州市泸县得胜仁和糊药厂
65	Ⅸ-1	"油符"疗法技艺	传统医药	遂宁市传统医学研究所
66	Ⅸ-2	传统彝医药	传统医药	凉山州西昌彝医药研究所
67	Ⅸ-3	嘉州中医滋脾疗法	传统医药	乐山市中医医院
68	Ⅸ-4	何天佐传统中医药正骨疗法	传统医药	八一骨科医院
69	Ⅸ-5	传统药浴疗法（新繁传统药浴）	传统医药	成都市新都区文化馆
70	Ⅸ-6	何天祺传统中医药疗骨法	传统医药	四川何氏骨科医院
71	Ⅹ-1	抬阁（晏场高台）	民俗	雅安市雨城区文化馆
72	Ⅹ-2	七里夺标民俗节	民俗	雅安市芦山县民族民间文化传承中心
73	Ⅹ-3	郪江镇城隍庙会	民俗	绵阳市三台县郪江镇人民政府
74	Ⅹ-5	羌族婚俗	民俗	绵阳市北川羌族自治县文化馆、阿坝州茂县文化体育局
75	Ⅹ-6	驼日节	民俗	阿坝州嘉绒文化研究会

序号	编号	项目名称	类型	申报地区及单位
76	X-7	"古尔果"（羌族转山会）	民俗	阿坝州茂县文化体育局
77	X-8	羌族成人冠礼	民俗	阿坝州汶川县文化馆
78	X-9	傈僳族婚礼	民俗	攀枝花市盐边县文化馆
79	X-10	仡佬族送年节	民俗	攀枝花市盐边县文化馆
80	X-11	苗族绷鼓仪式	民俗	攀枝花市盐边县文化馆
81	X-12	彝族嘎库甘尔习俗	民俗	凉山州布拖县文化馆
82	X-13	藏族服饰（尔苏藏族服饰）	民俗	凉山州甘洛县文化馆
83	X-14	苗族服饰	民俗	凉山州木里藏族自治县文化馆
84	X-15	女子踩桥	民俗	宜宾市屏山县文化馆
85	X-16	祭孔礼仪	民俗	乐山市犍为县文化馆
86	X-17	彝族维克达解习俗	民俗	乐山市峨边彝族自治县文化馆
87	X-18	人日游草堂	民俗	成都市杜甫草堂博物馆
88	X-19	郫县望丛赛歌会	民俗	成都市郫县文化馆
89	X-20	羌族服饰	民俗	阿坝州四川羌寨绣庄有限责任公司

（二）第一、二批扩展项目（共38项）

1	I-5	羌戈大战	民间文学	阿坝州茂县文化体育局
2	II-1	江河号子（嘉陵江船工号子）	传统音乐	南充市蓬安县文化馆
3	II-11	阿惹妞	传统音乐	凉山州甘洛县文化馆
4	II-18	四川洞经音乐（邛都洞泾古乐）	传统音乐	凉山州西昌市邛都洞泾古乐艺术团
5	II-1	薅秧歌（玄滩薅秧歌）	传统音乐	泸州市泸县文化馆
6	II-25	羌笛演奏技艺	传统音乐	绵阳市北川羌族自治县文化馆

序号	编号	项目名称	类型	申报地区及单位
7	Ⅲ-1	龙舞（盐亭梓江龙、泸县兆雅火龙、小金龙龙舞、李庄草龙）	传统舞蹈	绵阳市盐亭县文化馆、泸州市泸县兆雅镇综合文化馆、成都市青白江区文化馆、宜宾市翠屏区李庄镇社会事务服务中心
8	Ⅲ-2	灯舞（成都牛儿灯）	传统舞蹈	成都市大邑县文化馆
9	Ⅲ-11	锅庄（草地锅庄）	传统舞蹈	阿坝州阿坝县文化馆
10	Ⅲ-9	羌族萨朗	传统舞蹈	阿坝州茂县文化体育局、阿坝州汶川县文化馆
11	Ⅲ-6	狮舞（向家班狮舞、元坝狮舞）	传统舞蹈	乐山市市中区文化馆、广元市元坝区元坝镇生态与文化建设服务中心
12	Ⅲ-9	麒麟灯（荣县麒麟灯）	传统舞蹈	自贡市荣县文化馆
13	Ⅲ-11	花灯（回族花灯舞）	传统舞蹈	阿坝州松潘县文化体育局
14	Ⅳ-1	川剧（川北河川剧艺术、资阳河川剧艺术）	传统戏剧	南充市川剧团、自贡市川剧团、内江市川剧团
15	Ⅴ-3	竹琴（道琴）	曲艺	眉山市彭山县文化馆
16	Ⅵ-6	羌族推杆	传统游艺、杂技与竞技	阿坝州茂县文化体育局
17	Ⅶ-7	四川手工剪纸（西充剪纸）	传统美术	南充市西充县文化馆
18	Ⅶ-12	竹编（古城竹鸟笼制作技艺）	传统美术	成都市郫县文化馆
19	Ⅷ-1	蒸馏酒传统酿造技艺（苏东坡酒传统酿造技艺、醉八仙酒酿造技艺、崇州大曲传统酿造技艺）	传统手工技艺	四川省三苏酒业有限责任公司、泸州市千年酒业有限公司、成都市崇阳酒业有限责任公司
20	Ⅷ-2	自贡扎染工艺	传统手工技艺	自贡市天工艺术品有限公司
21	Ⅷ-6	藏族牛羊毛手工编织技艺（藏族毛纺织品编织技艺）	传统手工技艺	凉山州木里藏族自治县文化馆

序号	编号	项目名称	类型	申报地区及单位
22	Ⅷ-8	龚扇	传统手工技艺	自贡市龚道勇竹编工艺品有限公司
23	Ⅷ-11	毛笔制作技艺（柄林毛笔制作技艺）	传统手工技艺	绵阳市涪城区文化馆
24	Ⅷ-15	腐乳酿造技艺（唐场豆腐乳制作技艺）	传统手工技艺	成都市大邑县酿造厂
25	Ⅷ-17	醋传统酿造技艺（思泼醋传统酿造技艺、阆州醋传统手工酿造技艺、太源井晒醋酿造技艺）	传统手工技艺	四川省宜宾市思坡醋业有限责任公司、四川省阆中张飞牛肉有限公司、自贡市沿滩区文化馆
26	Ⅷ-28	民族乐器制作技艺（傈僳族口弦制作技艺、竹制口弦制作技艺）	传统手工技艺	凉山州德昌县文化馆、凉山州布拖县文化馆
27	Ⅷ-34	微刻（贾氏微刻）	传统手工技艺	宜宾市兴文县文物管理所
28	Ⅷ-35	丝毯手工编织技艺（手工打结丝毯编织技艺）	传统手工技艺	南充市阆中四川银河毛毯有限公司
29	Ⅷ-38	四川绿茶制作技艺（蒙顶黄芽传统制作技艺、叙府龙芽传统制作技艺）	传统手工技艺	雅安市名山区非物质文化遗产保护中心、四川省叙府茶业有限公司
30	Ⅷ-49	醪糟酿造技艺（木门醪糟酿造工艺）	传统手工技艺	广元市旺苍县文化馆
31	Ⅷ-51	酱油酿造技艺（"五比一"酱油酿造技艺）	传统手工技艺	泸州市合江县永兴诚酿造有限责任公司
32	Ⅷ-14	豆腐菜肴制作技艺（陈麻婆豆腐制作技艺）	传统手工技艺	成都市饮食公司
33	Ⅷ-7	羌族传统刺绣工艺	传统手工技艺	绵阳市北川羌族自治县文化馆、绵阳市平武县文化馆
34	Ⅷ-24	木雕（汉源涂家木雕）	传统手工技艺	雅安市汉源县文化体育局

295

序号	编号	项目名称	类型	申报地区及单位
35	X-15	彝族婚俗（彝族婚姻习俗）	民俗	乐山市峨边彝族自治县文化馆
36	X-17	彝族服饰（呷咪服饰）	民俗	凉山州木里藏族自治县文化馆
37	X-22	还山鸡节（尔苏藏族还山鸡节）	民俗	凉山州甘洛县文化馆
38	X-11	苗族踩山节（苗族花山节、古蔺踩山）	民俗	宜宾市兴文县民宗局、泸州市古蔺县民宗办

四、四川省第四批非物质文化遗产

（一）四川省第四批非物质文化遗产名录（共36项）

序号	编号	项目名称	类型	申报地区及单位
1	I-30	博葩（万物起源口头文学）	民间文学	凉山彝族自治州喜德县文化馆
2	II-65	傈僳族高腔	传统音乐	凉山彝族自治州德昌县文化馆
3	II-66	阿依阿芝（彝族女性叙事歌）	传统音乐	凉山彝族自治州越西县文化馆
4	II-67	牛牛合（"牛牛"调）	传统音乐	凉山彝族自治州雷波县文化馆
5	II-68	摩梭人阿哈巴拉调	传统音乐	凉山彝族自治州盐源县文化馆
6	III-49	笮山锅庄	传统舞蹈	攀枝花市盐边县文化馆
7	IV-14	曲剧（岳池曲剧、安岳曲剧）	传统戏剧	广安市岳池县文化馆、资阳市安岳县文化馆
8	IV-15	洪雅师道戏	传统戏剧	眉山市洪雅县文化馆
9	IV-16	羌族释比戏	传统戏剧	阿坝藏族羌族自治州理县文化馆
10	V-13	彝族克格（彝语相声）	曲艺	凉山彝族自治州昭觉县文物管理所
11	VI-17	藏棋	传统游艺、杂技与竞技	阿坝藏族羌族自治州阿坝县藏棋协会

序号	编号	项目名称	类型	申报地区及单位
12	VII-32	藏族尔苏图画文字	传统美术	凉山彝族自治州甘洛县文化馆
13	VII-33	峨眉山指画	传统美术	乐山市峨眉山市图书馆
14	VII-34	蚕茧纸轩丝绘画	传统美术	四川省非物质文化遗产保护中心
15	VII-35	羌族刷勒日	传统美术	阿坝藏族羌族自治州茂县文化馆
16	VIII-17	彝族泥染	传统技艺	凉山彝族自治州金阳县文化馆
17	VIII-118	摩梭人苏里马酒的酿造技艺	传统技艺	凉山彝族自治州盐源县文化馆
18	VIII-119	摩梭人青娜油制作技艺	传统技艺	凉山彝族自治州盐源县文化馆
19	VIII-125	川红工夫红茶制作技艺	传统技艺	宜宾川红茶业集团有限公司
20	VIII-126	七佛贡茶茶饼制作工艺	传统技艺	广元市青川县文化馆
21	VIII-127	东坡肘子制作技艺	传统技艺	眉山市东坡区文化馆
22	VIII-128	四川书画装裱修复技艺——蜀裱	传统技艺	四川省非物质文化遗产保护中心
23	VIII-129	藏香制作技艺	传统技艺	阿坝藏族羌族自治州壤塘县藏哇寺
24	VIII-130	羌族羊皮鼓制作技艺	传统技艺	阿坝藏族羌族自治州茂县文化馆
25	IX-15	峨眉伤科疗法	传统医药	成都中医药大学附属医院
26	X-73	安巴节	民俗	甘孜藏族自治州道孚县文化馆
27	X-74	摩梭人"若哈舍"习俗	民俗	凉山彝族自治州盐源县文化馆
28	X-75	彝族剪羊毛节	民俗	凉山彝族自治州金阳县文化馆
29	X-76	摩梭人服饰	民俗	凉山彝族自治州盐源县文化馆

序号	编号	项目名称	类型	申报地区及单位
30	X-77	彝族赛马习俗	民俗	凉山彝族自治州昭觉县文物管理所
31	X-78	瑞峰端午龙舟节	民俗	眉山市青神县文化馆
32	X-79	彭祖山三月三朝山会	民俗	眉山市彭山市非物质文化遗产保护中心
33	X-80	羌族夬儒节	民俗	阿坝藏族羌族自治州理县文化馆
34	X-81	涂墨节	民俗	阿坝藏族羌族自治州九寨沟县文化馆
35	X-82	穷度卜	民俗	阿坝藏族羌族自治州黑水县文化馆
36	X-83	木里"桑股"头饰	民俗	凉山彝族自治州木里藏族自治县文化馆
（二）第一、二、三批扩展项目（共26项）				
1	I-3	木姐珠和斗安珠	民间文学——第三批扩展	阿坝藏族羌族自治州茂县文化馆
2	II-1	江河号子（关河船工号子）	传统音乐——第二批扩展	宜宾市宜宾县文化馆
3	II-28	口弦（羌族口弦）	传统音乐——第一批扩展	阿坝藏族羌族自治州茂县文化馆
4	II—6	石工号子（福宝石工号子）	传统音乐——第二批扩展	泸州市合江县文化馆
5	II—4	川南山歌（珙县山歌、筠连山歌）	传统音乐——第一批扩展	宜宾市珙县文化馆、宜宾市筠连县文化馆
6	II—2	薅草锣鼓（打鼓草）	传统音乐——第一批扩展	乐山市马边彝族自治县
7	II—1	薅秧歌（柳街薅秧歌）	传统音乐——第一批扩展	成都市都江堰市文化馆

序号	编号	项目名称	类型	申报地区及单位
8	Ⅲ-11	锅庄（岚安锅庄、理塘锅庄）	传统舞蹈——第一批扩展	甘孜藏族自治州泸定县文化馆、甘孜藏族自治州理塘县文化馆
9	Ⅲ-11	花灯（芦山花灯）	传统舞蹈——第二批扩展	雅安市芦山县文化馆
10	Ⅲ-1	灯舞（牛滩马儿灯）	传统舞蹈——第三批扩展	泸州市泸县文化馆
11	Ⅲ-16	羌族羊皮鼓舞	传统舞蹈——第一批扩展	阿坝藏族羌族自治州理县文化馆、阿坝藏族羌族自治州茂县文化馆
12	Ⅳ-8	藏戏（木雅藏戏、理塘藏戏）	传统戏剧——第一批扩展	甘孜藏族自治州康定市文化馆、甘孜藏族自治州理塘县文化馆
13	Ⅴ-2	四川评书	曲艺——第三批扩展	成都市成华区文化馆
14	Ⅴ-2	四川清音	曲艺——第一批扩展	四川省艺术研究院
15	Ⅴ-1	四川车灯（车车灯）	曲艺——第二批扩展	宜宾市长宁县文化馆
16	Ⅶ-6	藏文书法	传统美术——第一批扩展	阿坝藏族羌族自治州阿坝县文化馆
17	Ⅶ-10	藏族唐卡（觉囊画派）	传统美术——第一批扩展	阿坝藏族羌族自治州壤塘县藏哇寺
18	Ⅶ-9	石雕（合江石雕）	传统美术——第二批扩展	泸州市合江县文化馆
19	Ⅷ-28	民族乐器制作技艺（彝族月琴制作技艺）	传统手工技艺——第二批扩展	凉山彝族自治州雷波县文化馆

序号	编号	项目名称	类型	申报地区及单位
20	Ⅷ-31	藏族金属手工技艺（佐钦藏族金属锻造技艺）	传统手工技艺——第一批扩展	甘孜藏族自治州德格县 四川康坝扎金属工艺有限公司
21	Ⅷ-8	麻布制作技艺（木里麻布手工纺织技艺）	传统手工技艺——第三批扩展	凉山彝族自治州木里藏族自治县文化馆
22	Ⅷ-20	传统民居营造技艺（木里藏族民居营造技艺）	传统手工技艺——第二批扩展	凉山彝族自治州木里藏族自治县文化馆
23	Ⅷ-38	四川绿茶制作技艺（雀舌手工茶制作技艺）	传统手工技艺——第一批扩展	泸州市纳溪区金凤山茶厂
24	Ⅷ-3	配制酒传统酿造技艺（保宁压酒酿造技艺）	传统手工技艺——第二批扩展	四川保宁压酒有限公司
25	Ⅷ-2	酿造酒传统酿造技艺[羌族咂酒酿造技艺、彝族燕麦酒古法酿造技艺、嘉绒藏区民间酿制阿让（蒸馏酒）技艺]	传统手工技艺——第二批扩展	阿坝藏族羌族自治州茂县文化馆、凉山彝族自治州会东县文化馆、阿坝嘉绒文化研究会
26	Ⅷ-1	蒸馏酒传统酿造技艺（永乐古窖酒传统酿造技艺、玉米酒传统酿造技艺）	传统手工技艺——第二批扩展	宜宾红楼梦酒业股份有限公司、北川马槽酒厂
五、四川省第五批非物质文化遗产				
（一）四川省第五批非物质文化遗产名录（共52项）				

序号	项目名称	类型	申报地区或保护单位
1	苏东坡传说	民间文学	眉山市非遗保护中心

序号	项目名称	类型	申报地区或保护单位
2	斯都呐嘎体	民间文学	凉山州普格县文化馆
3	自贡盐场号子	传统音乐	自贡市文化馆
4	九顶山山歌	传统音乐	德阳市绵竹市文化馆
5	马渡山歌	传统音乐	达州市宣汉县文化馆
6	花儿纳吉	传统音乐	阿坝州理县文化馆
7	霍尔古舞	传统舞蹈	甘孜州炉霍县文化馆
8	"垛"	传统舞蹈	阿坝州若尔盖县文化馆
9	新山傈僳族葫芦笙舞	传统舞蹈	攀枝花市米易县文化馆
10	夒坛戏	传统戏剧	巴中市南江县文化馆
11	木雅藏族"什结拉布"	传统戏剧	雅安市石棉县非遗保护中心
12	红原芒卓甲扎（红原马术）	传统体育、游艺与杂技	红原县邛钦马术演义有限责任公司
13	松溪内家拳	传统体育、游艺与杂技	南充市松溪内家拳法研究会
14	铁索飞渡	传统体育、游艺与杂技	绵阳市江油市文化馆
15	聋派指画	传统美术	绵阳市游仙区文化馆
16	玻璃吹塑技艺	传统美术	自贡市富顺县文化馆
17	川菜传统烹饪技艺	传统技艺	四川旅游学院川菜发展研究中心
18	江门荤豆花传统制作技艺	传统技艺	泸州市叙永县文化馆
19	东坡泡菜制作技艺	传统技艺	眉山市非遗保护中心
20	通江银耳生产传统技艺	传统技艺	巴中市通江县文化馆
21	土法榨油技艺	传统技艺	兴文县古宋粮油有限责任公司
22	水淘糌粑	传统技艺	甘孜州甘孜县文化馆
23	两河吊洞砂锅传统手工制作技艺	传统技艺	泸州市叙永县文化馆
24	彝族烟斗制作技艺	传统技艺	凉山州喜德县文化馆

序号	项目名称	类型	申报地区或保护单位
25	蒲砚制作技艺	传统技艺	成都市蒲砚文化发展 有限公司
26	丝绸传统织染技艺	传统技艺	南充市高坪区文化馆
27	蓝印花布制作技艺	传统技艺	巴中市恩阳区 非遗保护中心
28	唐昌布鞋传统制作技艺	传统技艺	成都市郫都区 文化艺术中心
29	雅安全手工工艺 软包皮拖鞋制作技艺	传统技艺	雅安金步文化创意 有限公司
30	白马毡帽擀制技艺	传统技艺	绵阳市平武县 非遗保护中心
31	黄氏吹糖人制作技艺	传统技艺	内江市市中区文化馆
32	木雅藏族服饰制作技艺	传统技艺	甘孜州康定市文化馆
33	水潦彝族草把龙制作技艺	传统技艺	泸州市叙永县文化馆
34	太极五子衍宗丸制作技艺	传统医药	太极集团四川绵阳 制药有限公司
35	"蛇难爬"消肿散	传统医药	达州市中心医院
36	南部杜氏中医	传统医药	南充市南部县文化馆
37	何首乌饮片传统加工技艺	传统医药	四川省川源药业有限公司
38	太素脉法	传统医药	广元市文化遗产保护中心
39	基勒俄足（羌族狩猎节）	民俗	阿坝州茂县文化馆
40	布依族"三月三"习俗	民俗	凉山州宁南县文化馆
41	什拉罗习俗	民俗	凉山州金阳县文化馆
42	汉源花椒生产民俗	民俗	雅安市汉源县 非遗保护中心
43	川南请春酒	民俗	宜宾市高县文化馆
44	甘棠耍火龙	民俗	达州市开江县文化馆
45	送蛴蟆	民俗	遂宁市蓬溪县文化馆
46	翔龙节	民俗	内江市威远县文化馆
47	天彭牡丹花会	民俗	成都市彭州市文化馆
48	元通清明春台会	民俗	成都市崇州市文化馆

序号	项目名称	类型	申报地区或保护单位
49	客家水龙节	民俗	成都市龙泉驿区文化馆
50	彝族历法与民俗	民俗	乐山市马边县文化馆
51	阆中春节习俗	民俗	南充市阆中市文化馆
52	秧勒节	民俗	甘孜州巴塘县文化馆

（二）第一、二、三、四批扩展项目（共37项）

序号	项目名称	类型	申报地区或保护单位
1	竹麻号子	传统音乐	乐山市夹江县文化馆
2	石工号子（华蓥山石工号子）	传统音乐	广安市华蓥市文化馆
3	唢呐艺术（桂兴唢呐艺术）	传统音乐	广安市前锋区非遗保护中心
4	唢呐艺术（童寺唢呐）	传统音乐	自贡市富顺县文化馆
5	傈僳族高腔（大麦地傈僳族山歌）	传统音乐	攀枝花市西区文化馆
6	龙舞（天兴龙贯山草龙）	传统舞蹈	泸州市泸县文化馆
7	锅庄（得荣九步锅庄）	传统舞蹈	甘孜州得荣县文化馆
8	锅庄（苟尔光楞琼格锅庄）	传统舞蹈	阿坝州金川县文化馆
9	川剧（叙泸河川剧艺术）	传统戏剧	宜宾市酒都艺术研究院
10	川剧（巴渠河川剧艺术）	传统戏剧	达州市文化艺术中心
11	灯戏（苍溪灯戏）	传统戏剧	广元市苍溪县文化馆
12	被单戏	传统戏剧	绵阳市安州区文化馆
13	傩戏（泸州傩戏）	传统戏剧	泸州市言合思动文化传播有限公司
14	四川竹琴（邻水竹琴）	曲艺	广安市邻水县文化馆
15	藏族唐卡（门萨画派）	传统美术	甘孜州白玉县文化馆
16	四川剪纸（巴山剪纸）	传统美术	巴中市通江县文化馆
17	石雕（隆昌青石雕刻技艺）	传统美术	内江市隆昌市文化馆
18	纸传统制作技艺（黄麻纸制作技艺）	传统技艺	达州市达川区文化馆
19	纸传统制作技艺（洪雅雅纸制作技艺）	传统技艺	眉山市洪雅县文化馆

303

序号	项目名称	类型	申报地区或保护单位
20	土陶制作技艺（荣县土陶）	传统技艺	自贡市荣县文化馆
21	土陶制作技艺（隆昌土陶）	传统技艺	隆昌市碧檀陶瓷有限公司
22	四川绿茶制作技艺（羌族罐罐茶制作技艺）	传统技艺	北川羌族自治县羌山雀舌茶业有限公司
23	酿造酒传统酿造技艺（两节山老酒传统酿造技艺）	传统技艺	四川两节山酒业有限公司
24	传统民居营造技艺（川南民居木作技艺）	传统技艺	宜宾市叙州区文化馆
25	传统民居营造技艺（彝族建筑技艺）	传统技艺	凉山州美姑县文化馆
26	传统民居营造技艺（摩梭人传统民居建筑技艺）	传统技艺	凉山州盐源县文化馆
27	木雕（觉囊木刻技艺）	传统技艺	阿坝州壤塘县藏哇寺
28	木雕（刘氏木雕）	传统技艺	雅安市芦山县文化馆
29	民族乐器制作技艺（彝族"胡惹"制作技艺）	传统技艺	凉山州雷波县文化馆
30	丝毯手工编织技艺（歧坪真丝地挂毯织造技艺）	传统技艺	苍溪县秀艺毯业有限公司
31	藏族金属制品加工技艺（花色青铜锻造技艺）	传统技艺	甘孜州白玉县文化馆
32	四川小吃制作技艺（双河凉糕制作技艺）	传统技艺	宜宾市长宁县文化馆
33	四川小吃制作技艺（军屯锅魁制作技艺）	传统技艺	成都市彭州市文化馆
34	藏医药	传统医药	阿坝藏族羌族自治州藏医院（阿坝藏族羌族自治州藏医药研究所）
35	传统正骨疗法（泸州王氏祖传正骨医技）	传统医药	泸州王氏骨科医院
36	传统正骨疗法（李氏正骨术）	传统医药	珙县巡场发科骨科医院
37	传统正骨疗法（峨眉僧医驳骨疗法）	传统医药	乐山驳骨堂骨科医院

主要参考文献

[1] 阿牛史日，吉郎伍野. 凉山毕摩[M]. 浙江人民出版社，2007.1.

[2] 陈思琦，李佳，李雨竹. 非物质文化遗产与文化创意产业融合发展实践[M]. 西南交通大学出版社，2021.1.

[3] 冯骥才总主编. 中国非物质文化遗产百科全书·代表性项目卷[M]. 中国文联出版社，2015.5.

[4] 冯骥才总主编. 中国非物质文化遗产百科全书·史诗卷（格萨<斯>尔、江格尔、玛纳斯）[M]. 中国文联出版社，2015.5.

[5] 顾江. 文化遗产经济学[M]. 南京大学出版社，2009.9.

[6] 国家文物局等编. 国际文化遗产保护文件选编[M]. 文物出版社，2007.10.

[7] 黄秀芳主编. 中华遗产杂志2019年全年典藏礼盒版[M].《中国国家地理》杂志社，2019.12

[8] 李树文等编. 非物质文化遗产法律指南[M]. 文化艺术出版社，2011.6.

[9] 林青. 非物质文化遗产保护的理论与实践[M]. 人民邮电出版社，2017.12.

[10] 刘锡诚. 非物质文化遗产保护的中国道路[M]. 文化艺术出版社，2016.5.

[11] 满珂主编. 非物质文化遗产：变迁·传承·发展[M]. 科学出版社. 2019.12.

[12] 麻国庆，朱伟. 文化人类学与非物质文化遗产[M]. 生活·读书·新知三联书店，2019.1.

[13] 彭冬梅. 非物质文化遗产数字化保护与传播研究：以剪纸艺术为例[M]. 山东人民出版社，2014.1.

[14] 宋俊华主编. 非物质文化遗产蓝皮书：中国非物质文化遗产保护发展报告（2020）[M]. 社会科学文献出版社，2021.6.

[15] 宋俊华，王开桃. 非物质文化遗产保护研究[M]. 中山大学出版社，2013.12.

[16] 苏秉琦. 中国文明起源新探[M]. 生活·读书·新知三联书店，2019.10.

[17] 王文章. 非物质文化遗产保护研究[M]. 文化艺术出版社，2013.5.

[18] 王文章主编. 非物质文化遗产概论（修订版）[M]. 教育科学出版社，2013.5.

[19] 魏力群. "小书大传承"中国非物质文化遗产通识读本：皮影[M]. 重庆出版社，2019.7.

[20] 文化部非物质文化遗产司主编. 非物质文化遗产保护法律法规资料汇编[M]. 文化艺术出版社，2013.9.

[21] 汪欣. 传统村落与非物质文化遗产保护研究 —— 以徽州传统村落为个案[M]. 知识产权出版社，2014.6.

[22] 汪欣. 中国非物质文化遗产保护十年（2003~2013年）[M]. 知识产权出版社，2015.5.

[23] 向云驹. 非物质文化遗产的若干哲学问题及其他[M]. 文化艺术出版社，2017.4.

[24] 向云驹. 解读非物质文化遗产[M]. 宁夏人民出版社，2009.5.

[25] 向云驹. 人类口头和非物质遗产[M]. 宁夏人民教育出版社，

2010.9.

[26] 杨红主编.非物质文化遗产：从传承到传播[M].清华大学出版社，2019.9.

[27] 杨红.非物质文化遗产数字化研究[M].社会科学文献出版社，2014.3.

[28] 于海广主编.中国的世界非物质文化遗产[M].山东画报出版社，2011.8.

[29] 苑利，顾军.非物质文化遗产学[M].高等教育出版社，2009.11.

[30] 张岂之主编.中国传统文化（第三版）[M].高等教育出版社，2010.4.

[31] 郑巨欣.文化遗产保护的数字化展示与传播[M].学苑出版社，2011.6.

[32] 中华人民共和国文化和旅游部国际交流与合作局主编.联合国教科文组织〈保护非物质文化遗产公约〉基础文件汇编（2016版）[M].中国数字文化集团有限公司，2019.3.

[33] 高山，谈国新.大数据驱动的非物质文化遗产管理范式转变研究[J].图书馆，2020（11）.

[34] 高金燕.媒介融合视野下非物质文化遗产的传承与创新发展[J].西北民族大学学报（哲学社会科学版），2020（06）.

[35] 高倬君.文化与科技融合视角下非物质文化遗产保护机制的模型构建[J].科研管理，2021，42（01）.

[36] 李腾巍.智媒体助力非物质文化遗产活态传播[J].出版广角，2021（01）.

[37] 马知遥，周晓飞.论媒介传播与非物质文化遗产传承[J].原生态民族文化学刊，2020，12（06）.

[38] 王明月.非物质文化遗产文化创意产业的衍生性：理论分析与实

践启示[J]. 四川戏剧，2020（12）.

[39] 萧放，王辉. 非物质文化遗产融入当代生活的路径研究[J]. 广西民族大学学报（哲学社会科学版），2021，43（01）.

[40] 郑奥成，郑家鲲，王学彬. 后疫情时代体育非物质文化遗产数字化传播的现实挑战与推进路向[J]. 广州体育学院学报，2021，41（01）.